D1610348

THE INCOMPLEAT SURVEYOR

By the same author:

THE HOUSING ACT 1935 (WITH T. J. SOPHIAN, 1936)

MEET THE PRISONER (1939)

THE CHILD AND THE MAGISTRATE (1942, 1950, 1965)

BRITISH JUVENILE COURTS (1948)

WHICH IS THE JUSTICE? (1969)

THE JUVENILE COURT—1970 ONWARD (1970)

NOTHING BUT THE TRUTH (1971)

The Author

Photograph:
David Campbell,
Saffron Walden.

The Incompleat Surveyor

being the reflections of

John A. F. Watson, CBE, JP

Past-President of the Royal Institution of Chartered Surveyors
Member of the Lands Tribunal 1957 to 1969

with a foreword by

THE RIGHT HONOURABLE LORD DENNING, PC
Master of the Rolls

THE ESTATES GAZETTE LIMITED
151 Wardour Street, London W1V 4BN

The Author's royalties on the sale of this book
have been given to the Royal Institution of
Chartered Surveyors' Benevolent Fund

Published 1973
© John Watson, C.B.E., P.P.R.I.C.S., J.P., 1973

Set in 12pt Bembo
Printed in Great Britain by
Western Printing Services Ltd., Bristol
and bound by the Pitman Press, Bath

TO MY WIFE
in memory of her father

Contents

List of Illustrations

Foreword

by

The Right Honourable Lord Denning PC

Master of the Rolls

John Watson has the gift of felicitous language. He has put this gift to good use. You will find it in this book. But elsewhere you will find it in the most unlikely places; for instance in his decisions in the Lands Tribunal. The subject matter of cases in the Lands Tribunal is dull beyond compare. Typical is the case where Lord Justice Harman said:

'To reach a conclusion on this matter involved the Court in wading through a monstrous legislative morass, staggering from stone to stone and ignoring the marsh gas exhaling from the forest of schedules lining the way on each side. I regarded it, at one time, I must confess, as a slough of despond through which the Court would never drag its feet, but I have, by leaping from tussock to tussock as best I might, eventually, pale and exhausted, reached the other side where I find myself, I am glad to say, at the same point as that arrived at with more agility by my lord.' (*Davy v. Leeds Corporation*, 1964, 1 WLR at page 1224.)

But into this depressing field John Watson, when he was a member of the Lands Tribunal, brought an exhilarating choice of words. He was able to give his reasons for his decisions clearly and yet entertainingly. His keen insight, his pungent criticism and his light touch enlivened the dullest of cases. It is worthy of note that in an anthology of legal prose, *The Language of the Law*,[1] there are extracts from five decisions by John Watson. The only rival is Mr. Justice Holmes, who has five also. Everyone else has only one apiece.

[1] Edited by Louis Blom-Cooper QC, assisted by Edward Jackson, 1965, Bodley Head.

John Watson has done many things which he describes aptly as 'God-bless-you jobs'—jobs for which one may be blessed by God, but not always thanked by one's fellow men. He has done great service as a magistrate, especially in the Juvenile Court. He is an acknowledged authority on the treatment of juvenile delinquents. He has done much for prisoners too, filling important roles in the National Association of Prison Visitors. He has served on important committees. All without reward save the satisfaction of work well done.

Yet all his life he has suffered from muscular dystrophy. He has overcome this disability with amazing fortitude. Forced by it to retire from the Lands Tribunal at the age of 65, he has continued to use his mind and his pen to the full. He has written books of first-rate quality. Now, from a wheel-chair, he has produced the story of his professional life and experiences. He calls it *The Incompleat Surveyor*, in contrast, he says, to Izaak Walton's *The Compleat Angler*. He need not have been so modest. As a Past-President of the Royal Institution of Chartered Surveyors, he is a past master of the surveyor's skills. The advice that John Watson gives the young surveyor is as complete as that which Izaak Walton gave the young fisherman. He intersperses it with lightsome talk, just as Walton did.

This book is instructive and yet entertaining, learned and yet witty, accurate and yet easy to read. It is just like him to take nothing for himself, but to give all his royalties to the Royal Institution of Chartered Surveyors' Benevolent Fund. If I may use his own expression, 'God bless you, John Watson'; you have given us a good book, fit to be read not only by surveyors, but by many besides.

Royal Courts of Justice,   DENNING
London.
September, 1973

Introduction
Double Life

Izaak Walton, author of *The Compleat Angler*, knew everything about angling and was a complete master of his subject. Not so the present author. Because of the complexity of a surveyor's activities, but also because of a peculiar circumstance I shall make haste to explain, I am *not* a complete master of my subject and only half a surveyor. Hence the title of this book.

You see I have lived a double life, having competed with my *alter ego* since I was twenty. For the avoidance of Latin I will call my *alter ego* the Other Chap. In 1922 I entered a London firm of chartered surveyors as an articled pupil; at about the same time the Other Chap entered (voluntarily) Wormwood Scrubs Prison. In 1926 I joined the staff of the late Sir Herbert Trustram Eve, who were engaged in the revaluation of Bedfordshire; conveniently for the Other Chap, who had got to like prison, Bedford Prison was round the corner. Then I went to help revalue Portsmouth, where there is another admirable prison; the Other Chap arranged a transfer. In 1928 I returned to London to become a partner in Ferris and Puckridge. The Other Chap, dogging my footsteps, got such a welcome on his return to the Scrubs that he attached himself to Pentonville as well and began to take an interest in borstal.

From 1957 until 1969 I was a member of the Lands Tribunal; from 1936 until 1968 the Other Chap was the presiding magistrate in a London juvenile court. I have had the honour of being president of the Royal Institution of Chartered Surveyors, and the Other Chap of being chairman of the National Association of Prison Visitors. I have been the manager of a great London estate, he the manager of an approved school. Today, because of our advancing years, we have retired from these things.

The Other Chap has enjoyed many advantages. Because he has never found a paid job I have always kept him, and I fear that he is a little spoiled. He has travelled abroad at public expense, been royally entertained and in the result is over-assertive. Should I wish to discuss some technical point with my surveyor brethren, the Other Chap won't let me. He switches the conversation to the psychiatric treatment of maladjusted juvenile delinquents before you can say 'knife'.

That brings me to our books. Between us over the years we have published seven. Five are by the Other Chap and only two—*The Housing Act 1935* (1936) and *Nothing but the Truth* (1971), on expert evidence—by me. In my judgment the Other Chap's most readable book is *Which is the Justice?* (1969),[1] even if one of his reviewers *was* a bit crusty. He cannot have known about our close relationship. How odd, he remarked, for the author of a book that ranges over his whole life to have made no reference to how he earned his living . . . Out of my way, Other Chap! I have accepted the challenge. *The Incompleat Surveyor* is the outcome.

It is not a textbook. Nor does it purport to be the full story of a professional career, much of which would be found boring. I concede, however, that it is largely autobiographical and I fear at times discursive. The immediate problem is where to begin.

It is good in most things to begin at the beginning, which is why the great generally begin their autobiographies with some

---

[1] Published by Allen and Unwin. The title derives from *King Lear*, IV, 6:
  'See how yon' justice rails upon yon' simple thief.
  Hark in thine ear: change places; and, handy-dandy,
  which is the justice, which is the thief?'

account of their infancy. On the face of it, it may seem of little relevance to the spiritual eminence of an archbishop that he had tantrums between three and five, and bit his nails from five to ten; or of deep significance that a cabinet minister, when he was a toddler, loved his gollywog more than his parents and at around seven had difficulties with his bowel action. But increasingly today the ordinary reader *expects* to be told these intimate things about the great and likes being told them; while the Freudian, gifted additionally with hindsight, laps them up and makes deductions.

One objection to my beginning a book in this way is that I cannot, on any ground I can think of, claim to be great. Therefore the reader is no more likely to be interested in my infantile peculiarities than in those of the man from whom he buys his newspaper. A more cogent reason is that the Other Chap, typically, got in first. He has told the story of our early days before the dichotomy in the opening chapter of *Which is the Justice?* And he has told it at considerable length: of the fatherless upbringing of an only child by a devoted mother and two kindly grandfathers; of a private boarding school which he endured and a public school where he was miserable; of a military career which was undistinguished if only because it lasted less than a month. It is possible that some of my readers will be interested in these happenings, but I cannot go through all that again; in the jargon of the television studio I will merely 'recap'. Other readers, including any who have read *Which is the Justice?* and find Chapter I repetitive, are recommended to skip.

This book is mainly about the adventures of a surveyor and I am grateful to a number of my friends, most of them compleat surveyors, for their wise advice and tonic criticisms while I was writing it. I also wish to acknowledge the help I have had from several of the books that are listed, with the names of their authors and publishers, in the Bibliography. Above all, I am grateful to Lord Denning, Master of the Rolls, for the honour he has done me by contributing a foreword and for the kind things he has said.

But *The Incompleat Surveyor* is not entirely about surveying. There are passages that have nothing to do with that subject and moments when, despite my efforts to restrain him, the Other Chap butts in. My purpose throughout has been to relate some experiences which have caused me to think and have led me to certain conclusions; whether they are valid conclusions the reader will judge for himself. If he finds anything I have written entertaining, I shall be pleased. If he finds any of it instructive, I shall be more so.

Elmdon Old Vicarage,   J.A.F.W.
Saffron Walden.
October, 1973

I

Early Days

Where born, to whom and when – the questing mind – words, words, words – foxhunting in Ireland – tactless small boy – childhood memories – unwillingly to school – A. P. F. Chapman – change of plan – military career.

Buzz . . . buzz . . . buzz . . . went the house telephone beside the fireplace in the drawing office. 'Bother!' said the chief draughtsman, Mr. William Smith. He laid aside his set-square, carefully wiped the ink from his ruling pen with the piece of rag he kept for that purpose, descended from his stool and crossed the room to answer it.

Voice: 'Is Mr. Watson in the drawing office?'

Mr. Smith: 'Yes'

Voice: 'Mr. Garrard wants him, so will he please come down? . . . And as Watson is new to the office perhaps you'll tell him where Mr. Garrard's room is.'

The date was in October 1922 and the drawing office a third-floor front room of a pleasant Georgian house on the north side of Charles Street (now Charles II Street) in the parish of St. James's, near the corner of St. James's Square. Like so many pleasant Georgian houses in London it has since been pulled down.

In 1922 the whole house, except for two rooms off the staircase, was occupied by an old and distinguished firm of chartered surveyors and land agents called Daniel Smith, Oakley and Garrard. Sir John Oakley was the head of it. The firm had been established early in the nineteenth century with the title Daniel

Smith, Son and Oakley. The original Oakley was Sir John's father, but little was known of Mr. Daniel Smith except that besides being a valuer and land agent he had been an 'upholder'. Later, upholders became 'undertakers'. Today, in the debased currency of the English language, they are 'funeral directors'. The two rooms between the ground and first floors were sublet to a worthy body, the Artists' Benevolent Association. People of eccentric appearance, encountered from time to time on the stairs, might have been apparitions but more probably were artists in need of benevolence.

But before going any further I must do what I undertook in my Introduction—recap. It is desirable to explain how it was that John Arthur Fergus Watson, aged nineteen years and a few months, came to be in Daniel Smith, Oakley and Garrards' office at all.

It is given to most of us to decide in general terms where we shall live and, barring accident, die. It is certain that a decision we cannot take for ourselves is where we shall be born. That depends upon the whim and circumstances of the preceding generation, and consciously at any rate we have no say in the matter. I was born on July 24, 1903 in the metropolitan borough of Greenwich a few hundred yards from Blackheath. I was born there because my father, J. G. Maitland Watson, a gunner captain, was Assistant Secretary to the Ordnance Committee at the Royal Arsenal in the borough of Woolwich, which adjoined the borough of Greenwich on the east. His father, Colonel Robert Samuel Watson, likewise of the Royal Regiment of Artillery, lived nearby.

At the turn of the century, and indeed until shortly before the outbreak of the Second World War in 1939, that corner of London differed in many ways from what it is now. Then, you could join the Roman road from London to Dover where it crosses Blackheath; climb Shooters Hill; pause at the summit beside the water tower to look back at the superb view with

Greenwich Observatory and the Royal Naval College in the foreground; descend the other side of Shooters Hill and on through the village of Welling: you were well on your way to the Kentish hopfields once you had passed the inn with the unexpected name, *We Anchor in Hope*.

The Roman road is still there. Shooters Hill and the water tower are still there. The view is the same, except that the great dome of the observatory has been demolished and the prospect on either side of the river is studded with monoliths. *We Anchor in Hope* is still there. But ahead, stretching nearly as far as the eye can see, is a vast suburban sprawl which you will need to traverse before reaching open country. The sprawl is intersected by A roads and M roads with their roundabouts, tunnels, fly-overs and other appurtenances. They are the Londoner's escape routes; is it any wonder he escapes at seventy miles an hour plus those extra miles an hour that he hopes the police won't notice? Such is progress. But it is not my purpose to be sentimental about the past, nor is this a guide book.

My father died in 1905 when I was eighteen months old. My mother, Mabel Watson, then aged twenty-four, had graduated before her marriage at the Royal College of Music and wisely decided to pick up the threads and continue with her profession. She also accepted her father's invitation to return to his house in Kensington and take me with her. That became my home, but my mother had a cottage in the country where we used to spend holidays and occasional weekends.

So it was that my maternal grandfather, James Weir, became a considerable influence in my life. Likewise my other grandfather, Robert Samuel Watson, whom I have already mentioned. The opening chapter of *Which is the Justice?* contains pen-portraits of my grandfathers who, in different ways, were remarkable men. I have little to add except to mention that they both lived to a great age and through an extraordinarily interesting period of English history.

3

James Weir lived through the whole of the reign of Queen Victoria. He was born in Edinburgh in 1832, the son of a Scottish lawyer and Writer to the Signet, and was educated at Edinburgh Academy, where he was a contemporary of James Clerk-Maxwell and nearly twenty years senior to Robert Louis Stevenson; he once told me that he remembered his parents going out to dinner in sedan chairs. He was a cultured man with wide interests. One, as I have recorded elsewhere, was an almost passionate regard for the purity of the English language; woe betide any member of his family who mispronounced a word, or misspelt it, or employed it in a wrong context. I have always loved words and I know where my affection for our language comes from. Another quality I hope I have inherited from my grandfather in some measure, and will pass on to my descendants, is the Questing Mind. He made it his business to try to understand everything that came his way, provided it was not so technical as to be outside his compass. 'My boy,' he would say to me, 'whenever you read or hear a word that is unfamiliar, or come across something of which you have no knowledge, don't let it pass. Go into the library, take down the dictionary or the encyclopædia *and look it up.*' He always did that himself. I can see him now, seated in his leather armchair and wearing an embroidered velvet skull-cap, a volume of *Encyclopædia Britannica* propped up before him.

My paternal grandfather was born in Ireland and came of a line of Irish squires, who had their roots in Cumberland but had settled in County Carlow (Catherlow as it was then spelt) in the seventeenth century. A hundred years later there were several branches of our family in Carlow and the neighbouring counties. In about 1675 nearly all the Irish Watsons became Quakers, but that did not prevent some of them, besides being landowners, being good men of business. For example, the Watsons of Ballingarrane in County Tipperary were bankers. My Watson ancestors and kinsmen seceded from the Society of

4

Friends at various dates during the nineteenth century. One of the first branches to do so were the Watsons of Ballydarton in County Carlow, who produced in three successive generations perhaps the most famous of all the foxhunting men in that famous foxhunting country.

John Watson of Ballydarton, besides being founder of the Carlow Hunt, is said to have had the distinction of hunting and killing the last wolf in Ireland at Baltinglass in 1808. His son and grandson maintained the family tradition by hunting the fox, Robert as Master of the Carlow and Island from his father's death in 1869 until 1902, and John as Master of the Meath from 1891 until 1908. Harry Franks, that most delightful of Irish land agents, told of the last time he saw the 'Old Master', as Robert Watson was affectionately called. The meet was at Ballydarton and Robert, in his eighties, had just been hoisted on to his horse. He called down to Harry: 'It may take three men to get me into the saddle, but once I'm there *it still takes the divil himself to get me out of it.*'

My grandfather was never a Quaker nor, so far as I know, did he ever hunt the fox although he may have done so in his youth. But his parents were Quakers and possibly they left the Society and came to England because their only son wanted to join the Army, which was contrary to Quaker principles.

Both my grandfathers had remarkable memories. Each of them, unlike many people who live to an advanced age, remembered every part of his life as clearly as any other. I think however, in common with most old people, they both enjoyed telling of their early experiences most. How I wish, when a boy, I had listened more attentively to what they told me and had asked more questions!

It is natural, and entirely right, that the young should look forward rather than backward. But not *all* the time. History, wrote Thomas Carlyle, 'is the essence of innumerable biographies.' There comes a moment in the lives of most of us, often too late, when we perceive more truth in his remark than in the later assertion by Mr. Henry Ford: 'History is bunk'. I think it sad, but possibly a sign of the times, that today too many young people show so little interest in the lives and doings of their forebears if only of two or three generations back; notwithstanding that the idiosyncrasy of each one of us—that admixture of strengths and weaknesses, hopes and fears, likes and dislikes, aims and frustrations—derives from theirs. How many of us possess family portraits such as paintings, silhouettes, daguerreotypes or photographs, the subjects of which we cannot even identify? To the more youthful of my readers I offer this advice. Seek out your oldest living relative, wake him up and don't allow him to go to sleep again until he has told you who these people were. Write their names and dates on labels, and stick the labels firmly on the backs of the portraits. Add a note of any particular distinction: that he or she was a town councillor or a magistrate, founded a firm, got drowned in the Serpentine, broke the bank at Monte Carlo, or (shortly to become a more commonplace achievement) went to the moon. I hope that as the years pass they will interest your children and your children's children. But, as the Victorian novelist used to say, I digress.

Naturally there are stories about my infancy and most of them pretty foolish ones. There always are. Only one is worth retelling, and that because it reveals at an early age a certain lack of tact that I have been accused of in later life.

I was about four, or possibly five, when my paternal grandparents came to London and stayed at an hotel in Bayswater. My mother and I had been invited to tea and there was a special attraction for me because my grandmother had mentioned to my mother, indiscreetly perhaps, that a 'black gentleman' was staying there. In those days people were less self-conscious about these things than they are now. I had been brought up on *The Ten Little Nigger Boys*, who today I suppose are unmentionable. If referred to at all, I presume they are described as *Ten Young*

6

John Watson M.F.H., of Ballydarton
1787–1869
Portrait by S. Catterson Smith (P.R.H.A., 1859–1864)

Gentlemen of Colour lest our children should grow up to become 'racialists'.

Little pitchers have long ears and I overheard what my grandmother said. I expect I asked some pertinent questions. I imagined she meant a negro, and I don't think I had ever seen a negro in my life although I was familiar with Man Friday in the picture books; how exciting to meet him in the flesh! So when we got to the hotel, and there was no one faintly resembling Man Friday, I was bitterly disappointed. But I had a roving eye, and while we were at tea in the public lounge I scrutinized all the other guests in turn. Presently I noticed, standing with his back to the fireplace, a gentleman of distinguished appearance who had possibly come from South America, which would have accounted for his rather swarthy complexion. If he was the black gentleman my grandmother had told me about, I thought it a poor do. However I decided to investigate further. Unobserved by my mother I left the tea table, planted myself in front of him, and surveyed him in silence for more than a minute. Then, in a shrill treble voice that could be heard all over the room, I spoke: 'Granny said you were *quite* black, but p'raps you are blacker under your clothes . . .'

It must have been a dreadful moment for my mother and indeed for everybody. Except the distinguished gentleman. He screwed his eye-glass into his eye, looked down at me with a charming smile and said, 'Ah, zee dear leetle chap! Ow I *vish* I could understan' vat 'e say!'

In September, 1911, when I was eight, I was sent to a boarding school at Seaford in Sussex. Some might say I was young to be sent away from home, but as I was an only child I think it was a wise decision.

St. Wilfrid's was a new preparatory school which only opened that term and I was one of the first boys. They taught us well, fed us well, punished us when they thought we deserved it, and showed a proper regard for all aspects of our spiritual and material welfare. On the whole it was a happy school, but I don't think it was entirely my fault that I was teased excessively. I have the misfortune to have been born with a large and oddly shaped mouth, which at St. Wilfrid's I was never allowed to forget. I had not yet reached the age when I could retort like Abraham Lincoln, overhearing an unkind remark about his appearance: 'Sir, I am as God made me.' Instead, I was apt to lose my temper and at St. Wilfrid's there was a well-known and terrifying phenomenon called 'Watson seeing red'.

Among my childhood memories certain things are in bold relief—does not that apply to us all? My nurse. Horse buses and the thrill of sitting next the driver on the roof. Ipswich where I got lost, and Hull where they pinched my fingers in a gate (I have avoided both towns since). Long sermons. The muffin man on Sunday afternoon. The hoky-poky man whose ices were taboo (*sure* to make the child sick'). Crossing sweepers. Foot warmers in railway carriages. *Peter Pan* and *Maskelyne and Devant*. Children's parties, all dressed up. Gas lighting. Learning to ride a bicycle. Balloons voyaging the sky. My first sight of an aeroplane and my first ride in a car. Scott in the Antarctic. The sinking of the Titanic. Outbreak of the First World War . . . .

We were still at war in the autumn of 1916, when I left St. Wilfrid's and went to Uppingham. Uppingham had long enjoyed a high reputation for its music, in my day under the direction of one of the Sterndale-Bennetts, and my mother had entered me at a time when she still hoped I might inherit her musical talent. Alas, her hopes were not fulfilled. I had piano lessons at St. Wilfrid's, but by the time I got to Uppingham we had both given up. Not that my instruction had been entirely wasted. I was able to play the piano for prayers in my house at Uppingham on the occasions when the regular pianist, W. S. 'Boosey' Elgood (later to become High Sheriff of Suffolk), took an evening off. He was not encouraged to do that often

8

because the only hymn I was able to play with both hands, and that from memory, was *Rock of Ages*. With constant repetition even a rock of ages tends to wear thin.

I was far from happy during the three years I spent at Uppingham, and they are the only part of my life I look back on with distaste. I expect it was largely my fault—but not entirely; I have since met other Old Uppinghamians of my period who have told me how much they disliked the place. There are others who feel differently, particularly if they were good at games, and they are to be envied. But not I think those people we meet occasionally who tell us that their schooldays were 'the happiest time of my life'. It leads me to reflect how boring the rest of their lives must have been.

It was unfortunate that I went to Uppingham—the same applied to all English public schools—in the middle of a war, when nearly all the younger masters were at the Front and old gentlemen had been dug out of retirement to do their work. A notable exception was the Reverend Reginald Herbert Owen who, at the early age of twenty-nine, had been appointed headmaster the previous year. He was not very popular in my time, mainly I expect because he was a new broom, but I am told that during the period of his headmastership he did a lot for the school. I venture no personal assessment of 'The Man', as he was called, because he hardly ever spoke to me, or I to him, except to say 'Good morning, Sir' as I doffed my hat in the High Street.

At Uppingham the supreme distinction was to be sent by your form master to the headmaster for good work. The Man shook you by the hand, told you that you were a 'good boy' and invited you to record the occasion by signing your name in a book he kept for that purpose. The supreme degradation was to be sent to him for bad work or grave misconduct; he then told you that you were a 'bad boy', caned you, and the only visible record of the event was on your buttocks. I was never sent to Reggie Owen to be caned, but went once for good work. On a

9

second occasion I was, as it were, selected for that honour, but another boy went in my place due to circumstances that I will relate.

It was the practice at Uppingham for the prefects (officially they were called 'praepostors') to take a large part of the responsibility for running the houses. It was unfortunate for me that in my house, called The Hall, so much importance was attached to proficiency in games; unfortunate, because never in my life have I been of the slightest use at any game involving a ball. The Captain of Games in The Hall was that brilliant cricketer, A. P. F. Chapman, later to become famous as Captain of England. Chapman was more than two years my senior and I used to fag for him—a job I did willingly because he was a delightful person. I was not in the least interested in cricket but had some talent for drawing and painting, and on Saturday afternoons when I was available an ageing art master, F. S. Robinson, used to take me sketching. I became available nearly every Saturday afternoon during one summer term as the result of an arrangement I made with Percy Chapman, whose brilliance on the cricket field was not matched by his prowess in the class room.

Every boy at Uppingham was required to write an essay on some given subject over the week-end for presentation to his form master on Monday morning. I had a certain reputation for writing essays, but was no good at games. Chapman was good at games, but no good at writing essays. Early in the term I shyly suggested to him that on the following week-end, when I particularly wanted to go sketching, I should write his essay in return for being excused cricket. He agreed with alacrity. I thought he was so kind that after returning from my sketching expedition I sat up late at night putting the finishing touches to the essay. I was rather proud of it when finished and left it in Chapman's study before going to bed.

On Monday, when I came back to the house at tea time, a

cluster of excited fags greeted me in the quad. Had I heard the *wonderful* news? Chapman's form master was so pleased with his essay that he was sending him to the headmaster for good work!

I admit that I was gratified. It is always satisfactory, if you have made a big effort, to see it bear fruit. In my study was a note from Chapman asking me to go and see him at once. I smoothed my hair and straightened my tie, and with a glow of pleasurable anticipation made my way to receive the thanks and congratulations of the great man. Alas for my hopes:

'You *bloody* little fool! You've heard what's happened? What the hell do you suppose I'm to do now? There's only one way out: you must write *all* my essays till the end of term.'

But Percy Chapman was a good sportsman in every sense of the word. For the rest of the term I played no cricket, did some pretty awful sketches, and for the edification of Chapman's form master produced a series of weekly essays, allegedly of Chapman's authorship, in a diminuendo of literary competence.

In a house where to excel at games was considered so important, my failure in that respect placed me low in the popularity stakes. I had little aptitude for making friends, took solitary walks and acquired a reputation for being 'mad'. That meant merely that you were an eccentric and as such to be handled, if handled at all, with caution. Partly as a result of these things (I say 'partly') I behaved oddly at times, some would say regrettably, but happily I was never found out. In the first chapter of *Which is the Justice?* a lot of my dirty linen, yellow with age, was washed in public. I see no reason to wash it again.

Long before I went to Uppingham it had been assumed by me as much as by my family that the Regular Army was my destination. I recorded earlier that both my father and grandfather had been soldiers, and so had two uncles; we were a family with a strong military tradition. At that time there were two main entries to the Regular Army. One was via the Royal Military

Academy at Woolwich (commonly called 'The Shop') and the other via the Royal Military College, Sandhurst. To join the Royal Engineers or the Royal Artillery, who were considered the 'brains' of the Army, you had to enter through Woolwich for which the examination was harder. My grandfather, being a gunner, had passed through The Shop, and so had my father. From my earliest years it was dinned into me that I must make every effort to do the hat-trick.

So at Uppingham, after a few terms on the Classical Side, I entered the Army Class. There I did reasonably well but not well enough, particularly in mathematics, for my master to think highly of my chances of passing into Woolwich. It was suggested that I should leave school early and spend the last year before the examination with an army crammer, which was not unusual in cases like mine. I was more keen to get away from Uppingham than into Woolwich, and as it was a valid means of escape I took it.

The next six months were uneventful but a relief. I lived at home in London and went daily to a firm of army crammers called Carlisle and Gregson. My examination was due in May 1921, or possibly June, but in the early spring I decided I did not want to be a soldier after all. During the 1914–1918 war, which had not long ended, we had had a surfeit of militarism and I dare say that had something to do with it. I think for me a more cogent reason was that at Uppingham I had been required to join the Officers' Training Corps and like so many things at Uppingham had disliked it. The only examination I have ever failed in was 'Certificate A', shortly before I left. I expect I did badly in the written part, but the practical was my undoing. The Brass-Hat who was my examiner asked me to name the component parts of a rifle, and when I described the nose-cap as 'the nozzle' I could see from the look in his eye that it was the last straw.

I felt however, having got so far, that I ought to take the

examination—if only because I did not want my father's family, who would be disappointed, to be able to say later that I had funked it. I told my mother of my decision and she was not disturbed, or I think surprised. I also told my paternal grandfather, Colonel Watson. He did not take me very seriously, tut-tutted a bit and said something kindly about pre-examination nerves; he was confident that once I had passed into Woolwich I would feel differently. I went ahead with my studies and my passing into The Shop, low in the list, was announced in the autumn of 1921. I wrote to the War Office resigning my cadetship a few days later. So began and ended my military career.

What should I do next? I don't think that anyone suggested a university, even if my mother could have afforded it. At that time a university education was much less common than it is now. Moreover I had not taken matric, which was a necessary qualification, and for some reason the Woolwich Entrance, although based on much the same syllabus and demanding a higher standard, was not acceptable instead. I felt that by changing horses in mid-stream I had made a pretty mess of things, and that the sooner I got down to learning how to earn my living the better.

II

Down on the Farm

Become a surveyor, *why?* – Hugh Webster – Apse Manor
Farm – Tommy Fisk – how old Bristol ate his 'nammit' –
'the smith a mighty man is he' – Robin, a spaniel (of a kind)
– equine love affair – sheep – crisis in a seaside town.

My idea was to become an architect. I had always loved buildings,
and interior decoration, and furnishings and design generally.
Also, as I mentioned earlier, I have always been rather good at
drawing. My mother sought the advice of an architect she
knew and consulted her brother, Charles Weir, who was a
solicitor. He in turn consulted Sir Aston Webb, who had
lately rebuilt the façade of Buckingham Palace and was also
responsible for the complicated white marble fountain in front
with lions at the four corners and Queen Victoria gazing down
the Mall. The consensus of opinion was that the architectural
profession was gravely overcrowded and I had better think of
something else. Naturally it was a disappointment, and I was not
yet old enough or experienced enough to protest that for a
young man, who is really keen, some degree of overcrowding
at the bottom of a profession is not of great consequence. There
is rarely overcrowding at the level he should aspire to, which
is the summit.

Charles Weir suggested as an alternative that I should become
a surveyor. I am sure he took pains to explain, but I remained
in considerable doubt about what a surveyor was. I gathered,
however, that he was connected with land and estate agency,
and as apparently I was not able to be an architect I thought I

might as well take my uncle's advice. And when he mentioned that when I was qualified his firm would probably be able to send me business, the die was cast.

In those days entry to the surveyor's profession was more likely to involve the service of articles than it does now. Articles normally lasted for at least three years. The articled pupil paid his master an annual premium, some part of which was returnable in salary towards the end of the third year if by that time his services were of value to the firm.

My uncle took a lot of trouble on my behalf. He began by approaching the late Mr. Hugh Webster,[1] as he then was. Webster was in partnership with Percival Tuckett, and Tuckett and Webster were a first-class firm in the City of London. But Webster advised that before going into a surveyor's office I ought to spend at least a year as a farm pupil, because all chartered surveyors in general practice, even if they were not country land agents, benefited by having some knowledge of agriculture. Later it was hinted to me that Tuckett and Webster had not wanted an articled pupil at that juncture and were anxious lest Charles Weir, an old client, should put pressure on them to accept me. If that was true, a year's farming staved off the evil day. If it was not true, it was excellent advice and I shall always be grateful to Hugh Webster for it. Webster was a nephew of Lord Alverstone, the Lord Chief Justice, whose family had owned estates in the Isle of Wight and who had taken his title from the village of Alverstone near Newport. His nephew still had contacts in the island, so at his instance I went there.

The parish of Apse Heath lies a few miles inland from Shanklin. The largest farm in the parish at that time, and the one that had by far the most attractive farmhouse, was Apse Manor.

The house was a long, low building with white-sashed windows and dormers in the tiled roof. The oldest part probably dated from the early years of the seventeenth century and it had

[1] Later Sir Hugh Calthrop Webster FSI, official arbitrator, 1926-1941.

16

been added to from time to time. And as is the way with so many old English farmhouses, allowed to grow naturally over the years, the result was lovely in the extreme. There was a dairy at one end and I think a wash-house. The other end joined on to the farm buildings, and it was difficult to judge from outside where the house ended and the buildings began.

In front of the house, in the shade of giant cedars, was a wide sweep of lawn. The lawn extended to the road which ran through the centre of the farm; and the boundary, invisible from the house because it dropped down to the road on a lower level, was an old stone wall. Near the top of the wall—that is to say, near the edge of the lawn—were several splendid stone urns of classical design. I suppose that they were nearly six feet high. No one seemed to know how they had got there or where they had come from, and I don't think Mr. Thomas Fisk, who owned the farm, was particularly interested. The urns had been embellished at one time with sculpted reliefs—of figures maybe, or foliage, or trees. But time and weather had taken their toll and most of the sculptures had been obliterated. Were they, I wondered, the source of inspiration for those exquisite lines:

> Thou still unravish'd bride of quietness,
> Thou foster-child of Silence and slow Time,
> Sylvan historian, who canst thus express
> A flowery tale more sweetly than our rhyme:
> What leaf-fringed legend haunts about thy shape
> Of deities or mortals, or of both,
> In Tempe or the dales of Arcady?[1]

It will be remembered that for a time Keats lived only four miles away at Ventnor.

Apse Manor was a mixed farm running to some six hundred acres. About a third was downland, excellent for sheep, which was known as 'Up Reach'. The buildings were extensive and

[1] *Ode on a Grecian Urn*: John Keats.

17

kept in beautiful order, as were the tied cottages for the stockmen and other labourers who lived on the place.

Tommy Fisk, as he was known to everyone in the Island, was a working farmer as opposed to what in those days was called a 'gentleman farmer'. The Fisks were an old Isle of Wight family who had gained their living from the soil for generations and had no reason to be ashamed of it—much the reverse. When I went to Apse Manor in 1921 I suppose Tommy Fisk must have been in his late fifties. He was a short spare man who wore 'sideboards', in those days less common facial adornments than they are now. He had a wife, a shy woman whom I scarcely got to know, a son who was a year or two older than I, and who eventually succeeded him, and a daughter. The whole family worked on the farm and Tommy kept them hard at it.

My mother had paid a premium for my pupilage, but I doubt if Fisk, a conscientious man, ever quite understood what he was expected to give in return. He himself taught me little. His method was to put me alongside one of his farm labourers, and when he thought I had been with one man long enough move me on to another. Except for a nod and a friendly inquiry how I was getting on when he came round the fields on his cob, which he did most days, he left me to myself. He certainly never attempted to teach me anything about the economics of farming, possibly because he never thought of it, but more probably because he was what the Scots call 'canny' and was reluctant to give me an insight into his financial affairs. But every few weeks, on market day, he would take me to Newport. He did not own a car and I don't remember any motor lorries on the farm; it was of course before the day of tractors. Fisk was a farmer of the old school who tended to decry any invention as 'new-fangled'. So when we went to Newport we went in his dog cart, lunched at *The Wheatsheaf* with other farmers and trotted home in the afternoon.

In truth Fisk's method suited me well. I may not have learned much about the processes of agriculture, but I learned a lot about the outlook of the countryman. To begin with, as was natural, the farm labourers looked with some suspicion on 'the young gentleman from London'. But the barriers were soon down and they came to regard me like any other youngster—albeit an extraordinarily ignorant one—who wanted to get the hang of things and was willing to become anyone's dogsbody if it would help him do so. For my part, as the months went by, I came not merely to like some of those men but almost to love them.

There was Hutchins, the carter, who taught me how to care for the horses, how to harness them to the plough or wain or waggon, and how to drive them. There was the cowman—I forget his name—who taught me to milk. And there was Bristol who, if he had donned a smock, might have walked straight out of a Morland painting. Bristol was not his proper name; he explained that he had been a sailor in his youth, had nearly always sailed from Bristol, and somehow the name had stuck.

I can see that old man now in my mind's eye. Shortish and sturdily built. Clean-shaven, at least during the early part of the week, except for a white fringe beneath his chin. Bristol always wore the same home-spun jacket; he scorned a waterproof and would throw a sack over his shoulders if it rained. He always had the same old scarf knotted loosely round his neck and in summer always wore the same dilapidated straw hat. He smoked a short clay pipe (never in the rickyard), tied his corduroy trousers tightly below the knees with string, and brought his food and other things wrapped in a red bandanna handkerchief.

Every working day throughout the year Bristol had two meals on the farm, under a hedge if it was dry or in the barn if wet. His first meal, taken punctually at ten o'clock, was 'nammit'.[1]

[1] I have never seen this word spelt. Someone in the Island once told me that 'nammit' derived from 'no meat'.

It consisted of the upper portion of a cottage loaf with a hole in it. The hole was filled with butter and on top of the bread was a lump of cheese. Bristol gripped these in his left hand using the crust, which covered the hole and had been preserved for that purpose, as a thumb-piece. And occasionally, fixed somehow between the joints of his fourth and fifth fingers, was an apple. Using a big clasp knife, he would proceed with his right hand to cut off a bit of each in turn and convey it to his mouth—bread, butter, cheese, apple . . . bread, butter, cheese, apple—until the last morsel was gone. His drink, from a bottle he kept in the recesses of a haversack, was cold tea. His dinner, taken at one, was a repeat performance except that a chunk of pickled pork replaced the cheese.

There can have been few jobs on a mixed farm like Apse Manor that old Bristol could not do. He was a highly skilled craftsman. He could plough a field as straight as a rule, sow a headland, cut and lay a hedge, thatch a rick, lamb a ewe. He did his best to teach me some of these things, but I fear he found me an inept pupil; you don't pick up in a few weeks or months the skills that a man in his late seventies has acquired laboriously during a life-time. He would watch me patiently with an amused twinkle in his blue eyes while I failed to accomplish in twice the time things which, when *he* did them, appeared so easy.

His weekly wage was around thirty shillings, and like all farm workers he lived simply. A large loaf cost fourpence-ha'penny, a pound of butter a shilling, a pint of 'mild' threepence and an ounce of shag threepence-ha'penny. Bristol grew all his vegetables in the garden behind his cottage and reared and killed his own pig; beef and mutton at one-and-sixpence a pound, except on high days and holidays, were beyond him. He was a humble man and by worldly standards poor, but he was a kind man and I am sure a good man. Long ago he plodded homeward wearily for the last time; may the good earth rest lightly on his bones.

The Author
Apse Manor Farm, 1922

I had not been long in the Island when Robin, the first of my dogs, came to me. I prefer that way of putting it to saying I bought him, for 'bought' would be a banal word to describe the beginning of such an intimate and delightful relationship. In fact he literally came to me, like a tornado, in an ecstasy of hysterical admiration, out of a shed into which his previous owner had locked him.

He was then about six months old and was alleged to be the first cross between a black labrador and a cocker spaniel. But a white chest and two white paws suggested that there might be more than one bend sinister on his escutcheon. He liked to think of himself as a spaniel, so I never argued the point. He had moreover a long feathery tail which he carried proudly—as would all spaniels if, as Lord Dunsany urged, their breeders could be restrained from the abominable practice of docking them.

We went everywhere together. Robin walked perfectly to heel, followed my bicycle, shared my dinner with Bristol in the shade of the straw stack, slept under my bed. When I was working in the fields he used to guard my jacket, which meant lie on my jacket after arranging it to his liking. The fact that I always came for my jacket sowed the idea in his doggy mind that, although obviously I was liable to forget something so lowly and unimportant as he was, anything I had worn or had had in my pocket and which therefore bore my scent was part of me, and if he waited long enough I was bound to return for it. He would wait outside a shop for almost any length of time seated on a glove, and once for nearly an hour he 'guarded' a matchbox beside a weighing machine on Waterloo Station.

Robin lived to be fourteen and was followed by Roger and Patch, both of them spaniels. Roger and Patch have appeared briefly in an earlier book, so it is only fair that Robin should have a mention in this one. Mark Twain said of a man he disliked: 'What business has that man to have a spaniel? *Spaniels should be a reward!*'

The pride of Fisk's life was his horses, and splendid beasts they were. Most of the cart horses were pure-bred Shires, but some were crossed with the longer legged Clydesdales and at least one was a Suffolk Punch. In addition there were the lighter draught horses, cobs and ponies. There was, and is, a first-rate pack of foxhounds in the Isle of Wight, but Tommy Fisk took his business of farming very seriously and I cannot remember that he ever followed them.

All the work of the farm was done by horses, except when the steam plough was hired to break up a particularly heavy bit of land. Because there were so many horses we had our own black-smith's shop and, appropriately, the blacksmith's name was Smith. In winter a forge is a nice warm place, and I made a habit of join-ing Smith at dinner time and remaining as long afterwards as he would have me on the pretext of 'helping'.

From time to time, when Fisk wanted to breed from one of his Shire mares, the stallion would pay us a visit. And I, an ignorant and inexperienced townsman, was the fascinated wit-ness of what in the country, at that time, was common enough.

A mare normally comes into season—in the Island they say she is 'horsing'—every three weeks during the summer months. The signs are unmistakable and on each occasion, during a period of about three days, she is disposed to accept a 'service'. Before there was motor transport the stallion came on foot. He was accompanied by his groom or 'tack man' who led but never rode him, lived with him, ate and drank and often slept with him, and who alone was to be trusted with the care of an animal which if provoked could be dangerous.

And what a magnificent animal he was! A superb example of equine strength, beautifully groomed and gaily caparisoned: the great head, the massive shoulders and deep chest, the burnished coat, the enormous bushy fetlocks, the mane and tail plaited with coloured silks, the matching plume flaunted above the withers, the glittering brasses . . .

Once he has arrived, no time is wasted. Two fields are separated by a stout fence, and a five-barred gate is an effective barrier notwithstanding it has been lifted temporarily from its hinges. The haltered mare is in one field and the stallion, likewise haltered, is led into the other. There are introductions over the gate, and the horse is quick to show an interest. Cautiously he makes advances, the prelude to a courtship that is charming to watch. Craning over the gate he whispers to the mare softly and flatters her, noses and nuzzles her, and eventually coaxes her by the seductive blandishment of biting her neck. Gradually—sometimes very gradually—she responds to these endearments, nosing, nuzzling and biting back.

The groom, alert and watchful, is in charge of the timing, and when he gives a signal the gate is drawn away. Now the horse's passion is at fever pitch. The mare, in an ecstasy of feminine abandon, invites him—bracing herself to withstand his weight. Then he rears and towers above her; neighing shrilly, nostrils distended, pawing the air with his unshod hooves. The groom leaps forward, and in a single gesture sweeps aside the mare's tail and guides her lover to his fulfilment. Seconds later the act is complete.

When I first went to the Isle of Wight my mother went with me. She wanted to see me safely installed and secured some respectable lodgings for me in Shanklin, where the only other lodger was a clerk in the Westminster Bank. Mrs. Jones was everything to be expected of a seaside landlady. But as time went on, being a farmer not a banker and still less a tourist, I became irritated by her frequent injunctions to 'wrap up warm'. I thought too, by contrast with the dinners that the farm labourers brought in their haversacks, that her vacuum flasks of coffee and neat parcels of thinly-cut sandwiches were effeminate. For her part, I expect she got rather tired of my muddy footmarks and Robin's, which were even muddier. She also took a not unreasonable dislike to the smell of ferrets I kept in a cage outside her kitchen window, which she fed on bread-and-milk supplemented by the dead sparrows that I had shot in her back-garden with an airgun. With no ill-feeling on either side we agreed to part, and for most of the time I was at Apse Manor I lodged with the blacksmith and his family in their tiny cottage in a village called Lake.

Squibb was the shepherd, a giant of a man with a bushy black beard. In the lambing season, which in the Isle of Wight is late autumn, he used to spend all day and night Up Reach in a wooden hut on wheels. In spite of his size and rather formidable appearance, Squibb like the others was a kindly man and I am sure there was never a more tender midwife. But I admit I never came to like his sheep. When the Creator designed the sheep it must surely have been an off-day. If there are sillier animals than sheep I have yet to meet them, although I realize it is not their fault. It is not *their* fault that besides having the same faces they all have precisely the same expression—though conceivably they think the same about us. It is not *their* fault that they invariably 'behave like sheep' and no sheep has ever been known to have an original idea in its head. It is not *their* fault that maudlin youths were said to make 'sheep's eyes' at their girl friends (today they 'chat them up'); and what could be more soporific than an imaginary count of sheep and yet more sheep going through a gate? It is no fault of the sheep that his dentures are so constructed that he cannot eat a mangold-wurzel (part of his staple diet) without leaving its saucer-shaped bottom stuck in the mud; one of my jobs was to work laboriously through the field prising them out after the sheep had left. It is not the sheep's fault that if he wants to relax and lies on his back he can no longer breathe and dies of suffocation; after a rough night another of my jobs was to go Up Reach and turn the silly things right side up. It is not the sheep's fault that . . . I could go on for a long time about sheep, but I admit being prejudiced. I am prejudiced because of a misfortune that befell me, twelve sheep and an Old English sheepdog called Bob.

On a bitterly cold morning in January twelve sheep needed to be moved a distance of four miles along a road that led through Shanklin. There was no market in that direction, and as I am sure that they were not going to the butcher I suppose their destination was another farm. For some reason Squibb was not available, so Fisk gave me the job of taking them—helped by Bob. He might well have entrusted the primary responsibility to the dog, with me (if I was needed at all) as his unskilled mate. For Bob, like most Old English sheepdogs, was extremely intelligent; he belonged to Squibb, but while working Up Reach I had got to know him. He was well-disposed towards Robin, who took no interest in sheep, and I have an idea that Robin looked on Bob as a wise if slightly eccentric uncle. But the younger dog was not in the least jealous when there developed between Bob and me the beginnings of that telepathy which exists between sheepdog and shepherd. On this occasion Robin had to be left behind, and Bob and I set off together down the main road. Under his watchful eye, compelled from time to time by a display of bogus ferocity, the sheep kept together in a neat bunch. My job, weighed down by a greatcoat reaching to the ankles and my neck encircled by my thickest muffler, was to bring up the rear.

In Shanklin our road passed Daish's Hotel on the sea front. It looked like snow, and in spite of all the clothes I was wearing the wind felt as if it were going through me. Opposite the hotel was a triangle of rough grass, owned I imagine by the municipality. Bob saw this piece of grass and, thinking he would take a short rest, decided to use it as a temporary parking place for our flock—if 'parking' is the correct word. The sheep were delighted and began at once to nibble the grass, as sheep do.

I was a bit footsore, besides being cold, and thought how agreeable it would be to slip into Daish's saloon bar for a quick one. I told Bob what I had in mind, and when he promised to keep a strict eye on the sheep until I returned I went in with

25

complete confidence. There was a good fire in the bar, and because I needed warming up I ordered a *crème-de-menthe*. It was suggested to me afterwards that for a shepherd *crème-de-menthe* is an unconventional drink.

Suddenly there was a lot of shouting and screaming outside and I feared there must have been an accident. I finished my drink and went out to see if there was anything I could do. As the King exclaimed in *Through the Looking Glass*, 'the horror of that moment I shall never forget!' Bob, whom I would have trusted almost with my life, had been untrue to me. I can only think that he too had felt the need for a drink and he had disappeared round the back of the hotel, possibly in search of the taproom.

No one, unless he has had my dreadful experience, can have any idea what twelve sheep, left on their own for five minutes, can accomplish in that short space of time. They had moved off sedately and in formation into Acacia Villas, a street at right angles to the sea-front, lined with what the estate agents call 'desirable residences'. Then, having successfully evaded the great shaggy animal whose sole purpose in life was to torment them, they had divided up. Singly, or in couples, they had forced their way through the trim hedges that formed the boundary between the front gardens of the desirable residences and the pavement, indented the beautifully kept lawns with hoof marks, trampled the rose beds, and when I arrived were browsing contentedly in the herbaceous borders.

Never can there have been a more hated person in Shanklin than I that morning! Indignant landladies, reinforced by their menfolk, came rushing out of the houses like the rats in Hamelin at the first notes of the Pied Piper. They were armed with walking-sticks, broomsticks, umbrellas and fire-irons, and what would have happened had it not been for Bob I dare not think. He arrived at full gallop from the direction of the taproom, and I could see from his expression that his conscience was troubling him. But he took in the situation at a glance, rounded up the sheep, and before some of the angry householders had exhausted their vocabularies had got them all back on the triangle. There they resumed nibbling the municipal grass exactly as though nothing had happened, and as if Acacia Villas was not a scene of ghastly devastation. As for Bob, he planted himself in front of me, wagged his stump of a tail and clearly expected to be congratulated. Need I say that there were complaints, offensive letters and threatened claims for compensation? Tommy Fisk was angry and I felt that in the circumstances there was nothing I could do but tell him the whole story. In the result, I was never allowed to take charge of sheep again.

Such was the first phase of my apprenticeship to the surveyor's profession. My year in the Isle of Wight came to an end and I returned to London. Clad in a black jacket and pinstripe trousers, I paid an unexpected call on Hugh Webster. He expressed himself as pleased to see me, but I resisted the temptation to yield to his suggestion that a second year at Apse Manor might be a good thing. Instead he gave me an introduction to Sir John Oakley. Sir John, at my initial interview in Charles Street, regretted that there was no peg in his office an articled pupil could hang his hat on. Later however Mr. Norman Garrard, the second partner, agreed to take me. And that is how, in October 1922, I came to be in their drawing office.

Buzz . . . buzz . . . buzz . . . went the house telephone beside the fireplace: 'Will Mr. Watson please come down?'

III

Articled Pupilage, the Lighter Side

Daniel Smith, Oakley and Garrard – Norman Garrard and his
advice about lunch – coffin on the roof – little-known facts
about the Horse Guards Parade – Sir John Oakley and his
lost file – orange silk pyjamas and the bank.

Were I asked to describe Norman Garrard to someone who had
never had the good fortune to know him, I should soon find
myself referring to his 'charm'. Charm: what a vague indefinable
thing that is! It can be superficial like a veneer, or transparent
like a glaze that fails to hide the common clay beneath; or it can
be the outward manifestation of a combination of human
qualities that we call character. His was of the last.

Garrard was short in stature but extremely good-looking.
His greying hair was brushed backward at the temples and, as
was fashionable in those days, he had a slightly drooping mous-
tache. Always impeccably dressed, I have heard him described—
I think aptly—as an elegant man. Although modest and rather
shy, he was readily approachable, especially by the young,
devoid as he was of pomposity or affectation. He had countless
friends and enjoyed good living, and he conveyed the impression
of wanting everyone around him to share in his enjoyment.

He was not a very clever man, as he himself freely admitted;
nor was he distinguished in the practice of his profession. Yet
he brought to his work, which consisted largely of valuation,
keen perception and sound judgment. The outstanding quality
of the man was his innate kindliness, whence derived the courtesy
that reflected his interest in, and his genuine sympathy with,

29

the likes and dislikes, hopes and fears, aspirations and disappointments of other people. Is it a wonder that he was greatly loved?

It was only later that I discovered these endearing qualities. But at my first interview, when I had found my way from the drawing office, at least I got an inkling of the sort of man he was. He was seated at a rather untidy writing-table in the centre of a comfortably furnished room. On one side he was flanked by an elderly man called Tom Torrance, his technical assistant who went nearly everywhere with him. On the other side was his secretary, a lady of uncertain age called Miss Gardner, who obviously adored him; she combined the duties of private secretary with those of counsellor, nurse, remembrancer and benevolent aunt. When he was about to leave the office she saw to it that he had his hat, his muffler, his overcoat, his gloves, his umbrella, the correct papers, Tom Torrance and the appointment he proposed to keep.

As I knocked and entered Mr. Garrard looked up. 'Well Watson, how *very* nice to see you! It's high time we spent a day together and Torrance and I taught you something. Isn't it Torrance?' Torrance, rather doubtfully, agreed that it was.

'I don't suppose you know we manage an estate belonging to Oxford University at Bexley down in Kent? Well, we do. I've not been there for some time and there are several little matters that need looking into. Aren't there Torrance?' Torrance, reluctantly, agreed that there were.

'Will tomorrow be convenient for you, Watson?' I made haste to say that it would.

'Capital! Then your job is to get busy at once and plan our day; you'll hire a car and make all the necessary arrangements. That's right, isn't it Miss Gardner?' Miss Gardner, suspiciously, agreed that it was.

'Now tell me: what is the most important thing in a day's work by a surveyor? Of course you know that?'

Regrettably I did *not* know, if only because as yet there had been no one to instruct me. The question without notice had me stumped. Could it be to remember to take with me a map, a notebook or perhaps a compass? I was pondering whether any of these answers would sound sensible when Garrard continued:

'Clearly you don't know. Now Watson, here's your first lesson in the duties of a surveyor and I hope you will remember it all your life. The most important thing in his day's work is *lunch*. Decide in advance at what time you will lunch, where you will lunch, and if possible what you will have for lunch. *Then build the rest of the day round it.*'

He was a superb raconteur. Too shy to excel as an after-dinner speaker, he was at his best at home over the port. He had an immense fund of stories, also of improper limericks in which if they were witty he took a childish delight. I remember he had three versions of the one about the gentleman from the Wiltshire town who had the misfortune to be anatomically unbalanced.

Garrard loved London and was a prominent member of the London Society, the Wren Society and the Pepys Club. It was a joy to travel across London beside him in a car or a taxi. (I never knew him travel by bus.) He asked me whether I could see two tall chimney stacks on the roof of a house in Kensington that we were about to pass, and obediently I craned out of the window and said I could. He then told me that until recently there had lain between those chimney stacks what from the pavement appeared to be a slab. In fact it was a stone sarcophagus containing a coffin, and in the coffin was the body of a man. A former owner of the house, who had some phobia about burial, had willed life-interests in his substantial fortune as long as the beneficiaries kept his body 'above ground'. They had dutifully carried out his wishes until the last of them died and the new owner declined to take over this macabre object with the usual tenant's fixtures and fittings.

Did I know, he asked me, how it had happened that the late nineteenth-century extension to the Admiralty on the north side of Horse Guards Parade was faced with red brick panels? I admitted I did not. He then explained that the original design by a distinguished architect of the period had been different. The façade of the new building was to have matched the stone façade of the Old Admiralty by William Kent, which fronts the east side of the Parade and runs through into Whitehall.

The plans and elevations had been submitted to the Lords Commissioners of the Admiralty and approved, but shortly before the work started the architect received a message from Windsor. It was to the effect that Queen Victoria wished to see the design and wanted him to go down to Windsor Castle for that purpose. He at once sent a telegram to his clerk, instructing him to collect the plans and elevations and meet him next morning at Paddington Station.

Everything appeared to go as he had intended. Arrived at Windsor, he was driven up to the castle and ushered into the royal presence. The Queen spoke some gracious words of welcome and told the distinguished architect how much she had been looking forward to seeing the drawings of the building that he proposed to erect in this important position. He bowed; the container was opened; the plans were unrolled. They were *not* the plans of the new Admiralty extension! Instead, by some inexcusable mistake, his clerk had given him the plans and elevations, mainly in red brick, of a mental hospital he had been commissioned to build on the outskirts of Dublin.

The wretched man stood speechless. Words failed him. What words could be found to account for such a ghastly happening? But mercifully the Queen spoke first: 'What a charming and original design! *So* clever of you not just to copy the old building on the east side of the Parade! We think your elevations beautiful and are greatly pleased.'

He no longer needed words, except perhaps to tell his clerk later what he thought of him; but he did need to devote a great deal more time and labour to this project. He returned to his

A. Norman Garrard
1868–1947

office and redrew the elevations to conform to those of the Irish mental hospital. 'And that,' concluded Garrard, 'explains why the extension of the Admiralty to the north of the Horse Guards Parade is faced with panels of red brick.'

Garrard's senior partner, and head of the firm since 1898, was Sir John Hubert Oakley, whom I mentioned in the last chapter. He was a very different type of man from Garrard, but in saying that I do not for a moment seek to disparage him. Oakley too was a kindly person, and although I never came to know him intimately he was consistently charming to me over a long period.

Like Garrard he was a handsome man, but taller and more powerfully built, and he had been a considerable athlete in his youth. He had a first-class brain and without doubt was the most distinguished chartered surveyor of his day; when I entered his office in 1922 he was fifty-six and at the height of his powers. He had been president of the Surveyors' Institution (as the Royal Institution of Chartered Surveyors was then called)[1] in 1918, its jubilee year, and had been awarded a knighthood. He was raised to G.B.E. ten years later. Sir John's reputation as a valuer was unsurpassed and his services as an arbitrator were in constant demand; on one occasion it had fallen to him to value what in effect was the entire city of Hong Kong to resolve a dispute between two government departments. He had also been a member of a series of royal commissions and governmental committees, of which one of the most important was the Irish Grants Committee between 1926 and 1930.

Sir John's room in the office was on the ground floor immediately under Norman Garrard's, and as it opened off the entrance hall he was more vulnerable to intruders than his partner. His private secretary, Miss Knox, who filled some but not all the

[1] From 1868 until 1881, it was called 'The Institution of Surveyors'; from 1881 until 1930, 'The Surveyors' Institution'; from 1930 until 1946, 'The Chartered Surveyors' Institution'; since 1946, 'The Royal Institution of Chartered Surveyors'.

roles assumed by her opposite number on the floor above, was Sir John's personal body-guard as well. Like Miss Gardner she was devoted to her boss, and I think she would gladly have given her life for him.

How grateful we old men should be to our private secretaries! Looking back on our professional lives, how on earth should we have managed without them? A private secretary has to cope with her employer, week in week out, all through the year—when he is tired, overworked or frustrated; when he is angry or ill-tempered; when he is depressed; worst of all, on those dreadful mornings when everything seems to be wrong for no other reason than that he has got out of bed on the wrong side. During the thirty odd years that I was in practice I was wonderfully well served in that respect; also by Bridget O'Brien, not my secretary but my housekeeper, who likewise bore the burden and heat of the day. Dear friends that they are, I should like to record in passing my appreciation of their loyalty and selfless devotion to my interests.

Miss Gardner and Miss Knox were of the same quality as those who served me. Partly because of Miss Knox's system of defences, but also because I was Norman Garrard's pupil, I seldom went into Sir John's room or undertook a job for him. When I did one of his jobs he was always courteous and appreciative, but I am bound to say that when I was a very young man I found him a little formidable. I expect that for his part he thought me an oddity, which was not surprising. It was in this period that the Other Chap[1] first went to prison, and Sir John found it difficult to regard as a serious aspirant to the chartered surveyor's profession a boy who appeared to spend most of his spare time mixing with criminals. When, having passed my Surveyors' Institution finals, I asked Sir John if he would kindly propose me for membership, I recall his remarking as he signed the form: 'I can't think what all this is *for*. I always thought you wanted

---

[1] See Introduction, *ante*, p. xiii

to become a prison governor or something of that kind.' In truth, he was not far wrong.

Then there was the unhappy occasion when I left his file, a fat one, on the top of a London bus. In those far-off days the upper decks of buses were open to the weather, and I think I must have left it on a seat. Wherever I left it, the wind took hold, blew it over the side and deposited it in the gutter of the New North Road. If it was not actually in the New North Road, I know for certain it was in that neighbourhood because of the addresses from which bits of the file came back. It had evidently disintegrated, and some of the bits, torn and muddy, were returned by worthy citizens from the goodness of their hearts; others by citizens perhaps less worthy because clearly they hoped to be rewarded. There were covering letters:

'Sir, Last evening when I cum out of the Pig and Whistle I found on the pavement . . .' 'Dear Sir John, I think these papers must belong to you. This morning, getting off a bus at the corner of the New North Road and Compton Avenue, I found them wrapped round a lamp-post . . .' 'Dear Sir Oakley, I begs to send your Lordship the enc. papers which as your name on them. I found them Tuesday down a manhole . . .' And so on.

It was very distressing. On discovering my loss I succeeded in bypassing Miss Knox and in sackcloth and ashes confessed to Sir John personally. Naturally he was displeased and said so, but on the whole he was nice about it, and I left his room buoyed up by the hope that with the passage of time I might earn his full forgiveness. The return of his papers (not even *all* his papers) over an extended period by the instalment system, the arrival of each instalment being the subject of a public announcement by Miss Knox, kept the wound open.

Oakley died in December, 1946, in his eightieth year. Whether it was because of the incident with the file which lingered in his mind, or for some other reason, I don't think he ever believed I had really grown up. The last conversation I had with him was a strange one. A few months before his death, on the 26 May 1946, I attended a meeting of the Council of the Royal Institution of Chartered Surveyors at which he was present. It was my first attendance as a new member of council and greatly to my surprise I was elected a vice-president. By tradition a vice-presidency normally leads to the presidency a few years later.

A day or two after the council meeting I met Sir John in St. James's Street at the corner of St. James's Place. He was walking slowly, leaning on his stick, down the hill towards his club. He stopped to congratulate me and was good enough to say he was sure that I would make an admirable president. Then he added something which amazed me. 'But you realize, don't you,' he added, 'that the whole thing was a mistake?'

I was silent for a few seconds while I collected myself. Then, respectfully, I ventured to ask him what the mistake had been. 'Why' he replied, 'surely you realize it was *that other Watson* they intended to elect? Most extraordinary! *Most* extraordinary! By some mistake they mixed you up.'

He congratulated me again and told me once more what a good president I should make. Then he patted me on the shoulder and resumed his progress down the street. 'Most extraordinary . . . *most* extraordinary . . . some mistake. . . .' The words were wafted back to me as he moved out of my hearing. Alas, he did not live until my presidency, but I hope I fulfilled his expectations. I never saw the grand old man again.

There were two more partners in the firm at the time I was serving my articles, both comparatively young. One was Ted Gillett, then in his thirties; basically he was an urban surveyor and undertook among other things a lot of urban property management. Sir Edward Gillett, as he now is, was president of the Royal Institution of Chartered Surveyors i n 1945-46, thus following in Oakley's footsteps. The junior partner was A. F. (Bim) Freeman. He was on the rural side, and as I was mainly concerned to gain urban experience I had little to do with him. Arthur Garrard, Norman Garrard's son, married Bim Freeman's daughter.

There were four pupils in the office besides me, although Arthur, who had been articled to that fine old firm of land agents, Nantes and Sanctuary in Bridport, would have been more accurately described as an 'improver'. Later he left his father's firm and, after being surveyor-general of the Duchy of Lancaster, became estates bursar to St. John's College, Oxford; he died in August, 1973. Holroyd (Roy) Chambers arrived a year before I did and was attached to Gillett. He is a son of the late Sir Theodore Chambers, the distinguished surveyor who became the first chairman of Welwyn Garden City. Roy until his retirement was surveyor to the Duchy of Cornwall. The third of my fellow pupils was R. H. (Reggie) Baucher—an Old Harrovian, extremely hard-working and, I am ashamed to say, a good deal better behaved in the office than I was. Reggie has recently retired from his partnership in Cluttons.

The fourth pupil was supernumerary. Lord Morven Cavendish-Bentinck was a younger son of the Sixth Duke of Portland and I really never quite understood why he came to us. He had been preceded as a pupil in the office by his elder brother, the Marquess of Titchfield.[1] I imagine that the Duke, in anticipation of his heir's succession to great landed estates, had wisely arranged for him to be taught something about estate management. Titchfield was very popular in the office and he has told me since how much he enjoyed his time there. Maybe it was that which led Morven to follow his example. But whatever the reason I am happy he did so, because Morven Bentinck was one of the most agreeable and sweet-tempered young men I have ever met.

He was a fine musician and a talented pianist; music was the supreme interest in his life. He died in 1951 at the age of fifty. I don't think Morven was very interested in surveying, and it was accepted in the office that he was free to come and go as he

---

[1] Now the Seventh Duke.

pleased. When he was not at a symphony concert or a music festival he would arrive in his little Wolseley car, park it in St. James's Square, apologize for his temporary absence and muck in with the rest. It was typical of Morven that he would cheerfully undertake the grubbiest jobs—searching for woodworm in the dark recesses of a cobwebby attic, or testing drains which involved a descent into the bowels of the earth.

Need I say that upstairs in the pupils' department Morven came in for his full share of leg-pulling? He took it all in good part, even on one occasion when I am sorry to say we behaved outrageously. Morven was artistic and had a nice taste in men's underwear. Returning one day after a long lunch hour, he had a parcel under his arm and (unwisely as it turned out) said he would like to show us what he had bought. He undid the parcel and displayed to our admiring gaze a suit of brilliant orange silk pyjamas. He then showed his purchase to Mr. Knowles, a long-suffering senior member of the staff who occupied a back room adjoining the drawing office. Knowles reminded him that they were due to go out together that after-noon. Morven apologized profusely for having forgotten the appointment, rewrapped the pyjamas, laid the parcel on a shelf—and out they went.

Within a minute of their departure the devil entered the room and said he had had an idea which he thought might appeal to us. Immediately under Knowles' room was the room occupied by the typists, and all the rooms at the back of the building over-looked a wide open space. It was bounded on the east by the backs of offices in Lower Regent Street, on the north by those of shops in Jermyn Street, on the west by those of clubs and insti-tutions in St. James's Square. Between the pupils and the typists there was a feud. The idea was that we should construct, out of wastepaper baskets, surveying instruments and other materials available in the drawing office, the effigy of a monster, dress it in Morven's orange pyjamas, attach it to the end of a 50 feet surveyor's tape—and scare the typists by dangling it outside their windows.

This devilish plan had no sooner been implanted in our innocent minds than we began to act on it, and the appearance of our monster was alarming in the extreme. We tied him to the end of a tape and, watched by the staffs of countless offices who had their noses glued to the windows, lowered him down the back of our building. At that moment Mr. Norman Garrard entered the room.

Of course he went out again at once, for he was too much of a gentleman to stay for a moment in a place where clearly he was not wanted. But someone lost his head and slammed the window shut. It may be that the sudden pull on the tape turned the monster topsy-turvy; whatever happened, the pyjamas, which were only lightly knotted fell off. We reopened the window and leaned out. Far, far below, a little heap of material coloured a brilliant orange lay limply on the flag-stones of an enclosed area to which the only access, as far as we could judge, was from the basement of the Westminster Bank.

It was most unfortunate. As tends to happen on these occasions, we bitterly regretted that we had been so impetuous, for what we had thought would be funny was now not funny at all. Somehow the pyjamas *must* be recovered, if possible before Morven Bentinck returned. The only way to get from our building into the enclosed area was by climbing down a stack-pipe, but we were young and agile in those days and could probably have managed it. The trouble was it was scarcely something we wanted to attempt in a glare of publicity, lest some well-meaning person should do what in that period was equivalent to dialling 999. But how could we do it secretly when we were under observation from all those office windows by idle people, who had nothing better to do in their employers' time than stare? We came to the conclusion that the only way was to stay late at the office, explain to the housekeeper that because of pressure of business we had to work overtime, and perform the operation under cover of darkness.

We were still debating the matter when Morven returned with Knowles and the situation was explained to them. Morven, not unreasonably, was angry that this 'foolery' should have resulted in the loss of his expensive new pyjamas. Knowles was angry that the foolery should have taken place in *his* room which by now was in considerable disorder. Morven thought nothing of the stack-pipe plan, and it was characteristic that instead of being offensive (had he not the right to be?) he was more concerned with the danger of someone breaking his neck. 'Nonsense!' he exclaimed. 'I'll have none of it. All that is needed is for one of you to go round the corner to the Westminster Bank, explain confidentially what has happened, and ask if they will kindly allow you to go through their basement to collect my pyjamas. They can't possibly refuse.'

That idea did not appeal to us. Admittedly there were dangers in the stack-pipe plan, but to call on a strange bank with such a strange story would surely arouse their suspicions, and the consequences might be more sinister than just being sent away with a flea in one's ear. However, the owner of the pyjamas was adamant. 'Come,' he said, 'which of you is it to be?' There was no answer.

Then one of the pupils had a better idea: 'Why don't *you* go, Morven?'

The effrontery of the suggestion shook Morven. 'Why of all people should *I* go?' he demanded. But we all thought it a good suggestion and flattered him by saying that he was so much more tactful than we were. We took full responsibility for what had happened, but after all they were *his* pyjamas. Someone remarked casually that it looked like rain. 'And damn it all,' we said, '*you're a lord* and we aren't; no bank can afford to be rude to a lord.'

He was silent for nearly a minute. Then, wearing his bowler

hat and an air of determination and firmly grasping his neatly furled umbrella, believe it or not, he went.

I have only Morven's account of what happened in the bank. In those days banks closed at three o'clock and he had some difficulty in getting in, but once inside all went smoothly. He presented his card to one of the clerks and asked if he could *possibly* see the manager on what he described as extremely private and personal business.

Now the managers of important banks dislike being called on without notice out of office hours, but of course there are exceptions, and an unexpected visit by the son of one of our wealthiest dukes, on extremely private and personal business, was one of them. Morven was bowed into the manager's sanctum and offered an imposing chair, and he sat down on the edge of it. The manager seated himself on the opposite side of the desk. There was a pause until the manager decided it was for him to begin.

'It is the greatest pleasure to meet you, my lord, even if at rather short notice. In what way can my bank assist your lordship? We shall be delighted to be of service.' [Was he going to open an account?]

His lordship was non-committal and explained for the second time that his business was extremely private and personal.

'All business brought to the Westminster Bank is regarded as confidential. If you will be good enough to tell me what the trouble is, you can have confidence in my discretion. [Was he hard up and wanted a loan?] Please, Lord Morven, tell me.'

Morven grew red and fidgeted with the handle of his umbrella, which he had taken in with him. Then he cleared his throat:

'I really am most *terribly* sorry. I just don't know how to explain. You have in your basement a small open area at the back of the building. [The manager, a little surprised, agreed that he had.] By an unfortunate accident, a most unfortunate accident, my pyjamas have fallen into it. And they are my *new* pyjamas,

41

orange ones made of pure silk that I had only just bought. Will you be so *very* kind as to allow me to go out through your basement door and pick them up?'

Morven could never remember exactly what the manager said in reply; I gather he was a little dazed. But he quickly recovered himself, for the honour of the Westminster Bank, which had promised to be of service, was at stake—and after all he *was* a lord. . . . Together they descended the basement stairs so that Morven might fetch his pyjamas. And fetch them he did.

IV

Articled Pupilage, the Graver Side

Examinations and all that – vagaries of valuation – 'Curiouser and curiouser' cried Alice – manorial land tenure – drainage and sanitation – baths, bogs, privies, pots.

The reader will have gathered from what I have written that the office of Daniel Smith, Oakley and Garrard in Charles Street was potentially an excellent training stable for young surveyors. The firm had a first-class general practice, it was not so large a practice as to prevent a pupil if he so desired seeing something of nearly everything that went on, and it was a practice conducted in accordance with the highest ethical standards. But to what extent, the reader may be asking himself, did these rather frivolous young men profit by all this? *Did they do any work?*

Actually we did, and the proof of the pudding was in the eating. All three of us, if I remember rightly, passed the qualifying examinations of the Surveyors' Institution at our first attempt. And later in our professional careers, although no one achieved the eminence of an Oakley, each of us found a respectable niche in the profession.

The Institution in those days had four sub-divisions of membership, and the syllabuses of its examinations (only two of them technical—Intermediate and Final) were geared to them. Sub-division I was 'Land Agency' and its principal or 'typical' subject was *Agricultural Valuations*. Sub-division II was 'Valuations' with *The Principles and Practice of Valuation* as its typical subject. Sub-division III was either 'Building' with *Constructive and*

43

Working Drawings as the typical subject, or 'Quantities'. Sub-division IV, highly specialized, was 'Mining'. In 1926, when I was elected a Professional Associate, the Institution had some 16,000 members; today there are more than 45,000.[1]

All three pupils had decided to read for Sub-division II, 'Valu-ations'. We learned the practical side by accompanying, and I hope occasionally assisting, one or other of the partners or some senior member of the staff; we learned the theory at the College of Estate Management, then in Lincoln's Inn Fields. The College offered two kinds of course. One was on the spot and necessitated an almost nightly attendance at lectures. The other was a correspondence course and copies of the lectures were posted to you. I chose the correspondence course because it seemed to me a good idea to have the whole of the subject-matter in typescript lest one went to sleep at a lecture, or by some mistake failed to turn up. Knowles, in his little room behind the drawing office, was a great stand-by. He had a thorough knowledge of theory and practice and was always ready to help. Indeed, if he feared there was a danger of your failing to satisfy the examiners, he would offer himself as a private coach.

Valuing is not, never was, and never will be an exact science. It is a subjective exercise. A valuation is no more than an opinion based upon an assessment by the valuer of influences that he personally has noted and weighed. As such, it is not 'a fixed and permanent part of the thing to be valued, but depends on outside factors, the chief of these being the desire to possess the property which exists in the minds of persons other than the owner and their ability to pay for it'.[2] The extent and intensity of the 'desire to possess' determine supply and demand. If supply exceeds demand, values tend to fall; if demand exceeds supply, they rise.

---

[1] Corporate members and associate classes in each case.
[2] *Modern Methods of Valuation of Land, Houses and Buildings* (2nd edn. 1949), D. M. Lawrance, H. G. May and W. H. Rees, p. 2.

It is a common fallacy among laymen that a thing—be it a building, a book or a bath tub—has only *one* value. It can have several. Consider, for example, in the field of real estate, the value of a rambling Victorian house for fire insurance compared with its value for estate duty. The first will almost certainly exceed the second and may greatly exceed it. To value higher for fire insurance (where the question is 'What could be the maximum loss in case of fire?) than for estate duty (where the question is 'What would it fetch if offered for sale?') would be legitimate and correct.

The average layman has no conception of the multifarious purposes for which today valuations of land and buildings have to be made. I have mentioned two, and here are some more. Letting; sale or purchase; mortgage; enfranchisement of a leasehold, capital-gains tax; rating; compensation for various happenings such as compulsory acquisition, an adverse planning decision, injurious affection, severance.

Valuation is obviously closely related to buying and selling. Some people give the impression of having been born salesmen; one suspects that they trafficked with their fellow babies at a profit to themselves in the daily feed of Glaxo. Others are incapable of selling anything to anybody, except at a price substantially less than what they paid for it. The late Mr. Claude Leigh, about whom I shall have more to say in a later chapter, was a valuer and a buyer and seller of landed property of the first order. He had what he and other valuers sometimes call a 'hunch'. As managing director of one of our biggest property companies, it constantly fell to Leigh to advise his board how much they should pay for this property which had been offered them, or for that property, or for the shares of another property company which they had an opportunity to acquire. He was well served by a competent staff. But time and again I have seen his top valuer lay before him an elaborate valuation on sheets of foolscap, in which every consideration and every contingency had been taken into account. Leigh, who had seen the property for himself, would scan it quickly: 'No, Lush, we are not paying so much as that.' Or alternatively: 'Buy it by all means if you can get it at that price, but if you can't we'll pay up to £x more.' And the amount of £x would make Lush gasp. Of course Leigh was not always right (what investor is?) but he was right more often than not.

The valuation of a property for investment purposes—still more of an estate or of a collection of properties—can be extremely complicated. Estimates have to be made under a number of heads: current rental value and the security afforded; future rental value, when obtainable, security again; capital expenditure likely to be incurred; development possibilities; facilities for a mortgage, the rate of interest chargeable, the resultant equity return—and so on and so forth. Claude Leigh did not under-rate the importance of these estimates and undoubtedly relied on them. But there were occasions when, like other experienced valuers, he relied even more on his hunch. What *is* a valuer's hunch? Certainly it is not a lucky shot in the dark; nor is it an instinctive conclusion deriving from some mysterious gift that others lack. I believe a valuer's hunch is best described as the product of a human computer. Besides a capacity for quick and accurate arithmetic, the computer has sound judgment and a long memory; feed him with the salient facts and he digests them instantly.

Today in certain classes of valuation—notably for compensation for compulsory purchase—the mental processes demanded of a valuer are much more complicated than in my youth. That is because of the assumptions which the law now requires him to make. A large part of the business of valuing in this field tends to be theoretical rather than practical, owing to a variety of statutory and common-law hypotheses that govern his approach. Most of these hypotheses relate to town-planning; planning determines user; user affects value. It is common

46

knowledge that planning permission for the development of a piece of land can vastly increase its price. Even the bare possibility of obtaining such planning permission can create a 'hope value' which the potential purchaser, and therefore the valuer, takes into account. But it is not always merely a matter of looking forward. Under modern legislation, particularly when valuing for the assessment of compensation, the valuer has also to look backward and base his valuation not on what *did* happen but on what *might have* happened.

Take, for example, a valuation made to fix the compensation payable to a landowner, whose land within the designated area of one of our New Towns is to be compulsorily acquired. The coming of the New Town and its expansion over a period of years have influenced the development of land, and consequently its value, for miles around. Yet Parliament has ordained that the valuer, in arriving at his figure for the land in question, must proceed on the hypothesis that the New Town has never been built, planned or even thought of. 'Curiouser and curiouser!' cried Alice in Wonderland. 'Curiouser and curiouser!' mutters the valuer, likewise in Wonderland, when he finds himself obliged by law to ignore the actual and peer behind the translucent curtain that divides the actual from the merely probable. My experience as a member of the Lands Tribunal taught me this lesson: given the most skilled, honest and conscientious valuer, his findings on the basis of some of these unrealistic assumptions are often only intelligent guess-work.

This dissertation on the subject of valuers and valuing may be thought irrelevant to my immediate theme. But I make no apology for two reasons. First, because what I have written may bring home to potential candidates for entry to the chartered surveyor's profession, and the parents of such candidates, that proficiency in the art of valuing is unlikely to be acquired quickly. Yet to a young man or woman with discernment and imagination, who will look upon these conundrums as a challenge and

47

is mathematically inclined, the principles and practice of valuation can be fascinating in the extreme. Others would be advised to leave this branch of the profession alone so far as they are able to do so. My second reason for including it is for instruction of the non-technical reader. I trust he will deplore, as I do, an insistence by the legislature upon the observance of hypothetical considerations that no layman can be expected to understand; laws which ordinary people of reasonable intelligence cannot understand are in general bad laws. Not only by the experts, but by all and sundry, justice should be seen to be done.

But the syllabus of professional examinations for Sub-division II of the Surveyors' Institution contained a number of subjects beside the making of valuations. For a non-lawyer there was quite a bit of law—of Landlord and Tenant, Vendor and Purchaser, Arbitrations. Other subjects were Imperial and Local Taxation, Town-planning (then in its infancy), Development of Building Estates, Drainage and Sanitation, and Enfranchisement of Copyholds. There was, and there still is, an omission that I have always thought regrettable. Although the candidate was required to master 'the powers and duties' of an arbitrator—which he was unlikely to become for a long time—he was not expected to learn anything about the principles and practice of giving expert evidence, a duty likely to befall him much earlier. Recently I noted with satisfaction that the Institute of Arbitrators has come to realize the importance of instruction in this matter.

Of all the subjects in the syllabus, the one I found the most interesting was Enfranchisement of Copyholds—with Drainage and Sanitation running a close second. The form of English tenure called copyhold, now extinct, was of great antiquity and is said to have evolved from the Saxon system of 'bondage'. The Normans probably admitted the bondsmen to fealty, the tenants were called 'villeins' and the tenure 'villeinage'. The obligation by a tenant to render service to the superior from whom he held was fundamental to the Feudal System. All land was held either directly from the Crown, or from an intermediary who himself held from the Crown. The villein was a tenant of the lord of the manor, and his title was a copy of the relevant entry in the manorial court-roll wherein all changes of occupation ('admittances' and 'surrenders') were recorded.

The copyholder owed certain services to the lord of the manor, who also enjoyed other privileges. Among the other privileges were rights to waifs (stolen goods waived by a thief during his flight), estrays (cattle found wandering), wrecks, the property of felons and suicides, treasure trove, tolls, markets and fairs, rights to warren and piscary (taking of game and fish) and authority to convene manorial courts.

Manors had 'customs' which were legally enforceable, the special customs of some manors dating from time immemorial. They included 'gavelkind', prevalent in parts of Kent, whereby on the death of a copyholder the inheritance passed to all his sons in equal shares. Another was 'borough English' or 'burgage', whereby the whole of the inheritance passed to the youngest son. It may be thought that the custom of burgage was a safeguard against the risk of the eldest son being illegitimate, which was not improbable if the lord of the manor had exercised what in France was known as *droit de seigneur*—assuming that that custom ever existed, which is doubtful.

In modern times the services due by a copyholder to the lord consisted principally of money payments on the happening of certain events. 'Heriots', nearly all of which were commuted into money, were originally paid in kind. On the death of the tenant, on a change of tenancy, more rarely on the heir to the lord coming of age, the heriot payable by the copyholder might comprise 'the best beast' or 'the second-best beast', or the best or second-best of his chattels. The selection was made by or on behalf of the lord and there was no appeal. Fines, sometimes

49

called 'reliefs', were paid in consideration of an admittance or surrender, or on the alienation by the copyholder of some part of his property under a licence to let. 'Rents of assize' or 'quit rents' were paid by most copyholders, the description 'quit rent' being appropriate when the amount of the payment had been arrived at by commuting all dues.

Under the Law of Property Act 1922 (often referred to as the *Birkenhead Act*) all copyholds and other special tenures of land were abolished subject to the payment of compensation, but because the Act needed amendment its coming into force was delayed until 1926. So it was that during the three years or more that I was studying for my examinations, late 1922 to early 1926, the subject of copyholds and their coming enfranchisement was under constant discussion. I found their history, which mirrored the history of England, absorbing, and in my examination probably gained more marks for this subject than for any other. For practical purposes during my professional life it has been of no value to me at all.

Drainage and Sanitation can be *fun*! And if the reader is a refined and superior person, who regards the subject as slightly sordid and is surprised by the description 'fun', I offer this advice. Lay aside this book for a moment, close your eyes, try to recall your childhood and that *memorable* day at the sea-side.

Was it at Cromer or Budleigh Salterton? Can you see in your mind's eye the wide expanse of virgin sand rising gently to the dunes? The line of waves, rippling and frolicking in the sunshine as they advanced—slowly, inexorably, each in competition with the last to be a little way ahead? The splendid castle you had built upon the beach? Its courtyard? Its moat? The inland lake, bounded by ramparts of indurate sand, which you had filled and replenished with countless buckets? The Grand Canal leading to the sea? Your feverish spade-work to repair the ravages of the incoming tide? That sigh of relief when just in time it turned? The reinforcement of the crumbling ramparts?

The satisfying spectacle of the flooded courtyard emptying by the planned route? The discovery that at least on one point your teacher was right: left to itself, water runs downhill? You enjoyed yourself immensely? Of course you did. Then don't tell me that the subject of Drainage and Sanitation, which is founded on that axiom, cannot be fun!

It is no part of the duty of a chartered surveyor, particularly if he is qualified only in the Valuations Sub-division, to design systems of drainage, refuse disposal or water supply. These are jobs for experts, but the surveyor in general practice is expected to have some superficial knowledge. A client has detected a bad smell. It may be a dead rat under the floor boards or an elderly lamb chop in a dark corner of the larder, but a bad smell needs to be investigated. Or something is wrong with the water system —the tank has overflowed and water is cascading down the front of the house. Or the boiler is making strange noises and your client fears it may blow up.

I tested many drains in my youth. One method is by a smoke test. The surveyor lights a smoke rocket, inserts it in the drain to be tested and seals both ends of the pipe. Then he sniffs. If he smells smoke there is likely to be a leak, and if a cloud of smoke rises from the rose garden there is no doubt about it. A water test is generally considered more effective. Soil drains are laid in lengths and a well-laid drain has a manhole or inspection chamber at each bend. The method is for the surveyor, equipped with a bicycle pump and what resembles a deflated balloon, to descend into one of the manholes. He stuffs the balloon into the pipe where it enters the manhole and blows it up, the lower end of the length of pipe to be tested being thus sealed. He then walks upstream, and with the aid of a hose pipe fills the pipe to be tested and the upper manhole with water. Having marked its level on the brickwork, he recalls the advice of the late Mr. Norman Garrard and goes to lunch. After lunch, if the level is the same and further tests have the same result, all is well and he is reasonably safe in attributing the smell to the dead rat or the lamb chop. But if the level of water falls, all is *not* well. Send quickly for the nearest plumber and put the whole of the responsibility on him.

'Domestic Sanitation' involves more than drainage. The expression covers all methods of removing from houses what the Institution's syllabus politely described as 'fluid refuse' and (another genteelism) 'solids'. The mechanics of modern drainage are outside the ambit of this book, but the reader may be interested, as I was, in the history of something of considerable importance to every generation about which the historians and novelists have told us little.

Until comparatively recently the almost universal standby for the disposal of human fluid refuse was the 'jerry' or 'chamber pot'. The first is short for Jeremiah and the connection is lost in antiquity; the second is simply a pot which is kept in a chamber, or room. Not only was there a jerry in every bedroom as a matter of course, but until well into the nineteenth century one was to be found in every gentleman's dining room. Sometimes there was a hidden cupboard in the reveal of a window, and every well-constructed Georgian sideboard had a pot cupboard in one end of it. Small pots were made for dining rooms, generally of pewter, but in grand houses they were sometimes of silver bearing the family arms. They turn up from time to time in the antique shops, where the Americans buy them at high prices for flower arrangement in their drawing rooms 'back home'. 'Carriage-folk' kept their chamber pots under the seats of their carriages. Judges, their extra-judicial functioning concealed by their voluminous robes, kept theirs under the bench.

These vessels had to be emptied, and Hogarth has depicted one convenient method of doing it. Servants do not appear to have found the duty distasteful and people generally were much less inhibited than we are now. Thus Samuel Pepys, on May 25 1663: 'Up and there hear that my wife and her maid Ashwell had between them spilt the pot[1] . . . upon the floor and stool and God knows what, and were mighty merry washing it clean. I took no great notice, but merrily.' A queer object for merriment, one may think, even in those days.

For coping with more serious matters (which children used to call 'big things') the ingenuity of mankind has been taxed over the centuries—primarily in improving the apparatus, but also in devising euphemisms wherewith to describe it. Even in medieval times the monks, to avoid the crudity of 'privy' and 'closet', invented '*necessarium*'. At about the same time we imported the French '*garde-robe*' (literally 'wardrobe': compare the euphemism 'cloakroom'). Pepys, when he needed to 'shift himself', repaired to his 'house of office'. Later we get 'convenience', 'lavatory', 'W.C.', 'toilet', 'bog', 'aunt' and 'loo'. 'W.C.' is said to be one of England's three principal contributions to a universal language—the others being 'bar' and 'sport'.

'Commode', which in France means an ordinary cupboard, acquired a special meaning here. Originally it was called a 'close stool', which was simply a stool having a pot beneath it. If it was intended to be portable, both were contained in a box with a hole in the lid; but if it was to remain permanently in one place, the contrivance was no more than a frame-work with a curtain drawn across the front. The principal manufacturers of close stools were the Royal Coffer Makers in the City of London. One specimen, made for the King, was covered with black velvet and embellished with fringes, ribbons and 2000 gilt nails. 'Groom of the Stole' is still a high office in the Royal Household, although its origin is forgotten. The great eighteenth-century English cabinet makers—Chippendale, Sheraton and Heppelwhite—followed the English practice in the use of the French word 'commode', and when they designed a close stool for a bedroom called it a 'night-commode'. It was intended, as Sheraton politely put it, for 'the accidental occasions of the night'.

[1] I spare the reader the diarist's lurid description of its contents.

The garderobe was rarely found except in castles and big houses. People who lived in smaller houses, like many country people today, were content to use an earth closet in the garden or the yard. The garderobe was usually built into the thickness of an outer wall, but it was sometimes located alongside a main chimney stack—presumably for warmth. Not infrequently (e.g. in the Tower of London) there was a garderobe near the banqueting hall, and a lot of the hidden chambers that are described by the guides to 'stately homes' as priests' hiding places were probably only garderobes. Inside the garderobe was a wooden or stone seat with one or more holes in it, and under the seat a vertical shaft—often a very long drop—which discharged into a stream or moat if there was one, or alternatively into a cellar. During the fourteenth century the monks of White Friars complained to the King that London's watercourses—particularly the Fleet and the Wallbrook—had become obnoxious, and Stow tells us that Sherborne Lane 'once by a long bourne of sweet water' had become known as 'Shitbourne Lane'. Cellars used for this unsavoury purpose had to be cleared at regular intervals and one of Pepys' many complaints about his next-door-neighbour, Sir William Penn, was that Sir William's 'turds' overflowed into his.

The water closet, as we know it, had its origin about the middle of the eighteenth century. But Leonardo da Vinci (1452–1519) is known to have designed some form of flushing system for the use of Francois I in his château at Amboise on the River Loire. And in 1596 Sir John Harington, a godson of Queen Elizabeth I, designed what was probably the earliest specimen of a valve closet, which was built near Bath. In 1748 the Duke of Bedford had a drainage system constructed at Woburn Abbey with four water closets 'at least one of which was within the house'. Then towards the end of the century Mr. William Hawkins of Fleet Street not only invented a closet with a valve mechanism, but decorated the inside of the pan with dainty pictures. Joseph Bramah, a contemporary of Hawkins, was a cabinet maker with a bent in the same direction and another pioneer. Eventually, in 1814, a Mr. Plair made the doubtful boast that water closets 'fitted up in the neatest manner' were in general use. So we progressed. There is, or was when I was a student, a remarkable exhibition of nineteenth and twentieth-century models in the museum of the Royal Sanitary Institute, ranging from 'long hoppers' and 'short hoppers' to what in the 1920s were the last word in porcelain suites.

If there is a long history of privies, closets—or whatever you choose to call them—there is an even longer history of baths. Until comparatively recently the cleansing of the human body was a secondary purpose. Francis Bacon, in 1635, listing the requirements of a person taking a bath, does not mention soap although it had been invented 300 years earlier. In ancient Greece the bath (a cold one) was ancillary to gymnastics, and the bath in the early English monastery (likewise a cold one) was in the nature of a penance. But the Romans had hot baths for relaxation, and when the Greeks copied the Romans old Tory clubmen in Athens lamented that their country was going downhill. The earliest English baths were made of wood and King John used one every three weeks. A reference by Chaucer to the heating of a bath over the fire is evidence that they were also made of metal.

Before the beginning of the eighteenth century a bathroom in a private house was rare. At Chatsworth, however, in 1700, there was a 'batheing room' containing a bath that had 'two locks to let in one hott, ye other cold water to attemper it as persons please'. They were commoner in France, where some of the great châteaux and royal palaces had splendid bathrooms. Louis XIII, like King John, was content with a wooden bath, but Louis XIV installed some fine specimens for his personal use, including a huge one of pink marble ten feet long by three feet deep. Later he decided he preferred the small bath in his bedroom and presented this monstrosity to the Pompadour.

It took 22 men to move it and it is still at Versailles. A bathroom in the Elysée was designed for Napoleon, who took a daily hot bath. It is on record that Wellington took a cold one.

In England, during the eighteenth and nineteenth centuries, we moved more slowly. In 1765 a lunatic asylum in Norwich had been provided with baths for the treatment of patients, but at the turn of the century there was only one bath in St. George's Hospital and it was never used. In 1812 the Corporation of the City of London refused a request by the Lord Mayor for a bath in the Mansion House. In 1837 there was not a single bath in Buckingham Palace; Queen Victoria in her younger days used a portable bath tub.

And so on down to the present. Increasingly, quite small houses are being built with two or more bathrooms and several 'toilets'. Soon it will be unheard of, as in the United States of America, for a bedroom in a respectable hotel not to have its private bathroom 'neatly fitted' with every known contrivance for the cleansing and relaxation of the world and his wife.

In dwelling so long on this subject I hope I have not bored my reader, but on the contrary have shown him that the subject of Drainage and Sanitation is not so dull as perhaps he thought. I hope still more that I have not offended him. 'To the historian,' wrote Siegfried Gierdon, 'there are no banal things.'[1]

Before ending this chapter I must return briefly to Charles Street, St. James's, before leaving it for good. I passed my final examination in the spring of 1926 and was duly elected a Professional Associate of the Surveyors' Institution in the autumn of the same year. The period of my pupilage, intended to be three years, was extended in order to give me plenty of time to find my first job. In the summer of 1926 I found it. At the ripe age of twenty-three I was fully fledged at last.

[1] Should the reader wish to pursue this subject he is referred in particular to *Clean and Decent* by Lawrence Knight, whence most of my information is derived (see Bibliography).

V

Rates, Rating and Ratepayers

History of rating – its economics – Robert Cobb – Bedford
valuation – Sir Herbert Trustram Eve – criminal interlude –
a *very* rude letter – interviews and a mink coat – Portsmouth
valuation – the Hampshire Halls.

The job I found was in a specialized field in which as yet I had
had no experience, because it was outside the professional ambit
of Daniel Smith, Oakley and Garrard. It was valuation for
rating, and it enabled me to play a small part in the first national
valuation of land and buildings by the rating authorities. The
Act that provided for it was the Rating and Valuation Act
1925, and its primary purpose was to promote more uniformity
in the assessments and consequently a fairer distribution of the
rate burden. The new valuation lists were timed to come into
force over several years and in preparation for them, with minor
exceptions, every brick and stone and every acre of land[1] in
England and Wales had to be valued.

A word at this point for the possible benefit of the reader
who is an ordinary householder and looks upon rates as one of
those distasteful and ever-increasing burdens he has to bear.
From time to time his house is revalued and its assessment raised;
every year the local authorities appear to spend more; rates are
impositions that never go down and nearly always go up. How
is the annual amount he is required to pay arrived at? When did
rates begin? Let me answer the second question first.

Rates, which is the name we give to taxes levied on the occu-
piers of land and buildings for purposes of local government,

[1] Agricultural land and buildings were not devalued until several years later.

had their origin nearly four hundred years ago. The 'general rate', that is levied today to meet the costs of a variety of public services—e.g. housing, education, roads, police, social welfare—is the lineal descendant of the 'poor rate' under the Poor Relief Act of 1601, commonly referred to as the 'Statute of Elizabeth I'. Under that Act the 'overseers', predecessors of the modern 'rating authorities', were required to set the poor to work; also—

> 'to raise weekly or otherwise by taxation of every inhabitant parson vicar and other,[1] and of every occupier of lands, houses, tithes impropriate or propriations of tithes, coal mines or saleable underwoods, in the said parish in such competent sums of money as they shall think fit . . . for and towards the necessary relief of the lame impotent old blind and such other among them being poor and not able to work, and also for the putting out of such children to be apprentices, to be gathered out of the same parish, according to the ability of the same parish'.[2]

As my reader who is a surveyor knows, the assessment of a property, or 'hereditament', for rating purposes is a reflection of its rental value in the open market. In broad terms it is the rent at which, if vacant, it might reasonably be expected to let from year to year. In respect of most classes of property, of which by far the largest consists of dwelling houses, the ratepayer, who is normally the occupier, is entitled to a deduction representing the annual cost of keeping the property in repair. The deduction is on a statutory scale and is the difference between 'gross value' and 'rateable value'.

For the benefit of the non-technical reader—and experience has taught me how little some ratepayers know about the way they are taxed—the rate in the pound or 'poundage' in any area (i.e. the amount payable per pound of the rateable value)

---

[1] Specific mention of 'parson' and 'vicar' immediately after 'every inhabitant' was possibly to make clear that the clergy were liable notwithstanding certain provisions of Magna Carta.
[2] 43 Eliz. I c.2 s.1.

is determined by a simple piece of arithmetic. The total of the local (spending) authorities' 'precepts'—i.e. their estimated expenditure for the following year—is divided by the total of the rateable values. If, for example, the precepts were to total £250,000, and the rateable values £500,000, the rate in the pound would be fifty pence. There is more than one reason why a demand for rates from an individual ratepayer may be higher, or lower, than in the previous year. Either the amount of his assessment has been varied; or the local authorities' expenditure has varied; or both have varied. In theory a general revaluation that has the effect of raising the assessments should not result in the ratepayers as a whole having to pay more, provided always that the local authorities' expenditure remains constant. If, for example, the total of the rateable values in the rating area were to be raised from £500,000 to £650,000, and the expenditure were to remain at £250,000, the rate in the pound would fall from 50p to 38p and the burden on the ratepayers would be the same. It is common knowledge, however, particularly when local elections are pending, that a high rate in the pound is thought a bad thing while a low rate may be thought a good one. A local authority that has a high rate in the pound may exercise economies for political reasons; but when as the result of a general revaluation the rate in the pound has fallen, and a modest increase is less likely to arouse comment, that consideration is not so cogent and there is a temptation to be extravagant.

Under the Act of 1925 the whole of England and Wales was to be valued for rating purposes and thereafter revalued at five-yearly intervals. The initial valuations were to be spread over several years and for administrative reasons the dates of the 'quinquennial revaluations' might be staggered between one area and another. Since the passing of the 1925 Act there have been occasions—for example during the war—when the revaluation has been postponed by legislation. Since the coming into force of the Local Government Act 1948, the duty of making, and if necessary defending, the assessments is that of the Valuation Office of the Inland Revenue. Formerly it had belonged to the rating authorities and that was the position when I got my first job.

We have seen that the overseers had been replaced by the rating authorities. In the provinces the rating authorities were the councils of the county boroughs, the boroughs, and the urban and rural districts; in London at that time they were the councils of the twenty-eight metropolitan boroughs and the Common Council of the City of London.

Under the 1925 Act it was for the rating authorities to decide individually how they should tackle the job, subject to a general oversight by officials called county valuers whose function was to ensure uniformity of valuation between one rating authority and the next. The rating authority, if it thought fit, might entrust the whole of the valuation to its own staff under the direction of its rating and valuation officer. Alternatively, it might delegate any part of the work to one or more private firms of rating surveyors, who when employed in this way became known as 'contract surveyors'. Contract surveyors were frequently employed by the rating authorities to value 'special properties' such as factories, departmental stores, gas and electricity undertakings, colleges and schools, breweries and public houses, and other hereditaments the assessment of which requires a specialist. Only in one county, as far as I am aware, did all the rating authorities combine to instruct a single firm of contract surveyors to value everything. The county was Bedfordshire and the contract surveyors were Messrs. J. R. Eve and Son, an old-established firm of rating surveyors with a national reputation who had their head office in Bedford. The senior partner at that time was the late Sir Herbert Trustram Eve, and I a lowly member of the large staff whom he recruited for the purpose.

I and two other young men of about my age, Ian Redfern and Reginald Ackland, lived and worked for a year or more in one of the firm's temporary offices that were located strategically throughout the county. Ours was in a pleasant little hotel called *The Bedford Arms* in the centre of the charming village of Woburn, nearly all of which belonged to the Duke of Bedford. There we were well fed and had comfortable quarters, and we made a large room on the first floor into an office. It needed to be a large room to contain among other equipment a complete set of the ordnance sheets of our 'diocese', which extended to a number of parishes in the surrounding countryside.

All three of us were 'referencers'. A referencer in the language of the rating surveyor is a junior assistant who makes the initial surveys of the properties to be valued. He identifies them by numbers on a large-scale map which relate to the relevant pages of his notebook. Then he describes each property, measures it and calculates the area. When measuring houses the referencer usually measures externally, so that the area includes the staircase and the thickness of the walls. The result is the 'reduced covered area' or 'R.C.A.'

A common complaint by ratepayers is that their houses have been assessed 'on the measurements', implying that nothing except their size has been taken into account. That is not true, as every rating surveyor knows. But to secure uniformity in the assessments of more or less similar houses a common denominator is called for. A square foot or a square yard of the floor area is a convenient unit. When, however, it comes to large detached houses of different architectural designs, a per-square foot or per-yard basis for arriving at the rental value is less reliable. And when it comes to very large houses, where the rental value is in inverse proportion to the extent of the accommodation, it is of no use at all.

When I was still a young man, but in practice as a rating surveyor, I was instructed by the owner-occupier of such a house. It was down in Kent, and although I have forgotten the exact figure the gross value fixed by the rating authority was about

£400. After going over the house I had no hesitation in advising my client that it was excessive; I was satisfied that no one would pay a rent of as much as £400 a year subject to the statutory conditions of tenancy that I recorded earlier. So I advised an 'objection', as an appeal to the local assessment committee was then called.

When the objection was heard a month or so later the rating and valuation officer, who had made the assessment on behalf of the rating authority, gave evidence to support his figure. He had measured the house internally from attic to cellar and tendered a valuation (a copy to each member of the committee) wherein he had valued nearly every room at a different price per square foot. I, on the other hand, had valued on a per-room basis subject to an 'end-deduction' for size, which resulted in my calculations being much simpler. The assessment committee, having listened patiently to both of us, reduced the gross value from £400 to £300 and my client was well satisfied.

Then the rating authority appealed to quarter sessions. In those days rating appeals were heard by an appeals committee formed of local justices. I had never given evidence at Kent quarter sessions and had no experience, as had the rating officer, of their likes and dislikes. I supposed that if he were to tender the same sort of valuation as he had tendered to the assessment committee, it would be because he knew that the appeals committee approved of that method. In that case, if I produced a valuation running only into a single sheet of foolscap, there was a danger that they would think I had not done my job thoroughly. So I got busy, went back to the house, measured all the rooms and produced a valuation every bit as long and complicated as the rating officer's. As, however, my unit prices were lower than his, and I had made an end-allowance, my answer was the £300 which the assessment committee had determined.

When I showed my valuation to counsel he was not happy about it. He saw my point about wanting to appear as thorough as my opposite number, but said he thought that to value a big house by such a method was unrealistic. Had I considered bringing in another rating surveyor to give supporting evidence, who might possibly have a different approach? I said I would think about it. Next morning I rang up Mr. Robert Cobb at his office in Cathedral Chambers, Rochester.

Bob Cobb, whose firm had at one time been associated with Daniel Smith, Oakley and Garrard, was nearly old enough to be my father. He came of a line of country land agents born and nurtured on Kentish soil. If the description 'old English gentleman' applied to anyone, it did to old Herbert Cobb, Bob's father, and in later life to Bob himself. There were no frills about the Cobbs, no affectations and no showmanship. Bob was typical—a bluff outspoken man who always said what he thought and left no doubt that any opinion he expressed, whether right or wrong, was honest. I told him about the case and asked him whether he would come to the sessions and support me.

'But did you say *rating*? I know nothing at all about rating and should not be of the slightest use to you. Where is this house anyway?'

When I told him he said that of course he knew the place, had known it all his life and used to go there a lot in the old days. He began to show an interest and asked me how much the rating authority's valuer had put on it.

Me: 'Gross value, £400.'

Cobb: '*Four hundred pounds!* Absolute nonsense! It would never let for anything like it; if I had to let it, the most I should expect to get is about £300.'

Me: 'Thank you very much, Sir. Will you please come to the sessions in Maidstone and say just that?'

I doubt if Bob Cobb had a high opinion of rating surveyors, but he had a lower one of a rating and valuation officer who could be so wrong. 'All right, John, I'll come.'

At the hearing things went as I had expected. The appellants began, and the rating officer produced his complicated valuation as on the last occasion and took the justices through it. Then it was my turn. I produced my complicated valuation and did the same. The case had been called on at half past ten and by half past twelve the court was beginning to look bored. Then counsel called 'Mr. Robert Cobb'. He asked Bob Cobb a few simple questions to establish to the justices what I knew already—that he had been familiar with this particular house for more than forty years. 'Now, Mr. Cobb, how do you think it should be valued, and what do you think its gross value should be?'

Bob Cobb replied: 'I'm not a rating surveyor, or an expert on rating as you are, gentlemen. [He leaned confidentially over the rail of the witness box.] All I can say is I have never heard anything so ridiculous as what these rating surveyors have been talking for two hours. They've been arguing about the rent a prospective tenant would pay for this large house. Who ever heard of a prospective tenant working out the rent he can afford to pay at 1s. 6d. a square foot on the drawing room, 1s. 3d. on the dining room, 1s. on the best bedrooms, £2 on each WC and £1 on the cupboard under the stairs?'

'Then, Mr. Cobb how would *you* value the house, and what in your opinion should the assessment be?'

'Sir, I value on the basis of my experience. The assessment committee were right—not a penny over £300.'

It was now past one and the chairman looked meaningly at the clock. The cross-examination of the witness was short, and I thought the final speech by the appellants' counsel a little perfunctory. The chairman looked to his right and left, and his fellow justices nodded.

'We need not trouble you,' he said to counsel. Then: 'Thank you, Mr. Cobb, you have been *most* helpful. The appeal is dismissed, the appellants will pay the costs and the gross value is confirmed at £300.' We went to lunch.

But this excursion into Kent was some years after I left Bedfordshire, and I must return to the Woburn office of J. R. Eve and Son.

Every few days one of the firm's valuers would arrive at breakfast-time and, accompanied by the appropriate referencer, inspect and value properties until late in the afternoon. It was an excellent experience for young men and I recall gratefully how patient the valuers were with us. The agricultural valuer in particular, an elderly gentleman called A. W. Merry, taught me a lot. He was head of Stafford, Rogers and Merry in Leighton Buzzard whom Sir Trustram had called in to help. Together we walked around the farms I had referenced, pausing occasionally while he plucked and examined a weed or crumbled a lump of soil in his fingers. In theory we walked 'round and across' each field, but happily he took short cuts. In the light of today's prices it is interesting to recall that the rental value of arable land in our corner of Bedfordshire ranged from about twelve to twenty shillings per acre per year.

Another way in which the rating referencer could learn about valuing was by studying the firm's *B.V. Instructions*, which arrived weekly from head office. As it would have been tedious to differentiate between one member of the staff and another, according to the types of property they were concerned with, a complete copy of the typescript was sent to everyone. Thus if you were working in and around a country village, as I was, your copy of *Instructions* included sections on referencing and valuing such properties as factories, warehouses, offices and shops. The subject matter was illustrated by hypothetical calculations, and taken as a whole it made an extremely useful text-book—practical and absolutely up-to-date.

Bedfordshire Valuation had some semblance to a military exercise and once we had an inspection by the Field-Marshal himself. Sir Trustram Eve arrived unexpectedly in his car with Mark Wilks, who was one of his junior partners, and a young assistant as A.D.C. Figuratively we all stood to attention while the great man inspected the office, examined our plans and turned over the pages of our notebooks. After making some minor criticisms he said kindly that he hoped we were comfortable and had no complaints, wished us well, re-entered his car attended by his staff officers, and disappeared towards Ampthill in a cloud of dust.

After an enjoyable year in Woburn I was moved to Bedford and became attached to the firm's head office. There I gained experience in the valuation of a much wider variety of rating hereditaments than is to be found in the average rural district. The Other Chap attached himself as a voluntary teacher and visitor to Bedford Prison, and we took lodgings in a pleasant Georgian square behind it. By an odd coincidence my old friend Frederick Gwilliam, who had been the deputy-governor of Wormwood Scrubs Prison during the four years the Other Chap had worked there while in London, was appointed governor of Bedford at about the time I got there. He had come ahead of his wife and family and we were two lonely men in a strange town. He had, moreover, the misfortune to take up his new post at a moment when more than the normal proportion of the prison population were mentally disturbed, and he assured me that several showed unmistakable signs of becoming violent. Worse still, the prison medical officer was on leave, and, as far as Gwilliam could ascertain, the prison contained no suitable accommodation or means of physical restraint for use in such an emergency. He told me that the Home Office, more psychologically minded than they used to be, were rather fussy about the treatment afforded violent prisoners. But a letter he had written them remained un-answered.

Any port in a storm. Gwilliam sought *my* advice and together we pored over a volume entitled *Instructions to Prison Governors* marked 'highly confidential'. Nowhere could we discover, if one of the prisoners were to become violent and unmanageable, whether the governor would be justified in adopting what I

66

advanced as a practical suggestion: to obtain a length of stout rope and employ his two heftiest warders—one to sit on the prisoner's head while the other tied him up. Eventually we adjourned the meeting, had a drink and took a punt on the River Ouse. There in the shadow of the alders, the shimmering surface of the water a mirror to the golden sunset, our companions the mosquitoes, the dragon-flies and an occasional water-rat, we lamented the plight of a prison governor who had no psychiatrist, no padded cell, no strait jacket, and whose prisoners were going mad.

In the Bedford office of J. R. Eve and Son I gained a much wider experience of rating referencing and the elements of valuation than in Woburn. But I missed the friendly atmosphere of *The Bedford Arms* where we had lived very happily and where, in contrast to head office, one's superiors were not continually looking over one's shoulder.

I saw something of Sir Trustram Eve and soon became conscious that he did not like me; I think he found me uppish and he was probably right. Partly for that reason I was no longer happy in my job and found the office a soulless place. I did not feel I was making progress, and when criticisms were made of my work that I thought unfair I made representations to Sir Trustram, who did not take them kindly. Eventually things came to a head and I wrote him a rude letter. It was fortunate I did so, because it enabled me to see a different and generous side of the man.

It was not just a rude letter, but a *very* rude letter! Something had happened that caused my quick temper to get the better of me, although at this distance of time I cannot remember what it was. I composed the masterpiece in my lodgings after supper, marked the envelope 'strictly personal', walked to the office, thrust it through his letter-box and returned home to bed. Next morning I awoke with a moral hang-over, conscious, as has often happened in my life, that on the previous evening I had gone too far. With alarm and despondency I received a message from Sir Trustram's secretary that he would like to see me at three o'clock in the afternoon, and on the stroke of three I knocked on his door in trepidation.

'Good afternoon, Watson, and kindly sit down. I had your foolish letter this morning and have read it. Your only possible excuse is that it is the kind of letter I sometimes write myself. But, to be fair, I have an advantage over you. I have a private secretary, and when I dictate and sign that kind of letter she carelessly forgets to post it. Next morning we nearly always agree that a better place for it than the posting box is the waste-paper basket. *You* have no secretary, but *there* is the waste-paper basket . . .' And crumpling my letter he tossed it in. 'Now,' he continued, 'we will talk this matter out.' We proceeded to do so and soon agreed in a perfectly friendly way that I should begin looking for another job at once, and that in both our interests we should part when I had found it.

I soon saw an advertisement of the type of job I wanted, for the great revaluation was not yet complete and there was a shortage of rating surveyors all over the country. The leading firm of general practitioners in Portsmouth, Hall, Pain and Foster, had entered into a contract with Portsmouth Corporation, the rating authority, to value a long list of 'special properties' in Portsmouth and Southsea. They advertised for an experienced rating surveyor to help them. I answered the advertisement, mentioning that I was on the staff of J. R. Eve and Son, and was invited to go down for an interview. I travelled to Portsmouth at once, where I was interviewed by Patrick Hall, then head of the firm, and his partner, Fred Foster.

I remember very little about that interview, but I expect, like most interviews, it was embarrassing for both sides. I hate being interviewed and do not pretend to be much good at conducting interviews. I forget to ask the right questions and am too gullible; also I think I lack the intuition needed by a really competent interviewer. Years ago I was discussing the conduct of interviews with the late Sir Nutcombe Hume, chairman and managing director of the Charterhouse Investment Trust. He told me of a method which he, or possibly one of his associates, sometimes employed when interviewing a seemingly bright young man who had applied for a job. It consisted of telling a story with an unexpected question at the end of it. There was more than one possible answer to the question, but the time he took to answer was an effective test of the speed of his mental reactions. The story has always stuck in my mind, and while young John Watson is at Portsmouth being interviewed I will tell it. If the reader would care to test his own reactions, he should take out his watch (preferably one with a second-hand) and lay it on the table in front of him.

Mr. Benjamin Lewis was an astute and prosperous furrier, who had his shop in a fashionable street of a certain provincial city. Mr. and Mrs. Conway were a well-to-do couple who were old and valued customers of Mr. Lewis, with whom they were on friendly terms. One morning Mrs. Conway was passing the shop and Mr. Lewis was standing in the doorway. She paused for a few moments and they chatted of this and that. Just as she was about to go Mr. Lewis said: 'I wonder if you have time to step inside? I have something here that I think might interest you.'

Mrs. Conway stepped inside, and at Mr. Lewis's bidding an assistant produced for her inspection the most exquisite mink coat she had ever seen. She exclaimed in admiration, and Mr. Lewis assured her that he would have to go a long way before finding another like it. The skins were perfectly matched, of a lovely pale colour with a silvery sheen, and Mrs. Conway reflected that it would be their silver wedding in three weeks' time. She tried on the coat and it fitted perfectly. She had always longed for a mink coat and it was with bated breath that she asked the vital question: 'How much?' 'To you, Mrs. Conway, fifteen hundred pounds.'

Her face fell: 'Oh dear,' she said, 'I'm afraid my husband would *never* pay as much as that for a coat . . .'

She took another look at her reflection in the mirror, and Mr. Lewis suggested that if only Mr. Conway could *see* the coat he might be as enthusiastic about it as she was. (Mr. Lewis had confidence in himself as a salesman.) Then Mrs. Conway had an idea. She had some National Savings tucked away somewhere and was sure that her husband had long forgotten they existed. She decided to take Mr. Lewis into her confidence and told him about them.

'Mr. Lewis,' she said, 'you *are* a man of discretion, are you not?' Mr. Lewis bowed. 'Supposing I were to write you a cheque for five hundred pounds and give it to you now. Would you ring up my husband at his office and ask him to come in and look at the coat? Of course, don't mention me. Then, if he asks the price, would you quote him a thousand pounds? I'm almost certain he would pay that.'

Mr. Lewis replied that he would be happy to collaborate in this innocent little subterfuge, and added that if Mr. Conway did not buy the coat at the reduced price of course he would return her money. Mrs. Conway wrote the cheque, handed it to Mr. Lewis with a slight twinge of conscience, and hurried home.

Next morning Mr. Lewis telephoned Mr. Conway at his office according to plan. He told him about the mink coat and Mr. Conway sounded interested. He said he would leave the office early that evening and call at Mr. Lewis's shop.

An attractive young girl modelled the coat, turning gracefully this way and that between the glass-fronted cabinets. Mr. Conway was visibly impressed. 'It is certainly a very nice coat: How much?' 'To *you*, Mr. Conway, a thousand pounds.'

'Mr. Lewis, you *are* a man of discretion, are you not?' Mr. Lewis bowed. 'I'll have the coat. Please have it packed at once and delivered, this evening if possible, to Miss Topsy Footlights,

care of the doorkeeper at the stage door of the Gaiety Theatre.'
Quickly! You are Mr. Lewis: what would you do?

But to return to Portsmouth, where I am happy to say my interview did not include a test of that kind. I liked the two partners and they appeared to approve of me. In my anxiety to get the job I am afraid I laid on my professional experience a bit thick. They were impressed by the fact that I had been articled to the great firm of Daniel Smith, Oakley and Garrard, and were clearly mesmerised by the name Eve; coming as I did from J. R. Eve and Son, it went without saying that I knew everything there was to know about rating. I for my part discovered that neither partner, nor so far as I could judge from what they told me any member of their staff, knew anything at all about rating. As they offered me the post at a much higher salary than I was then getting, I accepted with alacrity and returned to Bedford in triumph.

Next morning, as is my way, I began to have doubts. Mr. Hall had made it clear that I was to be in full charge of the job and had told me I might engage my own assistants, and I was to be allotted specially rented premises in the High Street adjoining the firm's head office. So far so good. But a glimpse of the list of hereditaments to be valued, that I had had during my interview, had perturbed me slightly even then. In Bedfordshire I had had some experience in the valuation of industrial properties and shops. But of the valuing of piers, docks, ship-building yards and slipways—because there is no sea in Bedfordshire—I had had no experience at all. However, I took comfort from the fact that I had friends in the rating world whom I could rely on to advise me. Were there not rating manuals and text-books? And *B.V. Instructions*, except in relation to piers, docks, ship-building yards and slipways, would be a tremendous standby. Such is the audacity of youth.

Alas for my self-confidence! I was shortly to receive a blow between the eyes that was cataclysmic and might well have led me to turn the Portsmouth job down. What occurred was this.

On getting back to Bedford I wrote Sir Trustram a letter in a very different vein from the last one. I told him about the Portsmouth offer and that I had accepted it, and asked him when it would be convenient for me to go. Possibly, in dwelling on the responsibilities I had undertaken, I was more enthusiastic than tactful. His private secretary replied asking me to go and see him again—and naturally I went.

On this occasion Sir Trustram was most cordial and asked me a number of pertinent questions, which I answered as best I could. When I had finished, although he was good enough to say that my appointment was a compliment to his firm, he was clearly convinced that at last a rather bumptious young man had bitten off more than he could chew. He added that if they needed me urgently, as seemed the case, it would be perfectly satisfactory to him if I left in ten days' time. I thanked him and was about to go when he called me back and referred to *B.V. Instructions*. He said they belonged to his firm and there was an absolute rule that a member of the staff, who was leaving, must hand them back without making any extracts. No doubt my face fell. 'But in your case', he continued, 'because of the importance of the post you have accepted, we will make an exception. Return your copy to me personally and write me a covering letter reminding me of our conversation. Subject to the deletion of our Bedfordshire prices [e.g. per square foot and per square yard] which are secret, I will have you supplied with a complete set. . . .' I thanked him again, this time effusively. The proposed deletion of the firm's basic prices was perfectly reasonable; it was instruction in method I should need in Portsmouth, not values in Bedfordshire. I returned to my lodgings, bundled up the typescripts and wrote him the covering letter he had asked for.

A week later *B.V. Instructions* came back and I was horrified by their appearance. Page after page of the typescript had been defiled by black blots. It was not only the basic prices that had been deleted; the hypothetical figures in the sample calculations had been blotted out too, making most of them unintelligible. I nearly wept over those ink blots. At the time I was inclined to blame Sir Trustram, but on reflection I doubt if the extent of what had been perpetrated ever came to his knowledge. Any other explanation would be inconsistent with the kind things he had said to me. I hastily wrote a letter to his secretary, protesting at what had happened, and a day or two later received a reply that if Mr. Watson needed figures to complete the sample calculations it was up to him to supply them. A possible explanation of this unhappy business was that some member of the staff had grossly exceeded his instructions—either from stupidity, or because he was jealous or bore me a grudge. Whatever it was, there was nothing I could do about it. I arrived in Portsmouth the following week with the good wishes of my friends and colleagues, their promises to help me if I got stuck, a couple of text-books on rating, and a bundle of dog-eared typescripts that were virtually worthless.

I have mentioned that the senior partner in Hall, Pain and Foster, when I joined them in 1927, was Pat Hall. The junior partner, Fred Foster, principally concerned with the estate agency side of the business, was a friendly person but I had little to do with him. The firm had been founded by Pat's father with the title Hall, Pain and Goldsmith many years before. There had been a disagreement between the partners which had ended in litigation, but Ernest Hall had come out on top. I was a bachelor, and I remember him warning me that an uncongenial partner was much more difficult to get rid of than an uncongenial wife.

When I came on the scene Ernest Hall must have been in his late seventies, but although retired he was still extremely active. His wife had been dead some years and he lived alone in a township on the Chichester Road with the hideous name of

Waterlooville, drove a large car (very dangerously) and poppe
into the Portsmouth office whenever he could find an excuse fc
doing so.

My arrival to undertake the rating revaluation was one c
the excuses. Although Pat often said to me 'You do realiz
don't you, that Father knows absolutely *nothing* about rating
the old man was determined to help. He was lonely and anxiou
to find something constructive to do. So Ernest Hall became m
principal assistant or I became his—I was never quite sure of th
precise relationship. He may not have known anything abou
rating, but there was little he did not know about propertie
and people in Portsmouth and Southsea. When I had to mak
an important valuation he would insist on accompanying m
driving his car rather erratically and slowing down from tim
to time; 'That's a fine new shopfront, my boy, don't you think
And when I agreed he would add with a twinkle: 'It was
who paid for it, I drove through the old one last March!'

I remember occasions, after his car had been seen entering th
forecourt of some big industrial undertaking, when the manage
ment gave him an almost royal welcome although the know
reason for our coming was to increase the assessment. He wa
immensely popular, and if Ernest Hall did not know everybod
in Portsea Island, everybody who was anybody knew hin
The only trouble was that, like most elderly people, he enjoye
reviving old memories and would engage in seemingly endles
conversations while I was champing at the bit to get on with th
job. But when we *did* get on he could be very helpful, for h
had an intimate knowledge of local values. And if around lunc
time he could contrive to be in Old Portsmouth, he woul
stand me a crab or a lobster salad at the famous old restaurant i
the High Street called Monks.

Later he left Waterlooville and went to live with his son an
daughter-in-law in Fareham. By the time the valuation wa
finished I had become a friend of the family, and our friendshi

ripened as the years passed. I often used to stay with them, and I happened to be down there shortly before leaving for a holiday in Ireland in the spring of 1930. Ernest Hall, whom by this time I had become very fond of, remarked that in all his eighty years he had never been to Ireland, so jokingly I suggested that he should come too. To my surprise he accepted and agreed to my condition that I should drive his car. We had a splendid trip. Our first stay was at Altamont, my cousin Feilding Watson's house in County Carlow; thence we drove across Ireland to Connemara and down the west coast. But there were a few embarrassing moments. An old lady whom I did not know, living in what was formerly the Watson house called Ballydarton, had invited us to visit her in order that she and I might discuss a matter of family business that I hoped might be resolved both to my advantage and Feilding's. But unhappily, so litigious are the Irish, she had just been having a law-suit with Feilding and his name was mud. When we left Altamont, Feilding suggested that in the circumstances it might be tactful were I to pretend that I had never met him, and on no account disclose that we had been staying under his roof. Ernest Hall was briefed accordingly, and I admit that some subterfuge was called for. It prompted the old gentleman to say on his return: 'I went to Ireland with John Watson and in twenty-four hours was made to tell more lies than I have told in the rest of my life!'

His only son, Patrick, was a man of parts, and it is sad that he should have died in 1941 while still in his forties. He was a scholar at Winchester; a county cricketer; an adept at 'real tennis', which he played on the ancient tennis court in Porchester Castle; a keen botanist with a penchant for wild orchids, violets and bladderworts; a connoisseur of eighteenth-century furniture; and an acknowledged authority on Old English wine glasses, of which he had a large and representative collection. In the time left over he earned his living as a very capable agricultural valuer and land agent.

75

But Pat's most attractive quality was his impish sense of fun. He made fun of things that would have worried most people, and in all the years I knew him I cannot remember him depressed. We hit it off at once and I was soon giving him my full confidence. The sad story of *B.V. Instructions* gained me his sympathy, and when I confessed to my anxiety about valuing piers, docks, ship-building yards and slipways, instead of reproaching me he teased me. Although he had not intended to interest himself in rating, whenever I had a problem he would weigh in and help me solve it. More than once I journeyed back to Bedford for the week-end, taking with me a long list of queries. My old colleagues were as good as their word and did their best for me, and I shall always remember gratefully the help I had from two of them. One was Charles Harman Hunt, then a valuer on Sir Trustram Eve's permanent staff and now a senior partner in Strutt and Parker; the other a peripatetic valuer on the temporary staff, called Norman Wailes, whom unfortunately I have lost sight of.

I remained in Portsmouth for rather more than a year, but the time came when all my valuations had been approved by Pat Hall and handed over to Portsmouth Corporation. Thereafter I returned to Portsmouth as often as was necessary to defend my figures before the local assessment committee. The valuation department of the Corporation did not appear to think my assessments unduly low, and judging by the modest number of objections the Portsmouth and Southsea ratepayers did not think them unduly high. Naturally I valued personally all the piers, docks, ship-building yards and slipways. And if any curious reader were to ask me how I did it, this is my answer. Like the late Sir Trustram Eve, I have my professional secrets.

VI

Principal and Principles

Ferris and Puckridge – Bill Gillett – *don't* jump the gun –
Sidney and Graham Motion – how to value a pub – background to housing – Octavia Hill – Claude Leigh – experi-
ment in private-enterprise housing – seaside camp – Christmas
ritual by the Thames.

In the early months of 1928, having left Portsmouth and returned to live in London, I entered into my first partnership.
The firm was Ferris and Puckridge, chartered surveyors, of 79,
Queen Street, round the corner from the Bank of England.
Its sole principal was Herbert Edward (Bill) Gillett, who used
to tell people he pronounced his capital G 'not soft as in "Gentleman" but hard as in "Bugger"'.

Because he had no partners, Bill could never afford to take a
day off from the office or stay in bed if he caught cold. But in
joining him at that juncture I made a mistake, for I was much too
young to go into partnership with anyone. True, I probably had
more experience as a specialist rating surveyor than most young
men of twenty-four, but Ferris and Puckridge were general
practitioners and, except as a pupil, I had had no experience of
general practice.

At least I was fortunate in my choice of a partner. Bill Gillett
was born in 1895, educated at Marlborough, and later articled to
the firm of land agents, established in Wiltshire in the eighteenth
century, of which eventually he became head. Seldom can
there have been a man more anxious to honour the traditions
of his profession, serve his clients and help his fellow members,
and less concerned to gain any advantage from doing so. I

77

remember him best for his extraordinary tolerance of people's failings and his reluctance to interfere in anything he conceived to be someone else's business. 'Live and let live' was constantly on his lips.

The mainstay of the business of Ferris and Puckridge in those days was valuation. Bill Gillett, who was not often instructed to make a very large valuation, was always up to his neck in lesser ones. His principal client was Lloyds Bank, and branch managers throughout London and the Home Counties kept him busy valuing securities for mortgages. He also made valuations for a building society of which he was a director, advised clients on sales and purchases, negotiated compensation for compulsory acquisitions, valued for probate, and undertook estate management mainly in the City and East End. To a man as supremely competent as he was, too few of the really big jobs came along. That was due to his innate modesty, an almost pathological inability to push himself, and a horror lest anyone should suppose that a professional man was looking for work. I used to urge him to be more self-assertive, but unsuccessfully. You can lead a horse to water; you can't make him drink.

Bill had no knowledge of rating and would often tease me about it. 'You rating surveyors', he would say, 'know nothing of *real* values and prefer to live in a world of your own.' But it was rating, naturally, that I was looking for and I think on the whole I was extremely lucky. If Fortune favours the brave, she also favours the intrepid. There was the aftermath of the Portsmouth valuation, which I was well paid for. A firm of rating surveyors, behind with their contracts, called me in to help them value a rural district in Essex. My old friend Alfred Savill, third son of Sir Edwin Savill, passed me all the rating that came into his office on a fee-sharing basis. And I, less sensitive and more mercenary than my partner, dropped hints when opportunities arose and collected clients of my own.

As for rating, so far so good. It was when other kinds of valuation came my way that inexperience landed me in difficulties. We could not afford any technical staff in those days and there was no counterpart to old Knowles, who had been such a redoubtable standby in Charles Street. Bill Gillett, though always ready to advise, was too busy to accompany me and hold my hand when I had some particularly difficult valuation to make. But mercifully I had other friends in London who went out of their way to help me, just as my Bedford friends helped me when I was in Portsmouth. What a nuisance I must have been!

I remember in particular some of the senior ones. Sidney Motion, for example, was then getting to be an old man. I had been instructed to value, of all things, a public house somewhere in North London. Now the valuation of licensed property, even more than valuation for rating, is a specialized business, and the most famous licensed-property valuers in England were the London firm of Sidney H. and D. Graham Motion. Obviously I should have passed the job to them. As, however, I needed the fee, I ventured to telephone Graham Motion, my friend and contemporary, to ask if he would lend me a hand. Graham, the most generous of young men, invited me to bring the papers and go to see him in his office next morning at eleven. I arrived, expectant, to find that Graham had forgotten the appointment and was out. I suppose I must have looked so downcast that his secretary, after asking me to wait a moment, ushered me into his father's room.

I had never met Mr. Sidney Motion before, and except that I had been announced as a friend of Graham's I doubt if he had the faintest idea who I was. But the fact that I *was* a friend of Graham's was quite enough for the old man, who suggested I should tell him all about it. I explained as briefly as possible, fearful lest I should disclose my ignorance or he should regard my intrusion, which was unintentional, as a piece of impertinence. Not so Sidney Motion: 'How very tiresome of Graham!

Have you brought the papers with you? Undo the file and let me look.'

I waited nervously for several minutes while he examined them. Then he rang and ordered a taxi. 'We'll go together and look at this pub and I'll tell you what I think.' And by the time we got back he had explained to me how it should be valued, what in his opinion its value was, and what I ought to say in my report. I stammered my thanks and timidly, no doubt stupidly, offered to send him my fee. 'Send me your fee?'—he nearly jumped down my throat—'*Send me your fee?* Go back to your office, dictate your report to your client and sign it, and never mention the matter to me again!'

But not all my hurdles were surmounted so easily. Inexperienced as I was, I encountered during the next few years an Aintree Course of hurdles, a fall at any one of which might have been disastrous. Gradually and at times painfully I acquired the skills of a chartered surveyor in general practice, or at least some of them. But I learned it all the hard way, which would not have been necessary if I had been more patient. A word of advice to my younger readers. After you have qualified in your profession, which is the first step, there are *no* short cuts. Obtain a solid grounding in the practical side before taking the bit between your teeth and launching out on your own. Never (the mixture of my metaphors is now climactic) try to jump the gun.

In the late autumn of 1929 I met Claude Leigh, founder and managing director of the Metropolitan Housing Corporation Limited (M.H.C.) whom I mentioned briefly in Chapter IV. M.H.C. owned thirteen large estates of houses and flats let on weekly tenancies and located in the poorer parts of London. Structurally they varied considerably. Some consisted of rows of pretentious villas with foliated stone mullions, tiled forecourts and aspidistras in their bay windows; other M.H.C. estates were high blocks of late nineteenth-century tenements. I was introduced to Leigh as a competent rating surveyor. My task was to inspect all these properties and value them for rating, examine the new assessments which were about to be published, and contest any I thought excessive. The basic fee, a handsome one in those days, was a thousand guineas. So began my association with Leigh, which lasted until his death. First he was my client—which was good. Then we became close friends—which was better. Eventually I married his daughter—which was best of all.

He was born in 1888, the son of a surveyor and estate agent who had a modest business in the north-east of London, and was educated at one of the City of London Foundation Schools and later at a private school in Putney. On leaving school he joined his father, but soon lost interest in working for clients. He became instead an investor in real estate, and throughout his life made a point of never describing himself as a professional man. While in his twenties Claude Leigh had taken an interest in what used to be called 'working-class' houses or, if the quality was above average, 'artisan' houses; some people refer to them as 'weekly' houses, which means houses let at weekly rents. And when I write 'houses', unless the context implies the contrary, I include maisonettes and flats. To begin with, at any rate, Leigh's interest in this class of property was wholly commercial, and I must digress for a few pages to explain how it arose.

The final decade of the nineteenth century, in which Leigh was brought up, is sometimes referred to as 'The Gay Nineties'. It is certain, however, that they afforded little gaiety for a large section of the population. Until the Industrial Revolution most English families lived in villages and country towns. The staple industry was agriculture, and many of the farm-workers occupied tied cottages owned by the landowners. Then came the great social and economic change—a vast migration from the country districts into the coal-mining and rapidly expanding industrial areas. There was an ever-increasing demand for houses in these parts of Britain, and the heyday of the speculative builder had arrived.

There are two ways in which a family can come to occupy a ready-made house. One is to buy and the other to rent it. But for this army of migrants, except the few who were so fortunate as to have capital, buying a house was out of the question. So the speculative builders sold the houses to investors, and the investors became landlords. And, as both were out for the maximum profit, the houses were as crowded and their construction as cheap as the builders could contrive, and their rents as high as the landlords could get. But wages were low and many families, desperately in need of accommodation, were unable to pay the rents demanded. So they 'doubled up' and shared accommodation that was not intended to be shared at all. 'Thousands of dwellings', wrote R. L. Reiss, 'were constructed which were slums from the time they were first occupied. During this period there was practically no government or local control and a builder could do what he pleased.'

Things went from bad to worse. The first building byelaws, made under the Public Health Act of 1875, were ineffective. It was not until 1885 that the public was made aware, and its conscience stirred, by the report of a royal commission. This was followed by the passing of the Housing of the Working Classes Act 1890. But the Act was only permissive. It empowered the local authorities to close individual houses that had become uninhabitable, and many local authorities did so because it cost them nothing. It also empowered them to clear slum areas and build new houses for letting in place of the old ones; this they ignored because it could only have been done at a financial loss to the ratepayers. In the meantime one effect of the operation of the new byelaws had been to push up the cost of building, and the speculators now found it more profitable to provide a superior type of accommodation for higher income groups. Except for the philanthropists (the name of Peabody springs at once to mind) it was nobody's business to house that section of the population which existed below the poverty-line and was sometimes called the 'Submerged Tenth'.

It is not surprising that in these circumstances working-class or artisan housing, whichever they chose to call it, became an unfashionable investment, except by some of the newly-rich industrialists who needed to maintain a pool of labour. Literally and metaphorically, it stank. It is shameful to have to record the ownership during my lifetime of a seven-storeyed block of tenements in that part of Bermondsey that was described horrifically by Charles Dickens in *Oliver Twist*; he gave it the fictitious name of 'Jacob's Island'. A later writer alleged that Wolseley Buildings was the worst block of tenements on the riverside. It belonged to a distinguished Speaker of the House of Commons.

In 1914 came the First World War. There was practically no building while it lasted, and because of a shortage of labour and materials the existing slums deteriorated further. So far did the demand for accommodation exceed the supply that, but for the passing of the first of the 'Rent Acts', a rapacious owner of this class of property could have got almost any rent he liked.

The Rent and Mortgage Interest (War Restrictions) Act 1915 was the first of a long series of Acts of Parliament that has continued until the present time. Their provisions, constantly amended, have been too complex for me to attempt to summarize them. But running all through this legislation has been the principle that tenants of houses below a certain value, as long as they behave properly, need to be protected from eviction by their landlords and from capricious increases in rent. Under the 1915 Act the rent of every house under a prescribed rateable value was frozen at the pre-war rent plus a percentage: that was called the 'standard rent', the tenancy became known as a 'statutory tenancy', and the house a 'controlled house'. Once, however, the landlord of a controlled house was able to regain possession (e.g. on the voluntary departure, or, subject to conditions, on the death of the statutory tenant) it became decontrolled. The statutory tenancy was then replaced by an ordinary contractual tenancy determinable by the landlord after giving proper notice, and there was no longer any restriction on the rent chargeable.

The coming into force of the 1915 Act had several immediate results. One was that an estate, consisting wholly or mainly of controlled houses, became a more secure investment than it had been formerly. The level of rents might be low, but that had probably been reflected in the purchase price. A tenant having the benefit of a statutory tenancy had powerful inducements to co-operate with his landlord. In the knowledge that he would have to pay more for decontrolled accommodation if he moved, he was reconciled to staying put. He kept the house in decent order for his own comfort as a long-term resident, and was careful to pay the rent regularly lest his landlord should apply to the county court for an eviction order.

The war ended, but rent restrictions did not. The nation was now housing-conscious, and there followed several Housing Acts designed to remedy conditions that the public were ashamed of. Under the Act of 1919 it became the duty of local authorities to meet the housing needs of their districts, and subsidies were provided to enable them to do so. The *Chamberlain Act* of 1923 contained a limited provision for extending these subsidies to private developers who were disposed to build. The *Wheatley Act* of 1924 increased the subsidies to local authorities and was specifically designed to help them cater for the poorest tenants.

Claude Leigh was then in his mid-thirties. He had not served in the war because of bad eyesight and since leaving school had watched, sometimes critically, this sequence of events. He prided himself on being a 'business man', had imagination and drive, despised inefficiency and disliked the idea of subsidies unless he was satisfied that there was no alternative.

I did not know Leigh in that period, but from what he told me later I think this is the way his mind worked. He was not interested in the housing of the affluent and the upper social classes; in his mind he divided the rest of the population broadly into three groups.

Group 1 was what are commonly called the middle classes, consisting mainly of families whose incomes, although they may be modest, are secure. Increasingly at that time, and since, the tendency of these people was to want to own their own homes. They were assisted financially by the building societies, a movement which had begun in a small way during the first half of the nineteenth century and since about 1870 had made great strides. A further tendency by Group 1 was to move out of the congested city centres and build or buy their new homes in the rapidly expanding suburbs. But in those days Town and Country Planning was in its infancy, and the result in many areas was thoroughly bad planning (if there was *any* planning), 'ribbon development' and 'suburban sprawl'. Pioneers in the field of housing, some of whom had been operating for more than a generation, were unable to counteract these evils. Bournville, on the outskirts of Birmingham, was a product of the genius and foresight of George Cadbury and dates from 1870; Hampstead Garden Suburb from 1903; Letchworth, which embodied the garden-city principles of Ebenezer Howard, from 1903; in the early 1920s Welwyn Garden City, in the same tradition, had just begun. Claude Leigh was neither a town-planner, nor an architect, nor an economist, nor a social reformer. He claimed no more than to be an efficient man of business. The housing of Group 1 was interesting and of national importance, but no business of his.

At the other extreme and at the bottom end of the social scale was Group 3. The aged and impoverished, the chronically sick, the retarded and unintelligent, the alcoholics and the drugtakers, the young and irresponsible, the idlers, the procrastinators and lay-abouts, the unemployable and occasionally the criminal, the 'just unlucky'—these were, and are, the Submerged Tenth.

'The poor ye have always with you. . . . ' For nearly two thousand years that has proved true. And there is nothing to be gained, but much to be lost, by closing our eyes to the fact that a section of the poor, often through no fault of theirs, are incapable of existing in a civilised society except with the constant support, financial and otherwise, afforded willingly or unwillingly, of their fellow men. Nowhere is that truth more evident than in the matter of housing. We can demolish slum houses, widen streets, dig drains, abate overcrowding, clear and redevelop large sites— it is impossible, and in our lifetime is likely to remain impossible, to rehouse these people on anything approaching an economic basis. In the past we did little for them, which was nice for the taxpayer. Today we recognize the need to do a great deal for them at the taxpayer's expense. 'At the taxpayer's expense' implies subsidies. Leigh, as I have said, disliked subsidies and made no claim to be a philanthropist. Even a philanthropist, seeking a solution to this facet of the housing problem, could only have touched the fringe. A business man, *qua* business man, could do nothing.

Between Group 1 and Group 3 was Group 2, and that was the group that Leigh had his eye on. It was a vast hinterland, occupied for the most part by people living in undistinguished houses and flats interspersed with more or less grim blocks of multi-storeyed tenements.. These properties were not yet in the category of slums, and there was no immediate prospect of the local authorities treating them as such. On the other hand it was a class of accommodation that the average reader of this book would not want to live in. Many of the houses were in poor repair, and nearly all were deficient in those things that even in the early nineteen-twenties were provided in council houses as a matter of course— ventilated food cupboards, modern grates, stoves, sinks and cooking appliances generally, to say nothing of hot-water systems

Claude Leigh
1888–1964

Photograph:
Anthony Buckley,
London.

and baths. Notable exceptions in Group 2 were properties owned by conscientious landlords such as charities, colleges, public bodies and some of the great private landowners. A few houses were easily recognized as owner-occupied by their superior condition. As for the rest, nobody except perhaps the local sanitary inspector knew or cared who owned them. Some, individually or in small batches, belonged to a neighbour who collected the weekly rents himself. Others, in bigger batches and occasionally on large estates, belonged to an absentee landlord who employed an agent to collect the rent and do only such repairs as were absolutely necessary. The absentee landlord was not proud of his investment. As far as possible he tried to forget it, and postpone indefinitely the tour of the 'family property' that his conscience told him he should have made long since.

Claude Leigh foresaw that these houses, unless something was done and done quickly, were without doubt the slums of tomorrow. What *could* be done? Here in brief was his master plan:

1 A public company to be formed under competent business management by a board of directors having vision and imagination;

2 The company to pay a dividend on its ordinary share capital attractive to the commercial investor;

3 The company to acquire estates of Group 2 houses and flats in Greater London;

4 Its policy to be to recondition and improve its properties and maintain them in good order.

5 The management of the estates to be enlightened, in the sense that the company would concern itself for the welfare of its tenants and provide 'social services' to promote it.

The intentions were clear enough. The burning question was whether, if No. 2 was fulfilled (the payment of a dividend on its

87

ordinary shares attractive to the commercial investor) it would be economically possible to fulfil the others.

Metropolitan Housing Corporation Limited (M.H.C.) was floated as a public company in March, 1929, and fully subscribed. Its authorised capital of £1,000,000 was divided into 1,000,000 one pound shares of which 650,000 were issued. The first chairman was Mr. Thomas Gilbert Scott and the managing director Mr. Claude Leigh, and the object of the corporation was primarily to acquire the share capital of a company called Metropolitan United Estates in which Mr. Leigh was principal shareholder. The assets consisted for the most part of artisan houses and flats, together with a few shops and business premises in suburban positions. They were situated in Battersea, Camberwell, Fulham, Islington, Kensington, Lambeth, Lewisham, St. Pancras, Stepney, Westminster and the City of London, and they had been valued by Messrs. Knight, Frank and Rutley at £924,503. The following is an extract from the prospectus:

'Mr. Leigh has agreed to act as Estate Manager, and his organization, which has been built up over some twenty years, will be at the disposal of the Corporation. The Directors are of opinion that Mr. Leigh's experience shows conclusively that it is possible to re-condition weekly-rented property, maintain it in a proper state and at the same time show a satisfactory return on the money invested. Mr. Leigh is a successful pioneer in the organization of welfare work for the benefit of his tenants, thereby encouraging good will between landlord and tenant. Such co-operation ensures the maintenance of comfortable homes for the tenants, a minimum of expense in the collection of rents, cost of repairs and other overhead charges, and therefore the maximum return on capital.'

The 'maximum return on capital' meant the maximum dividend on ordinary shares, and it was decided at the outset that this must not be allowed to fall below 8 per cent. There were people, accustomed to the low dividends paid by the quasi-philanthropic housing associations, who protested that this was excessive. It is a matter I shall return to later. Claude Leigh was a large shareholder, but I am convinced that his refusal to contemplate any lower rate of interest was not from a desire to line his own pocket. In seeking a solution to this aspect of the housing problem he was not interested in philanthropy or quasi-philanthropy; the wells of charity would run dry. Nor was he interested in State subsidies. The remedy he proposed was a business proposition, which to succeed must remain viable. If the dividends were not made sufficiently attractive the public support he relied on would not be forthcoming, and the exercise would be brought to a halt as surely as a car that has run out of petrol.

A company called Reps Limited had been formed in 1928 to carry out all works of repair and reconditioning on Claude Leigh's artisan estates. It became a wholly-owned subsidiary of M.H.C. with its headquarters in Camberwell and depots in various parts of London. A third company, also a subsidiary of M.H.C., was formed in 1934. Claude Leigh (Management) Limited took over the management of the estates from Leigh personally, although in practice it was continued by the same staff under his direction as chairman. I accepted a seat on its board with special responsibility for rating assessments, rating appeals and Schedule A taxation.

Leigh's scheme for improving the corporation's properties had been launched before I got there. When a house or a flat became vacant, and in consequence decontrolled, his policy was to put it into good repair and at the same time make such improvements as were practicable before reletting. Interest on the cost of the improvements was included in the decontrolled rent. When, however, a statutory tenant wanted an improvement, and the corporation was willing to comply, the economics were less simple. Until the coming in force of the Rent Act of 1933 a landlord was forbidden to make *any* increase in the rent of a controlled house, whether he had improved it or not.

Leigh overcame this difficulty by introducing the M.H.C.

'Improvement Scheme' for the benefit of its statutory tenants. The improvements were listed and the amounts of the weekly 'hire charges' shown against them. Here are some of the improvements: a ventilated larder where previously there had been no larder; a bath (generally in the scullery with a table-top over it) where previously there had been no bath and still less a bathroom; an ingenious contrivance whereby, if there was no hot-water supply, bath water could be heated in a gas copper and syphoned across; an up-to-date WC: a deep porcelain-enamelled sink, replacing a shallow one of brown earthenware; a modern cooking stove; a 'contemporary' chimney piece in the living room (much admired by the tenants) consisting of a slow-burning grate enshrined in a castellated edifice of glazed bricks—and so forth. There were 'Ideal flats' where all these things were displayed and the tenants invited to come and see them. And the hire charges payable by the statutory tenants, though accounted for separately, were added to their weekly rent.

The Improvement Scheme was never challenged, but I doubt if it was strictly legal. The answer to the critics, who complained that some of the hire charges were excessive, was that no statutory tenant had his house or flat improved unless he had asked for it and knew in advance what it would cost him. If it was a fiddle, it was a legitimate fiddle—a co-operation between landlord and tenant to the advantage of both.

But a true and lasting co-operation between landlord and tenant is achieved only by mutual confidence and an appreciation of each other's points of view. That brings me to housing management, and it is important before I proceed further that the reader should have some knowledge of what in this context 'management' entails.

The pioneer of housing management was Octavia Hill, who was born in Suffolk in 1838. Later she came to London, where she began by teaching in a 'ragged school'. In 1852 she opened a school of her own. In 1865, shocked by the conditions in which the children lived, she purchased an overcrowded court of slum houses near her home in Nottingham Place. 'Nearly every family', she wrote later, 'rented but one room . . . knowledge of sanitary matters had hardly penetrated at all, gross ignorance prevailed.' And in defining 'management' she included the following: 'Repairs promptly and efficiently attended to, references completely taken up, cleaning sedulously supervised, overcrowding put an end to, the blessing of ready-money payments enforced, accounts strictly kept, and above all, tenants so sorted as to be helpful to one another'. Her biographer adds: 'A further requisite [of good management] and quite as important, she considered to be the power of dealing with people at once wisely and kindly; through all the work, however strictly carried out, should run the golden thread of sympathy and kindliness'. From this small beginning her field widened. Increasingly private owners gave her their houses to look after, and in 1884 the Ecclesiastical Commissioners entrusted her with a large part of their estates in South London. She died in 1912. The Institute of Housing Managers, formerly the Society of Women Housing Managers, was formed in 1916 to carry on the work in her tradition.

In 1938 the Central Housing Advisory Committee[1] took evidence on the subject of housing management, mainly on municipally owned estates. In reporting to the Minister of Health, they recorded the evidence of the Society of Women Housing Managers at some length—in particular their stipulation that the social and the business sides of management should be undertaken by the same person and that that person should be a woman. The society had said that the rent collector had a business excuse for calling at every house, and had claimed that the regular visitation enabled her to keep a watchful eye on its condition; further, that it enabled her to get to know the tenants, perceive their problems and help solve them.

[1] Of which the author was a member.

I had had no personal experience of 'Octavia Hill' management at that time. I have had a little since and I know it to be admirable. But whereas it is a comparatively simple matter to introduce it when the houses are newly-built, say by a local authority or by the development corporation of a New Town, it is much more difficult when, as on the M.H.C. estates, there is a system of management by a male staff in being. It is just not practicable, even if it were desirable, to scrap the existing system and begin again. Leigh did what he thought the next best thing. He superimposed the social services, which he had come to recognize as essential to good management, on what was there already.

It had not been his policy to collect rents at the door. There was a rent office on every estate and the tenants were expected to pay them over the counter. Some tenants prefer it that way and for the landlord, in the short run if not in the long run, it is more economical. A rent collector called only if a tenant was ill, or was known to be infirm and house-bound, or got seriously into arrears. If a house needed repairs or redecoration the tenant was expected to report the matter to the rent office, and the superintendent instructed Reps if he considered the work necessary.

On two of the M.H.C. estates, the first in Camberwell and the second in Fulham, and later on a third estate in East London, Leigh provided a building he described as a 'social centre'. It was close to the rent office, suitably equipped and furnished, and each centre contained an assembly hall, one or more smaller rooms, a library and a canteen. In charge was a resident woman social worker called the 'estate matron'. Her duty was two-fold. Every weekday at the same hour she was available to any tenant who cared to come and see her; she also maintained contact with the superintendent, who kept her informed of any social problems known to the rent office and of any tenant who he thought might benefit by being visited. The other part of the matron's duty was to supervise a variety of social activities in the centre, mainly in the evenings and at week-ends, in which the tenants were encouraged to take part.

A unique side-line of the M.H.C. management was the annual summer camp in Norfolk. In the 1920s I used to go camping in the summer with borstal boys, from Portland Borstal Institution, in a remote bit of country a few miles west of Lulworth Cove. The camps were enormous fun and I have described them at some length in an earlier book.[1] Camping in the countryside under canvas is a splendid experience for young people; it brings out all the best in them—*and* the worst.

It occurred to me that some of the Cockney youngsters on the M.H.C. estates might benefit from a week or two in camp, preferably at the seaside. Some friends of mine in the Carlton Club, who felt as I did, had raised enough money to establish an organization for young campers on the Norfolk coast. Its headquarters were at the Old Hall in the village of Ingham. For an inclusive charge per head they undertook to accept three hundred of our tenants' children in batches of a hundred, each camp to last ten days. The camps were to be in August and they agreed to provide tents, a marquee, a portable kitchen complete with cook, ground sheets and necessary equipment, and all meals. My job was to arrange transport from London to the camp and bring a staff to run it.

Claude Leigh and his fellow directors of M.H.C. thought it a good idea. The cost per child was a little over two pounds, and we agreed that the parents should be required to contribute ten shillings. A camp fund was opened at each of the three social centres and the money was paid in advance by dribs and drabs. We ran three camps. There was one for boys, ages ranging from about ten to about fourteen; a second camp for girls in the same age-group; and a mixed camp for younger children. The entire operation was carried out voluntarily by members of the staff of Claude Leigh (Management), some of whom had had no

[1] *Which is the Justice?*—Allen and Unwin, 1969.

experience of camping. They were a splendid team. The second-in-command was my friend, and at that time my principal assistant in the office, Walter Philp. Molly Marchant (now Mrs. Shotton), for many years my private secretary, has a great love for and understanding of young people and ran the girls' camp. The mixed camp for the younger children was the responsibility of the estate matrons.

Early on the appointed day a big motor coach drew up outside each of the three social centres and the campers, wildly excited, piled in. There was a stop somewhere on the Newmarket Road for a picnic lunch for those who had a taste for it. (Every child as he entered the coach had been given a brown paper bag to be sick into, and by this time many of them had been used.)

The boys' camp was my department. We reported at Ingham Old Hall on our arrival, and then drove to the camp field beside the sea at Palling. Our first job was to divide the campers into four groups of 25, the members of the groups being identifiable by coloured discs which they were required to attach to their clothing and wear throughout the ten-day period. Each group, in charge of one of my helpers, was allotted tents in one of the four corners of the camp field. In the centre of the field was the flagstaff, and near to it a marquee which at meal-times could accommodate the whole lot at one sitting. Next to the marquee was the cook-house, a ridge tent containing an old-fashioned kitchen range with a tall iron chimney protruding through the roof. The wash-tent and latrines were at a discreet distance. Finally, there was the tent which I occupied as commander-in-chief, so placed that I could see and hear nearly everything that went on.

The first night in a boys' camp is always much the same. You are lucky to get *any* sleep and your only consolation as you toss and turn in the small hours, listening to the seemingly endless chatter from the other tents, is the certain knowledge, born of experience, that on the ensuing nights the whole camp

94

will be sound asleep before ten. The first night is different. In spite of a long and tiring day, no one wants to settle down. After a first mad rush through the sand dunes, to make sure the sea is really there, there is the unpacking. There is always the boy who has left his suitcase in the coach, and the miserable creature who has already lost his pocket money on the beach. There is always the boy who by some accident had not been assigned to a tent and whom no one wants, and there is always the boy who has toothache. Singing and talking continue far into the night, and the sun is rising when at long last the weary leader closes his eyes. At that moment a small boy fully dressed (the time being half past four) appears in the doorway of the tent: 'Please, Mister, is it time for breakfast?'

To supervise these London children and keep them out of mischief was no light undertaking. It was quite different from taking a school to camp, or a club, or a scout troop, or the members of any disciplined or semi-disciplined body. Our boys and girls, unless they happened to attend the same school or live in the same block of dwellings, did not even know each other's names. And at the beginning of camp, with a few exceptions, neither I nor my helpers knew them either. The exceptions were those who came last year, although it was hard to fit names immediately to some of the familiar faces that detached themselves from the mass and claimed instant recognition. But there was Jackie Jones, our champion swimmer, who had grown at least six inches; Charlie Brown, his mate, who had again brought that dreadful mouth organ; Bertie Allen, who nicked the vicar's raspberries and caused all that trouble; Bobby Smith, who raised a family of field mice in the pocket of his jacket—and a dozen others grinning all over their attractive faces and proffering sticky hands. Every year, advised and aided by these veteran campers, we made our own rules and devised a code of conduct (*pace* the child psychiatrists) based on a system of rewards and punishments. The rewards were eatables and the punishments deprivation of eatables. For serious misbehaviour a boy was confined to his tent. In an extreme case—it seldom happened—he was put on a train and sent home.

There was any amount for them to do in the daytime. In the morning after breakfast they made their beds and tidied their tents. (A daily prize in the form of Mars-bars for the tidiest tent in each group.) Next the tidying of the camp field. The London child is inherently untidy and ever since his third birthday, when he got a whole lollypop to himself, has been allowed to cast its wrapper on the floor. So the whole camp turned scavenger, lining up on one side of the field and then advancing slowly across it like devouring locusts. Not a scrap of paper or a particle of tinfoil, not the tiniest bit of orange peel, remained in their wake; for a king-size bar of chocolate was the coveted prize for the boy who collected most. Judging took place beside the litter bin, not without argument, and the prize was awarded. The ceremony usually ended with the victor departing proudly to his tent, munching his chocolate and scattering its wrappings to the winds of heaven.

The chores finished, there were rounders, football or stump cricket. The naturalists went in search of crabs and starfish, and I remember a boy bringing back a dead and bedraggled sea gull which he announced his intention of taking home to stuff. The wide sandy beach stretched as far as the eye could see, and the bathing was said to be safe if we took proper precautions; precautions or not, it was a continuing miracle that no one got drowned. After dinner, and a blessed hour of compulsory rest, there were cross-country rambles and organized expeditions to Hazeburgh lighthouse. And for those who could afford it, boating on the Broads near Stalham, where white sails glide mysteriously through green fields.

The day wears on and the sun sinks low over the Norfolk landscape. In twos and threes these tired, grubby, happy youngsters drift back to camp. Supper all together in the marquee; then out once more into the camp field. It is dark now and there is a hush as we stand in a circle for prayers. A verse or two from the Bible, 'Our Father', and Cranmer's glorious collect—'Lighten our darkness we beseech thee O Lord . . .' Then: 'Off to your tents everybody. No ragging and if it rains *don't* touch the canvas. Good night all, and sleep well.' Suddenly you find that you are alone.

The average English working-class child is brought up in certain traditional beliefs. One of those beliefs is that fresh air is dangerous, and he has a conviction, fostered by his mother ever since he was weaned, that to open his bedroom window is to catch his death of cold. At night in camp he does his best to reproduce the climatic conditions that obtain in his bedroom in Walworth by lacing up the doorway and hammering in the brailing pegs until the tent is virtually air-tight. He is also frightened of the dark, this child of the lamp-lit streets, and his fears are not allayed when someone starts the perennial rumour that the camp is haunted—' 'aunted by a lidy all in w'ite, 'oo walks across the field at twelve o'clock carryin' 'er 'ead in 'er 'ands'. Another reason for sealing up your tent is lest you should see this ghastly apparition.

My helpers and I did our best to instil a few hygienic ideas in the short time available. The fact that the tent doorways, so tightly laced the night before, were often found open in the morning occasioned surprise. But the road to hygiene has its pitfalls. I learned that to my cost when, with the best possible intentions, I had offered a generous prize for the boy who at an inspection when the camp ended was found to have the cleanest teeth. There was keen competition, and, as some of their teeth had been extremely dirty when they arrived, I listened every morning with satisfaction to the scrubbing noises that came from the wash tent. The camp was nearly over before I discovered that only *thirty* boys had brought tooth brushes, which they were hiring out to the other *seventy* at a penny a scrub.

One of our biggest problems was what to do when it was wet. The under-twelves in particular tended to become restive. One evening, when it had rained all day, I saw a danger of the younger boys getting out of hand before bed-time; so I assembled the whole camp in the marquee and made an announcement: 'I'm going to read aloud some horror stories by a man called Edgar Allan Poe. They're so frightening that no one under twelve is old enough to listen. Everyone under twelve will have to go to bed early, so go to your tents the under-twelves—and please keep quiet.' There was a reluctant exit to a chorus of 'O Sirs.'

I then proceeded to read from Poe and had scarcely begun when I became conscious—which was exactly what I had expected—of a rustling in the long grass along the sides of the marquee, deep breathing, and occasionally a hastily suppressed giggle. Eventually there was a complete and unaccustomed silence, and I knew that all the under-twelves were now huddled together under the brailing. I read two of the less gruesome stories, but *The Murders in the Rue Morgue* and *The Mystery of Marie Roget* were gruesome enough. It was voted by everyone a most enjoyable evening, and if some of the younger boys made their tents doubly secure and had nightmares I don't suppose it did them any harm.

When I embarked on this long digression I was describing the work of the estate matrons in Claude Leigh's social centres. I had a great respect for those matrons, who were humane and dedicated women. They put everything they had into their work and within a limited field undoubtedly did good. The limitation of the field was a defect of the system. There were tenants in urgent need of advice and help whom no one knew about, and others who would probably have welcomed visits but feared lest their neighbours should see the matron coming and draw adverse conclusions. It underlined the importance of the Octavia Hill principle that all tenants, except those who are emphatic that they do not want it, should be visited regularly.

But the outstanding defect of the Claude Leigh system was its cost. The annual cost of the M.H.C. social services on *three* of their estates was not a large proportion of the rents received from *thirteen* estates. But if the cost of the services had had to be found from the rents of the three estates only, nothing on these lines could have been attempted. It followed that to provide anything approaching the same standard of social services on the other ten estates, much as Leigh would have liked to do so, was out of the question.

The dividend was the trouble. Once established, it became the almost obsessional concern of everyone within the organization to maintain it. Outside the organization were people who disparaged the social services on the three estates, which were publicized, as window dressing. Expenditure on repairs was also affected by the amount of the dividend and the same critics condemned the condition of many of the Corporation's properties as sub-standard. In Fulham, they scoffed, everything in the garden might be lovely, but it was different in Newington Butts. There was some truth in that. Sorrowfully I record my own conclusion. Leigh cut his coat according to his cloth, and so long as the M.H.C. project had to remain on a commercial footing, which he was so afraid of losing, there was never enough cloth to make a proper job of it. To attempt, in this context, to reconcile the uncompromising *demands of business* with the urgent *social needs of people* was to attempt the impossible. As a profitable commercial enterprise, efficiently conducted, the project made its contribution to the nation's housing needs. I would not go further than that.

On the outbreak of the Second World War all rents of this class of property were again frozen, but the cost of repairs and improvements went up steadily. Even as a commercial enterprise, the project became unworkable. During and after the war nearly all the artisan estates belonging to M.H.C. were sold and many of the tenants, financed by building societies, bought the houses they lived in. In this inflationary world they are unlikely to regret having done so.

But that was not the end of M.H.C. For some years before the war it had been widening the scope of its investments and intended to pursue that policy when it ended. A new company, Metropolitan Estates and Property Corporation Ltd. (M.E.P.C.) was formed in 1946 and acquired its assets. M.E.P.C. has holdings in nearly every class of real estate, but never so far as I am aware, except perhaps fortuitously, has it bought any more artisan dwellings. Claude Leigh became its president, on his retirement as chairman and managing director in 1961. When he died in 1964 M.E.P.C. had a capital of £50 million and was the fourth largest property company in Great Britain.

To conclude this chapter, a few lines about Claude Leigh as a person. No narrative by me would be complete without some description of this unpredictable, often contrary, argumentative, kind, generous and lovable man.

He began with nothing and made money. He enjoyed making it ('Of course I do—what am I in business *for*?') He enjoyed spending it ('You can't take it *with* you!') Most of all he enjoyed giving it away. Because he had money he was able to enjoy those things a rich man can afford—a big house, his racehorses, backing a play. In short, he enjoyed expensive living and made no secret of the fact. And he had a not inexpensive second wife. Within the man burned a flame of idealism; had she fanned that flame and shared his enthusiasms, she could have helped him greatly in his work. The marriage ended in divorce.

But, more than *things*, Claude enjoyed *people*. He liked meeting new people, getting to know them, listening to their views, advancing his own and observing their reactions, helping them in one way or another if the need arose. He was genuine and unaffected, and there were few faults he despised more than pomposity or humbug. You always knew where you were with him. These were the qualities that gained him his wide circle of friends and led so many, in his household as well as in his office, to devote their lives to serving his interests. But he was far from being a passive man. He held strong opinions on most subjects (frequently he changed them) and loved an argument. He loved an argument so much that you sometimes suspected he had deliberately adopted an indefensible standpoint for no other reason than to promote one. But he never argued with rancour, and the fiercest argument would end by his patting you on the shoulder, offering you another drink, telling you how much he valued your friendship—and what fun it all was!

He supported many public charities. He was especially interested in hospitals and was deputy chairman of the Princess Beatrice Hospital in Fulham. He was interested in boys and girls, and was honorary treasurer of the Royal Albert and Alexandra School. He supported Jewish charities, went to Israel several times and handsomely endowed two kibbutzim. There were private charities no one knew about: paying the cost to a young doctor, whom he admired and respected, of studying for a research fellowship; or to a clergyman, whom he liked, the cost of his son's education at a public school. When he contributed to the funds of an organization, he expected it to be as efficient as his own, and when possible he would go to see what it was doing and how his money would be spent. On at least one occasion he went to extreme lengths in applying a test.

During the inter-war period Claude was asked if he would support financially some project by one of the largest London hospitals. He was inclined to do so, but had heard a rumour that its casualty department was not as efficient as it might be. He resolved to find out. Late one night, in the company of an embarrassed friend (me), he smeared his clothes with mud and limped, groaning, into the casualty entrance. He explained that he had fallen in the street outside and feared a broken arm. As he resisted any attempt by a nurse to help him off with his jacket, and declined to be touched by anyone except a doctor, the nurse told him that in that case he had better lie on the couch and wait. Surreptitiously Claude looked at his watch, and fortunately for the finances of the hospital the doctor took only four minutes to come. The patient was well satisfied, leapt to his feet, congratulated the doctor on the efficiency of his department, and vastly to that gentleman's surprise handed him a substantial cheque which he asked him to convey to the treasurer next morning.

I think I was also the only person ever permitted to witness his Christmas ritual. Shortly before midnight on Christmas Eve he would put on an old overcoat, stuff his pockets with Bank of England notes and make his way to Westminster Bridge. Thence he walked slowly up the Embankment to Blackfriars. He would pause on the way to hand a note—sometimes several—to anyone who appeared cold, or hungry, or lonely, or whom for some other reason he felt sorry for. The beneficiaries included tramps, drunks, lay-abouts, prostitutes, probably a few criminals, and ladies and gentlemen (as astonished as they were respectable) waiting for their last bus home. 'Happy Christmas!' he would say, 'here's a present for you.' Turning quickly on his heel, he passed on.

Later I chided him about this extraordinary method of almsgiving. I asked him how he could possibly know whether the strange assortment of people among whom he had distributed all this money were deserving? I added that I thought the whole business totally inconsistent with the gospel of efficiency he was always preaching—and so on.

'Yes, John, I expect you're absolutely right, but I *do* enjoy it. *And anyway, whose money was it—yours or mine?*'

He married again in 1945 and there is no doubt about the happiness of his old age. In January, 1964, he and his wife went on holiday to Jamaica, where he was taken ill and died. He had always loved the sunshine and at his request was buried out there.

VII

A London Estate in War-time (I)

Lieut. Colonel P. F. Story – Marquess of Northampton and
his trustees – appointment as agent – estates in North London
– Clerkenwell – Canonbury, historical note – evacuation –
Blitz – mend and make do – *truite au bleu* – C. C. Walkinshaw
– Canonbury Youth Centre.

In September, 1939, I was negotiating for a tenancy of a pleasant
little early nineteenth-century house in Trinity Church Square,
Southwark, 'in the suburbs near the Elephant', where the sea
captain lived in *Twelfth Night*. At that time I had more interests
south of the River Thames than north of it. Since 1936 the
Other Chap had been sitting a day a week as chairman of the
Southwark Juvenile Court, the Sessions House was in Newington
Causeway round the corner, and I was spending several evenings
a week in one or other of the Oxford and Bermondsey boys'
clubs. I had lived the previous winter in Bermondsey, sharing
with three young men, who were doing the same job as I, a
disused public house called *The Jolly Waterman* which overhung
the river about a mile east of Tower Bridge. The immediate
result of the outbreak of war was to bring all business to a
standstill. But a month or two later I reopened negotiations, and
before Christmas I moved into Trinity Church Square with my
housekeeper, Bridget O'Brien, and my dog.

In March, 1940, which was still the period of what was later
called 'the phoney war', I read in *The Times* of the death of
Lieut. Colonel P. F. Story, who had been agent for the Marquess
of Northampton's estates in North London. Born in India,

103

Philip Story had been one of the first volunteers to join Kitchener's Army in the First World War and had been commissioned in the Royal Engineers. He served in the Ypres Salient and on the Somme, won the D.S.O. and Bar, and was made a Chevalier de la Légion d'Honneur. In 1919 he resigned his commission to take up the Northampton agency. Although he became a chartered surveyor I never knew him well, but well enough to recognize a man of the highest integrity. I knew moreover that the Northampton estates consisted largely of working-class houses.

I had decided that this side of urban estate management interested me more than any other branch of the surveyor's profession. I had, however, been driven to the conclusion, while concerned with the M.H.C. estates, that an enlightened management of working-class property was incompatible with insistence on what any ordinary business man would expect by way of return. From all accounts the Northampton estates were in sympathetic ownership, and the welfare of the tenants was considered more important than the profit. The Fifth Marquess, who died in 1913, had been a splendid man. A chairman of the L.C.C. Housing Committee and a president of the Ragged School Union, he had taken a keen interest in housing and in education. *The Times* said of him that, as a large London landowner, he never forgot that the ownership of property 'had its responsibilities as well as its rights'. The management of his family's estates was just the sort of job I had been looking for, and I applied for it.

But I was unwilling to make it my full-time occupation, as had my predecessor. Once upon a time most landowners—especially country landowners—employed a full-time estate agent[1] or, as he is called in Scotland, a factor. Today that is less common. Because of the complexity of modern legislation an

---

[1] By 'estate agent' I mean a surveyor or land agent who *manages* an estate. 'Estate agent' as a sobriquet for 'house agent' or 'flat agent'—i.e. a person who sells or lets houses or flats—is a deeply rooted genteelism.

owner is generally better served by a firm of surveyors consisting of specialist partners, any one of whom can be called in to advise as occasion demands. I recommend a young man to think carefully before he accepts a full-time agency unless it is in the service of a government department, a local authority, or some other body which is permanently established. The full-time agent, as the years pass, inevitably loses touch with the run of the mill of his profession. Except in regard to legislation and new procedures that specifically affect his management, he gets rusty. Then something happens—the employer dies, the company whose estate he looks after is taken over or wound up, or for some reason the estate is sold, and he finds himself out of work and ill-equipped to return to private practice if he has to.

Before meeting Lord Northampton I had sent him a list of my activities. I was a partner in Ferris and Puckridge and determined to remain so in order to retain my independence. I was a director of Claude Leigh (Management) Limited and, although I was quite ready to resign my directorship, the beginning of a war with possibly terrible consequences was hardly the moment for that. I was a member of the Central Housing Advisory Committee to the Minister of Health, and it might be thought that if ever the Minister needed advice it was now. And there was the Other Chap's weekly session as a juvenile court magistrate, which he was not prepared to give up in any circumstances. Lord Northampton, rather wryly but perfectly understandably, said he could not help wondering how much time I should have left to devote to *his* business. I replied that if I were appointed I would promise always to put the service of his interests first, but that that was as far as I could go. Clearly he would have preferred another full-time agent like Story, but in wartime the field was restricted and I got the job.

Story had been responsible for the management of two estates in North London, but only one of them—and that estate was in two sections, both in the metropolitan borough of

Finsbury—belonged personally to the Marquess. In 1931 he had made a voluntary settlement of the other estate, which was in Canonbury in the metropolitan borough of Islington, and had appointed Baring Brothers, the merchant bankers, trustees. Having thus alienated the family properties in Canonbury, he had no say in their management and as far as that estate was concerned I was employed by Barings. This, however, did not preclude me from discussing matters affecting Canonbury with Lord Northampton, who continued to take a personal interest.

The Marquess and the trustees had a joint estate office in Northampton Square, Finsbury, which was the headquarters of the management, and they shared the payment of my salary in proportion to the amount of work entailed on their respective estates. The same applied to the staff in the estate office, who, though some of them were elderly, were a loyal and efficient team. They numbered about twelve. The senior members had been in the same employment most of their lives and at least one of them had served the Fifth Marquess. A. W. Prior was chief clerk and the agent's secretary. A. Pottier, a chartered surveyor, was the valuer. J. H. Ryder was the accountant. A. B. G. Reeve was the rentals manager. Nobbs and Eastoe were building surveyors. Nash was the draughtsman. The junior member of the staff, unusual even in those days, was a male shorthand-typist. All repairs on the estates were undertaken by local firms of contractors.

It became evident within hours of my arrival that the system of management, though it might appear high-powered in relation to the size of the estates, was a little old-fashioned. There were unanswered letters on my writing table. Prior, seated opposite with his pencil poised above his notebook, invited me to dictate the answers. I obliged and Prior bowed himself out. Later in the morning, when he brought me the answers beautifully typed, I signed them without comment, but could not help wondering whether a gentleman so venerable and of such distinguished appearance as my secretary had typed them personally. Next day I found an opportunity to inquire discreetly of Pottier what the custom was. Pottier was visibly shocked by the implication of my question. 'Mr. Prior, Sir, never types letters. The Colonel always *dictated* his letters to Mr. Prior; Mr. Prior *re-dictates them to Mr. Maidment.*'

An addition I made to the staff in Finsbury was Miss Tresise, an extremely competent member of the Society of Women Housing Managers, who collected the rents and looked after the weekly tenants. She had no counterpart in Canonbury, where we had a branch office, but was always available for consultation if the need arose. The policy on both estates was to collect the rent from door to door unless a tenant preferred to come weekly to the office and pay it there.

Both sections of Lord Northampton's personal estate were in the ward of Finsbury called Clerkenwell. The northern section lay between Goswell Road and St. John Street, and was centred on Northampton Square which I have mentioned. This was an attractive square of late Georgian houses, most of which had been turned into offices or workshops. Clerkenwell had long been the home of the English clock and watch making industry, and in Northampton Square and nearby streets (one of them is Tompion Street) were small firms that had been there for generations. They specialized in making parts for watches, clocks and clock cases—generally of superb craftsmanship. Old Carter, for instance, who occupied an office-workshop on the entrance floor of a house on the corner of the square, was a first-grade cabinet maker. But he had fallen on bad times, largely I imagine because increasingly clock cases were machine made. He was a dear old man, but not an entirely satisfactory tenant. For one thing, he was nearly always in arrear with his rent. For another, contrary to the conditions of his tenancy, which forbade his sleeping on the premises, the room I entered when I called to see Carter was his office-workshop-bedroom. He slept on a mattress under the counter, and if I arrived before he had made his bed the breach of his agreement was very obvious. When that happened I pretended not to notice; but he knew I knew, and I knew that he knew I knew.

The southern section of the Clerkenwell estate lay on either side of Rosebery Avenue. It included Wilmington Square, another pleasant square of the same period as Northampton Square, and behind Finsbury Town Hall the busy little Exmouth Market. Here were yet more clock and watch makers, of whom the most famous were (and are) Thwaites and Reed of Bowling Green Lane. I remember their inviting me to come and see the great astronomical clock from Hampton Court Palace which they had in for repair, and recently I read that they had secured the contract for maintaining the clock in the Palace of Westminster that is commonly, but erroneously, called Big Ben.

For some years before the outbreak of war most of the Clerkenwell estate had been allocated under planning law for industrial development. Therefore it had been the policy, when opportunity arose, to clear sites for that purpose. In war-time no kind of redevelopment was practicable and all preparation for it stopped. What with the big gaps between some of the terraces, groups of houses standing empty awaiting demolition, to say nothing of houses in the residential streets that were empty because the tenants had been evacuated, the general appearance of the estate was dismal—but not so dismal as it was to become later.

The trustees' estate in Islington consisted of the ancient manor of Canonbury, less the western portion which had been sold off. It extended to about 100 acres. The boundaries of the manor were clearly defined: on the north St. Paul's Road and on the south Islington Green. In A.D. 1253 its then owner, Ralph de Berners, gave the manor to the Priory of St. Bartholomew of West Smithfield and it remained their property until the dissolution of the monasteries by Henry VIII. Hence the name Canonsburgh, or Canonbury. Prior William Bolton, between 1509 and 1532, was responsible for building the houses in which the canons lived, which later became known as Canonbury House. Much of Bolton's work remains.

Except for Canonbury House there were no buildings of any importance at Canonbury until the nineteenth century. Most of the estate was planned and leased for development between 1820 and 1850, and the planners did their work well. A few commercial buildings had been erected since, but when I went there ninety per cent of the estate was residential and appeared likely to remain so. Its lay-out was admirable, with wide roads and generous gardens behind the houses. Most of the larger houses were detached or semi-detached, but the smaller ones were in terraces and nearly all had basements, ground and at least two upper floors. Until the end of the First World War Canonbury remained what its developers had intended—a stolidly respectable middle-class suburb. Later, however, the neighbourhood 'went down'. That was partly due to the advent of the motor-car, which created a demand for houses further out, but more particularly I think to the increasing difficulty in getting domestic servants. If you had to do your own chores, a modern two-storey villa was preferable to one of these rather gaunt houses with their high ceilings and several flights of stairs.

Most of the ground leases, granted nearly a century earlier, had been assigned, and it was the exception rather than the rule to find a lessee living on the premises. When you did, he was usually occupying only part of the house and subletting the rest; more often he was an absentee landlord, who sublet the entire house, and there was a different family on each floor. Much of the sanitary accommodation was shared, and if no one had an exclusive tenancy of the garden no one bothered to look after it. And when in 1942 the iron railings in front of the houses were requisitioned and removed, supposedly as a contribution to the war effort, the appearance of the estate deteriorated further.

Near the middle of the estate on high ground is a complex of buildings of considerable historic interest and architectural merit. They include Canonbury Tower, which is the most important example of Tudor architecture in North London. It would appear that Prior Bolton's building consisted of three, or possibly four, blocks around a central courtyard. To the south was a walled park, or 'pleasaunce', with small hexagonal towers at the corners. To the north was the monastic fish pond. In about 1770 the south block was pulled down and replaced by 'five elegant new villas' fronting an internal cul-de-sac. Numbers 1 to 5 Canonbury Place are charming examples of their period. Behind them are long gardens in what was once the pleasaunce, and their front windows overlook the garden of the Tower with an ancient mulberry tree in the centre of the lawn. There may be a more enchanting little corner of old London; if there is, I have yet to see it.

No one knows why Prior Bolton built the Tower. It is 66 feet high and 17 feet square, and constructed of the narrow red bricks characteristic of the period. There is a central staircase and some important rooms in the gabled building adjoining. The view of London from the roof of the Tower is superb, and probably the explanation is simply that Bolton thought his canons would enjoy it.

In 1539 the manor of Canonbury escheated to the Crown and thereafter was granted to a series of court favourites. Among them were Thomas Cromwell, later Earl of Essex; John Dudley, Earl of Warwick; and the Duke of Northumberland. In 1556 Queen Elizabeth I granted it to Thomas, Lord Wentworth. In 1570 Wentworth sold it to Sir John Spencer, citizen and cloth-worker and Lord Mayor of London 1594-95, for £2,000. Spencer was rich, and although the structure of Canonbury House remained much as in Bolton's day he made many im-

Canonbury Tower
A drawing by the author

provements. They included several finely panelled rooms, some splendidly carved chimney-pieces, and ceilings of elaborate plaste work.

Sir John Spencer had only one child, Elizabeth, who was his heiress. To his dislike she was courted by William, Lord Compton, who lived at Tottenham, and he disliked it still more when the young couple eloped. According to tradition, Elizabeth was lowered early one morning from a window of Canonbury House in a baker's basket and Sir John, up betimes, mistook Lord Compton for the baker and commended him for being so early about his business. When he learned the truth he cut off his daughter with the proverbial shilling and said he never wanted to see either of them again. But Queen Elizabeth intervened personally on their behalf and there was a reconciliation. Sir John Spencer died in 1610 and was given a magnificent funeral 'where some thousand men did assist, in mourning cloaks or gownes, amongst which were 320 poor men, who had every one of them a basket given them, stored with . . . provisions'. Later Lord Compton was created an earl and the Marquesses of Northampton are his descendants.

The author[1] of a privately printed booklet, called *Canonbury House*, remarks that Elizabeth Compton 'appears to have had a pretty conceit of herself'. Some years after marrying Lord Compton she wrote him a letter listing all the things she expected him to provide for her. She was to have coaches; carriages; saddle horses; jewels, twenty gowns 'six of them excellent good ones, eight of them for the country, and six other of them very excellent good ones'; chairs; stools; carpets; beds; silver warming pans; £2200 'to put in my purse'; and a retinue of indoor and outdoor servants including a gentleman-usher, six or eight other gentlemen, two coachmen, women-attendants, laundresses, chambermaids and washmaids. The letter concludes: 'So now that I have declared to you what I would have, and what that

---

[1] Henry W. Fincham F.S.A., revised edition 1926.

is that I would not have, I pray that when you be an earl to allow me £1000 more than I now desire, and double attendance. Your loving wife, Eliza Compton.'[1]

But in spite of all this grandeur, Canonbury House did not remain their home for long; perhaps it was not grand enough. But it remained in the family and during the Commonwealth the Third Earl of Northampton lived there. Thereafter it was let to a succession of tenants, and during the eighteenth century appears to have been let in parts. The most distinguished of the tenants, from about 1616 to 1625, was Francis Bacon. Another tenant was Oliver Goldsmith. A third was Washington Irving, who wrote his *Tales of a Traveller* at Canonbury and hoped to be inspired by Goldsmith's muse.

When I first went to Canonbury, the estate, as I have indicated, was a depressing sight. Many of the middle-class tenants sitting at rack rents had been evacuated during the previous autumn, their houses stood empty and their gardens were overgrown. In Canonbury Square, west of the Tower, Story had converted a number of old Georgian houses into flats and more than half were empty for the same reason. It was the same in Canonbury Place. The Canonbury Gentlemen's Club, installed in the Tower by the Fifth Marquess, consisted of a handful of elderly members who seldom went there in war-time. Only the Francis Bacon Society, whose office and library were in an upper room of the Tower (Who knew but that the Writer of the Plays himself might have slept in it?) was as active as ever under the direction of an erudite and charming old lady called Miss Pott. War or no war, she went there regularly, invited me to go to see her, lent me books, and was clearly bent on seducing the new agent from the ranks of the misguided Shakespearians.

One of the first things I did at Canonbury, with Lord Northampton's approval, was to remove Sir John Spencer's panelling and chimney-pieces from the Spencer and Compton Oak Rooms

[1] The letter is preserved in the British Museum: Add. M.S. No. 4176, fol, 57.

112

in the Tower and send them for safe-keeping to Castle Ashby, his Northamptonshire seat. To the disappointment of Miss Pott and her disciples, we found nothing behind the panelling except a couple of old leaden pistol bullets. As it was taken down, section by section, they hoped to discover at any moment the manuscript of *Hamlet* in Bacon's hand. There was nothing we could do about the ceilings beyond making sure that they had been photographed in enough detail to make it possible to repair them if they were damaged.

Almost the first high explosive bombs to fall on London, in the spring of 1940, fell on the Clerkenwell estate. They did extensive damage in Wilmington Square, but mercifully there was no loss of life. Lord Northampton came to London at once and offered to take back to Castle Ashby any of the older tenants who would like to go. Some, but not all, accepted his invitation and were billeted there until the war ended.

That was the beginning of the blitz. It was at its worst from about June 1940 until June 1941, when it eased off and the bombing became intermittent until the 'baby blitz' of February 1944. One thing to be said for the blitz, compared with the buzz bombs that came later, was that it only troubled us at night and the All Clear sounded at the first sign of dawn. People then emerged bleary-eyed and dishevelled from the air-raid shelters in their gardens, the communal shelters in the streets, or the subterranean regions of Essex Road tube station. They were remarkably cheerful in the circumstances, exchanged their morning bomb-stories, got their breakfasts, and went to see what else had been knocked down.

On the night of May 29, 1941, during the second great raid on the City of London, the offices of Ferris and Puckridge in Queen Street were destroyed by fire bombs, and nothing remained of the block next morning except a pile of smoking rubble within blackened walls. Our suite had been on the second floor, and too much space had long been occupied by old files and deed boxes. Before the war Bill Gillett and I agreed we ought to get rid of some of it; the trouble was that, both being by nature hoarders, we could never decide what should go and what should be kept. Hitler made the decision and we lost the lot.

The Northampton estate office was in Clerkenwell, only a short distance north of the City and nearly as vulnerable. So we rented a temporary office in Southgate, a northern suburb, and arranged for the more important estate records to be sent there. The staff went too, except those who were needed on the spot— for example, the building surveyors. Most of the staff lived on that side of London, and by doing as much of the clerical work as possible at Southgate we helped solve their transport problems. I myself took a tenancy of a house at Cuffley, not far from South-gate, and was able to get enough petrol to travel to and from the estates by car.

Obviously, however, this was an inconvenient arrangement. Towards the end of 1941, when the bombing had become less intense, I advised my employers that we should bring the staff back to the estates and as far as possible house them under one roof. I advised further that, with the prospect of a great many houses in Canonbury reverting from ground leases during the next few years, the interests of good management required that the main estate office should be in Canonbury rather than Clerkenwell. It was agreed that my headquarters should be Number 1, Canonbury Place, the largest of the 'elegant new villas'. I then told the trustees that I should like to live as close as possible to the estate office at least until the war ended, and thereafter Number 2, an exquisite little house next door, became the agent's official residence.

Need I say that the management of a great estate in the middle of London in war-time was a depressing business? We were full of plans for post-war redevelopment and it was not in my nature to take kindly to a situation in which, having made my plans, I was unable to begin to carry them out. Another difficulty was that our post-war plans hinged on how much of the estates would be left when the war ended, and it was impossible to forecast week by week what would remain standing and what would have been destroyed. In the meantime, thanks to the efforts of a loyal and competent staff in conjunction with local builders, we pursued a policy of 'mend and make-do'. Only temporary repairs were practicable as long as the war lasted, and because of recurrent bombing some of the properties had to be repaired again and again. The most grievous part of the burden was born by my rent collectors and the staff of the weekly-rentals office. They knew all the tenants personally, and often after the estates had been bombed there was a melancholy toll of injury and death.

All through this difficult period I had every possible support from the owners, and I should like to put on record what model landlords they were. They gave me a wide discretion and it was understood that in an emergency my duty was to act first and tell them about it later. I cannot recall any suggestion that I made for the welfare of the tenants generally, or of any individual tenant, that they turned down. As their agent I held several *ex officio* quasi-philanthropic appointments that had formerly been held by Story. I was a trustee of Lord Northampton's 'Charitable Trust', which existed for the benefit of local and other charities. I was also chairman of the Northampton Estates Society, which had been established by his father under the Friendly Society Acts to encourage thrift among his tenants.

The frustrating thing about estate management in war-time was one's inability to break new ground or achieve anything constructive. The only works I did on the estate, that might be described as constructive, was the conversion of a cellar under a block of flats into a mortuary at the request of the Town Clerk; and the digging of a pond at the end of my garden at the request of the Fire Brigade, who wanted a supply of 'static water' lest the mains should be destroyed.

A common way of providing static water was in the basement of a bombed building which, cemented and filled, looked like a big swimming bath. Alternatively the water was stored in huge and hideous open tanks made of cast-iron plates which quickly became rusty. We had as yet no bombed buildings in or near Canonbury Place, and apart from their ugliness the iron tanks would have been useless after the war. The need for static water afforded me an admirable opportunity of digging a formal pond that would be decorative in itself and in which, unless unhappily the Fire Brigade had cause to drain it, I could plant water lilies and keep goldfish. Later we dug two more ponds and surrounded them with old York paving. Water lilies were not difficult to come by, but the goldfish were small and very expensive; it seemed that they were bred in Japan.

A secondary use for the pond in my garden—I admit it was an afterthought—was to augment our food supply. In the old days a popular dish at the Savoy had been *truite au bleu*. In the centre of the restaurant was a large ornamental glass tank in which trout, unaware of their imminent fate, swam happily around. The waiter handed your order to a water-bailiff in evening dress who, with remarkable dexterity, netted a good-looking trout and bore it off to the chef. Why, I asked myself, at a time when the fish shops had nothing to offer but salted cod and whale steaks, should I not perform the same operation on a larger scale? It would be patriotic—and I liked trout.

It was a simple matter to couple up the domestic water supply so as to provide a continuous flow of water through the pond. It was more difficult to obtain the trout. But I made inquiries in all directions and eventually located a hatchery in Sussex. There can scarcely have been a keen demand for their product in the middle of the war and they said they would be delighted to supply as many trout as I wanted, suggesting an average weight of half to three-quarters of a pound. That seemed big enough for my stretch of water, so I ordered a couple of dozen for a start.

They travelled in a large circular zinc container with a ventilating cowl on the top. I met them at Victoria Station and with some difficulty got them across London to Canonbury. With the trout, besides the invoice, was a card of instructions of which the most important was that they were to be fed on horse meat. We carried them in their container to the edge of the pond, unscrewed the lid and tipped them in.

For the first few days they did not need to be fed. That was because they lived on the goldfish, a catastrophe that I had not anticipated. I had imagined that, especially in war-time, trout and goldfish would sink any differences there might be between them and live contentedly side by side. It did not work out that way. As soon as a trout felt hungry he selected, like the water-bailiff in evening dress, a good-looking goldfish. He then gave chase. Round and round the pond they went at high speed, the trout a grey shadowy form beneath the surface; the brightly coloured goldfish, as clearly visible to his pursuer as he was to me, stood no chance. Suddenly the goldfish vanished, which meant that the trout had swallowed him whole. Bridget, my housekeeper, who had cherished the goldfish and looked on them as pets, was horrified. But there was nothing she or I could do, and before long the trout had the pond to themselves.

In the meantime we had been looking for horse meat. No horse meat, as such, was to be bought in North London. Fortunately, however, my trout revealed an unexpected liking for Wall's sausages which were said—I had no reason to doubt it—to contain pork.

When they had had time to settle in, I gave my first dinner party. Bridget, with no show of enthusiasm, had spent the day over her cookery books because the main course was to be *truite au bleu*. We opened a precious bottle of gin, had cocktails on the lawn, and when I judged the time was ripe I armed myself with a landing net and advanced on the pond.

If the reader has never caught a trout with a landing net, in a pond seven feet square by four feet deep, I advise him not to bother to try. The evening wore on. After an hour or so, during which each of my guests in turn had a go at netting his dinner, we agreed it was hopeless. Bridget was vastly relieved. In spite of her expressed desire for vengeance for the deaths of 'her' goldfish, she was disgusted by the whole enterprise and remarked with satisfaction that there was a tin of Spam in the larder.

Suddenly I thought of another method which, even if it were ineffective, was more sporting. I ordered my guests from the water's edge to give the fish a chance to calm down. Then I went indoors and put up a trout rod, complete with line and 4x cast, and tied a fly to the cast. For the second time I advanced stealthily—to fish the evening rise.

A new difficulty presented itself. The garden was long and narrow, the pond was at the end of it, a mulberry tree was half-way down. It was impossible to cast *down* the garden because of the overhanging branches. It was impossible to cast *up* the garden from beyond the pond, or across from either side, because the boundary walls were too close. The only way was to enlist the co-operation of my next-door-neighbour and next-door-neighbour but one. Standing on the wall which divided their gardens, I could see at least part of the pond. After a few false casts across my neighbour's garden and over our wall, avoiding the hollyhocks, I succeeded in laying my fly on the surface of the water. The trout, agreeably surprised and bored no doubt with their unbroken diet of Wall's sausages, rose as a man. The goldfish were avenged and the *truite au bleu* was first-class. I must return, however, to less agreeable but more important matters.

We have seen that Canonbury House, during more than four centuries, had a variety of occupants. First the Canons of St. Bartholomew; then on the dissolution of the monasteries a series of royal favourites; then a Lord Mayor of London, whose daughter and heiress was married to the First Earl of Northampton; then distinguished men of letters; finally a tenants' club.

I have mentioned that before the war I spent a winter in South London working in my evenings in the Oxford and Bermondsey Boys' Clubs. But my experience was limited. It was negligible, for example, compared with that of Basil Henriques, founder and first warden of the Bernhard Baron Settlement in Berner Street E.1 (now Henriques Street), or of that other great man, the Hon. Arthur Villiers (incidentally a partner in Barings), of the Eton Manor Clubs in Hackney Wick. In war-time, however, what with the blackout and a necessary curtailment of all forms of transport, it did not require much experience to perceive the need for something of the same kind in Islington, albeit on a smaller scale.

I was fortunate in two respects. During the period of Story's agency, at the invitation and with the financial support of the Marquess, an old friend of mine, C. C. Walkinshaw, had provided certain organized social services for the benefit of young people on the Canonbury Estate. 'Walks', as he was known throughout North London, was warden of the Mary Ward Settlement in Bloomsbury and a fellow magistrate in the Metropolitan Juvenile Courts; he was as anxious as I to expand the activities of what had been known hitherto as the Canonbury Guild. The other respect in which I was fortunate was that Canonbury Tower and the buildings alongside it, including King Edward's Hall, which had been built by the Fifth Marquess for the tenants' club, were vacant. It was decided, with Lord Northampton's approval, that they should become a youth centre under Walkinshaw's general direction. It was further decided that I, who lived opposite and took an active interest, should become its president.

Walks and I agreed at the outset that the age-group we ought to cater for ranged from fourteen or a bit less, to seventeen or a bit more; that it should be a mixed club for boys and girls;

119

and that if possible it should be open every night of the week.

Pressure was put on us by Lord Northampton to widen the age-group. He said he thought too little was being done for children of school age (the leaving age was then fourteen), and he would have liked us to make contact with children of seven and eight and keep them within the social organization of the estate until they grew up. That was a counsel of excellence, but under war conditions and in our limited accommodation it was impracticable. Under-thirteens need to be treated differently from adolescents and their leaders need a different type of training. Lord Northampton's suggestion would have necessitated two separate organizations under the same roof, which, at a time when there was an acute shortage of club leaders and voluntary helpers, was something we could not possibly have coped with.

A more practical criticism of our proposals, again by Lord Northampton, was that boys and girls should not be encouraged to take more than a platonic interest in one another until they were seventeen; and in the meantime, if they were to have clubs, that they ought to have separate ones. I resisted that criticism, but mainly on the ground of expediency, for under normal conditions I am inclined to think he was right. Girls tend to mature about two years earlier than boys of the same age, and one of the difficulties in a mixed club is that adolescents, particularly the younger adolescents, differ in their attitudes from their contemporaries of the opposite sex. A girl of fourteen or fifteen, if only subconsciously, is already looking forward to, and preparing herself for, the fulfilment of her supreme function of wife and mother; it is not unnatural that an at early age she should begin to look on boys as potential partners. The average boy of the same age does not think that way at all. Girls to him are 'silly things'; *his* interests are—or should be—in boxing, running and football. 'Experience has shown', wrote Basil Henriques, 'that the finest qualities of manhood are created when the young adolescent boy is being trained with members of his own sex.' The danger in a mixed club is that the girl, displaying a perfectly natural physical interest in the male sex, arouses in the young boy feelings which nature intended to remain dormant for the time being. It militates against the training process. Walks and I were resolved as far as possible to provide separate activities for the boys and girls as well as those which they could share. But I replied to Northampton that if we established a mixed club and later the girls' side were to be discontinued, the boys' side would continue much as before. If, however, the boys' side were to be discontinued, the girls' side would pack up at once. I went on to say that if, under existing conditions, we did not provide an agreeable meeting ground for the sexes, an alternative, at any rate for the girls, was necking in a dark alley-way or copulation behind a hedge in the blackout.

Walks and I, more than most people, had had an opportunity of observing at first hand the dangers and temptations that beset the adolescent girl in war-time. The number of such girls being brought before the Metropolitan Juvenile Courts was increasing by leaps and bounds. Most of them were brought, not for criminal offences, but on the statutory ground that they were in 'need of care or protection'. Not infrequently the girl had run away from home, had had sexual intercourse with one or more young soldiers, and become pregnant or infected by venereal disease (sometimes both), before being picked up by the police. I do not for a moment suggest that we solved this problem locally by establishing a mixed boys' and girls' club in Canonbury Tower. I claim no more than that we helped a little towards its solution in the most adverse circumstances.

Once the centre had been opened its membership grew rapidly. The most we could accommodate was a little over three hundred, and a large proportion of the members attended every night. We certainly met with difficulties, one of which

121

was to find competent instructors and helpers. However, we managed to establish a first-rate carpentry group in one of the denuded oak rooms; there were boxing, table-tennis and a billiards table, darts and of course a canteen. Outdoors, although we never got so far as forming our own football team, there were practice runs through the darkened streets. A valuable and popular activity by the older boys was fire prevention. Canonbury Tower had been classified as an 'historic building' and the Islington Borough Council and the Fire Brigade gave all the help they could. The Town Clerk presented me with a white tin hat and excused me from being enrolled as an air-raid warden so that I should not have to leave the estate. We had our own motor fire-pump in charge of a specially trained team of boys. It was stationed permanently in Canonbury Place and their duty was to start the engine and run out the hoses immediately the Alert sounded.

In the Tower we had a mixed debating society and a mixed drama group, and when an opportunity arose I asked my friends to come and give lectures. I remember in particular that remarkable woman, Constance Spry, addressing the girls on 'flower arrangement'. There were few flowers to be bought in the shops, and she amazed us by what could be achieved with the aid of a few jam pots filled with wild flowers picked in the deserted estate gardens—never, she impressed upon us, to be referred to as 'weeds'. But admittedly the girls preferred dancing before everything and one of my tasks, qua their president but also qua estate agent, was to persuade them to cut down the blare of the gramophone which could be heard for several hundred yards in all directions from King Edward's Hall.

Another of our difficulties was in the vital question of leadership. The club leader was paid out of Lord Northampton's Charitable Trust, but in war-time experienced and efficient leaders, like instructors, were hard to come by. In the early days of the centre we were plagued by doubtless dedicated, but extremely left-wing, leaders who insisted that a youth centre must be run on strictly democratic principles. That meant, as far as I could see, that the leader abrogated all personal responsibility in favour of a 'democratically elected' management committee of boys and girls to whom all decisions were referred. Tory as I am, I allowed myself to be humbugged by that nonsense and inevitably, as I ought to have foreseen, things went wrong. The most aggressive and self-assertive members got themselves elected to the committee. Mild admonitions by the leader were ignored. There was a lack of any kind of discipline and the members of the centre appeared to do exactly as they liked. Tenants on the estate justifiably complained of disturbance by these 'hooligans', whom the new agent, to add to the wretchedness of war conditions, had planted in their midst.

In despair I went to consult Henriques. I asked him whether it would be a good thing to close the centre, at least temporarily, and possibly reopen it later if and when the members came to realize how much they were missing.

'By all means', said Basil, 'close this club or youth centre or whatever you call it. *But don't reopen it.* Wait a couple of months until things have settled down. Then announce the opening of a *new* club which no one who happened to belong to the old one has a right to join.' He went on to give me a little lecture on so-called democracy, and assured me from a lifetime's experience that it was quite impracticable in any organization of teenagers. 'Of course,' he said, 'afford them every reasonable opportunity to decide and choose for themselves and let it appear that the administration is democratic, but for goodness' sake ensure that there is a benevolent autocrat in reserve to descend from heaven like a *deus ex machina* if need be.'

Basil's advice was pretty drastic. If we were to close the centre, the club leader would resign—not that that would matter much. Most of the helpers would disperse and that would be a loss. Tenants on the more distant parts of the estate, especially parents, would deplore the closing of the centre, and conversely there were tenants within sight and hearing of the Tower who would oppose any resumption of its use for the same purpose. At a time when heaven knows we had enough difficulties to contend with, it was a bore to have to begin all over again. A personal problem was my dual role. As president of the Canonbury Youth Centre and largely responsible for its conception, I was desperately anxious that it should be a success; as agent for the trustees, I was responsible for the well-being of the estate tenants and their interests had to come first.

The problem, I suppose, was one that we all have to resolve occasionally. Things are going wrong and look like getting worse. Two alternative courses are open to us. One is to take no action, on the ground that it would be unwise to interfere, and hope that eventually things will sort themselves out—as they sometimes do. The other course is *to do something* even if it turns out—as it sometimes does—to have been precipitate, tactless or misguided. I can only judge for myself. Looking back over my life and regretting my many mistakes, I am driven to the conclusion that far more of them were due to doing *nothing* than to doing *something*. The reader's experience may be the converse of mine, and I do not venture to advise.

Perhaps, therefore, it was not surprising that after a conference with Walkinshaw I decided to do as Basil had suggested. I told no one else of my intentions, least of all Lord Northampton. In spite of further warnings the state of ill-discipline in the Tower persisted; so one evening, supported by a few stalwarts, I went over from my house and turned the whole boiling lot into the street. The doors were then locked and notices were posted: 'THE CANONBURY YOUTH CENTRE IS CLOSED'.

It remains to add that the 'new' centre opened a few months later, flourished exceedingly, and that when the war had ended and the panelling and chimney pieces had been restored to the Tower, alternative premises were found nearby. I need hardly say that the new centre opened under wiser and less 'democratic' leadership, with a management committee of whom the nucleus had been hand-picked. It was recognized, moreover, that the centre was not a democracy but a benevolent autocracy—and *I* was the benevolent autocrat.

VIII

A London Estate in War-time (II)

Buzz bombs and V rockets – an embarrassing journey – eight-teenth-century candlesticks – Dutch courage and where it led – good things in war-time – bad things – dreadful things – peace but no plenty – a selling up – advice to a young land agent.

The final months of the war, after the Normandy landings, are memorable. But for us Londoners the thrill of the spectacle of the Allied Armies, moving slowly but steadily across Europe was countered in some measure by the effects of the German campaign of retaliation (*Vergeltung*) that we were called on to endure. I refer to what Sir Winston Churchill, in *The Second World War*, describes as 'the pilotless bombardment'.[1]

On the evening of June 12, 1944, my old friend Sir Charles Petrie, the historian, came to dine at Canonbury. I think his wife must have been in the country, as there were only the two of us and he had accepted my invitation to stay the night. In war-time, because of the difficulty of getting home after dinner in the black-out, there was much to be said in favour of the prin-ciple enunciated (for quite a different reason) by Mr. Jorrocks: 'Where I dines I sleeps.'

I hope I gave Charles a good dinner in spite of the limitations imposed by the meat ration. I fear we had nothing more exciting to accompany it than Algerian Burgundy (Wine Society ration, six bottles per member per month). But in addition I had brought up from the cellar one of my few remaining bottles of port.

[1] Most of the technical details in this chapter are condensed from Volume IV, Chapter III.

It was a warm, still evening, a little cloudy, and the french window overlooking the garden was open. Round about midnight, having nearly finished the port, we were thinking in terms of bed and were about to rise from the table when the sirens began to wail. This was not unusual, for although the violence of the blitz had abated we still had air raids—sometimes nasty ones—from time to time. What *was* unusual on this occasion was that, instead of the interval which normally elapsed between the last wail of the sirens and something happening, there was an immediate burst of gunfire to the south. Even more unusual was the sound of an aircraft flying low and apparently towards us, the roar of its engine drowning the noise of the more distant guns. We hurried to the window, but could see nothing. The roar grew louder and the aircraft, to whomever it belonged, passed near to us. Suddenly the noise stopped and there was silence for perhaps a minute. Then came the rumble of an explosion and our windows shook.

They had scarcely stopped shaking when there was a knocking on the door between my house and the estate office, which I usually kept locked, and I hurried to open it. It was Card, the office keeper, on duty that night as a fire-watcher. He was an elderly, quiet man who had always been imperturbable, no matter how many bombs were falling around. Even Card was in a state of excitement.

'*Wonderful* news, Sir! Just seen an enemy bomber shot down. On fire it was, with flames pouring out of the back. One of our shells must have hit it, because just as it went over the engine stopped. That bang you heard was its bomb load exploding when it came down. I suppose some poor chaps must have copped it, but, by God Sir, what a splendid shot!' Charles and I returned to the table and emptied the port decanter, and I hope we gave old Card a glass. Then we went upstairs and to sleep.

In the papers next morning there was no mention of this achievement by our anti-aircraft defences. Nor on the day following. But that was no surprise, because in war-time there were many things that for strategic reasons or 'the avoidance of alarm or despondency' we were not told. Most of the news calculated to create alarm or despondency came to us over the German radio, with sinister embellishments, in the excellent English of the persuasive gentleman whom we nicknamed Lord Haw Haw. After the war he was convicted of high treason and hanged.

The lack of any official exultation over the 'shooting-down' incident on the night of June 12–13 was because in truth it was not a shooting-down at all. The aircraft, that had roared so noisily above us until it glided down to wreak havoc further on, was the vanguard of Hitler's allegedly secret weapons. The Germans called it the V1. It was followed about three months later by the V2. Mercifully the V3, a multiple gun with barrels 400 feet long, whence it was planned to fire a six-inch shell into the centre of London every few minutes, failed to work, and someone had the unenviable job of informing the Führer to that effect. Over here we called the V1 the 'doodle bug' or 'buzz bomb' because of the noise it made. It may be thought that the second name was the more apposite; the doodle bug is a noisy insect but harmless, and these things were not.

Two days passed before the buzz bombs arrived in strength, and I can remember few nights more exciting than that of June 15–16. During the twenty-four hours, beginning at midnight on the 15th, more than two hundred came over London. Sometimes, when an air raid was in progress, I used to go to the top of Canonbury Tower and 'keep observation' (as the policeman says) from a small square room under the roof with windows in three walls. I went there that night, accompanied by two fire-watchers from the boys' club.

That was not so brave as it may sound. The Tower is a massive piece of masonry with thick walls, and the windows in the observation room were positioned high enough to enable you to duck and keep out of a possible line of fire if trouble seemed to be coming your way. The chances of a direct hit on a building only seventeen feet square were negligible, and in case the lower part of the building were to catch fire I had installed a 'Davy' fire escape which would enable us to lower ourselves in slings down the outside. I always felt safer at the top of the Tower, capable of seeing what was going on, than in a basement wondering what would happen next. Also if one is frightened—and I admit that at times I *was* frightened—there is no better antidote than being in charge of young people and having to set an example.

From the top of Canonbury Tower I could see all the buildings that went to make up Canonbury House: the fire-watchers at their stations on the roofs; the fire hoses unrolled across the garden; the pump, its engine running noisily, in Canonbury Place. I could also see the whole of the Canonbury estate, and although Lord Northampton's Clerkenwell estate was too far away to distinguish its boundaries, I knew where it lay and could see at once if anything untoward occurred.

During the night of June 15-16 I stayed up the Tower till dawn. Then I came down, assuming illogically that once daylight had come we should enjoy the same respite from pilotless bombing as we had become used to during and since the blitz. While up the Tower I had kept a record. The flames emitted by the buzz bombs made them look in the distance like fire-flies, and it was thrilling to watch our anti-aircraft shells bursting round them. Suddenly the flame would go out, but it did not follow that a shell had gone home. More often it meant that the engine of the bomb had stopped automatically and the diabolical contrivance was on its downward glide; a minute or so later the sky was illumined by the explosion when it hit the ground. We noted the time when each bomb was sighted, roughly the direction it was taking, and approximately where it burst. I wrote all this in pencil on the whitewashed wall of the Tower beside the window, and I remember reflecting that it might create a further interest in this ancient building for future generations. Regrettably, due to some mistake, when the inside of the Tower was redecorated after the war, my record was painted out.

Before giving any further account of Hitler's secret weapons, it may possibly be of interest to my younger readers if I explain briefly what they were and how they were fired.

The enemy's great research station and factory for rockets and guided missiles was at Peenemünde, an island in East Germany at the mouth of the River Peene. We had known of its existence for a long time, and for many months before the first of its products made an appearance it had been a regular target for our bombers. The V1 was smaller even than a single-seater aircraft, was powered by a jet engine and carried a ton of high explosive in its nose. It was launched by catapult from one of the specially constructed and well camouflaged ramps or 'ski sites' which were dotted about the Pas de Calais. Once the machine was in the air its course was controlled by a magnetic compass, and the distance between the launching ramp and where it was intended to explode was regulated by a propeller. The propeller was driven by the passage of the machine through the air, and after a predetermined number of revolutions it tipped the controls and the descent began. Sometimes, by accident or design, the engine cut out and the machine came down in silence, but not always. A buzz bomb exploded on impact, generally without penetrating the ground.

It was revealed after the war that all the buzz bombs intended for London had been aimed at Tower Bridge, which the Germans looked on as a focal point. Only a proportion got as far. But some went further and the church tower at Heydon, a Cambridgeshire village near my present home, nearly fifty miles north of London, was demolished by a V1 which appeared unexpectedly out of the clouds. A major difficulty for our fighter pilots, chasing the things across the sky and trying to shoot them down, was the speed at which they travelled—about 400 miles an hour. And the damage they did when they hit the ground was an obvious reason for trying to shoot them down outside London. That is why, by June 21, our defences had been moved from Central London and resited on the North Downs, and only a month later the entire defence organization was redeployed on the coast.

In the meantime the Allied Armies were gradually over-running the launching sites, and early in September, prematurely as it turned out, Herbert Morrison, the Home Secretary, announced 'The Battle of London is won.' From then onward, although we were troubled intermittently by buzz bombs, the V2, against which by comparison there was no defence, troubled us more. In all about 8,500 VIs were launched against London; of those about 1,000 crashed soon after being launched and about 2,400 got through. The total of civilian casualties caused by the VIs were 6,184 killed and 17,987 seriously injured.

The V2 was a rocket weighing about twelve tons, and it carried about the same weight of high explosive as a VI. Its thrust was developed in a jet from the combustion of alcohol combined with liquid oxygen. It began by rising vertically from the launching pad to a height of about six miles; then automatic controls increased its speed at an angle of 45 degrees. Eventually, when the speed was sufficient for the pre-determined range, the supply of fuel was cut off. 'The missile then flew in a gigantic parabola, reaching a height of about fifty miles and falling about two hundred miles from the launching point. Its maximum speed was about four thousand miles an hour, and the whole flight took no more than three or four minutes.' The first V2 fell at Chiswick on September 8 and during the next seven months 500 descended on London. The total of civilians killed and seriously injured by the V2 were 2,724 and 6,476 respectively.

It will be noted that on average the V2 caused twice as many casualties as the V1, although the size of their war heads was about the same. It was due to the different methods of approach of the two weapons. You could hear a V1 coming, often from a long way off, and had time to take cover; and if you were able to find cover below ground you were relatively safe unless it made a direct hit. The V2, being a rocket, fell silently out of the blue and if, as the saying was, it had your name on it, that was that.

The best protection from the V1 was a deep air-raid shelter or a tube-railway station. Failing one or other of these, a basement. I remember on my way round the estates scurrying uninvited down basement steps. If there was neither a shelter, nor an underground station, nor a basement, and we heard a buzz bomb coming, we were officially advised to lie down. Winston Churchill's chauffeur, having motored up from Chequers on the third day of the V1 bombardment, was surprised to see people lying face downward in Parliament Square. But a trouble with the English is that we are so self-conscious and the delicate question, when a buzz bomb was coming, was who should lie down first. There was the cautionary tale of the lady who was wearing a new suit and for fear of spoiling it decided to remain standing. The buzz bomb landed and 'she vanished without trace'.

One evening I was due to stay a night with my friend and later my partner, Fred Ragg, at his home in Surrey. I was travelling in one of those green electric trains from Waterloo and there were four of us, obviously all business men commuting, in the four corners of a first-class compartment. When the train stopped beyond Surbiton, we thought nothing of it and went on reading our evening papers. And when the buzz bomb was heard approaching, we concentrated even more intently on the news to show each other how cool we were. Suddenly, when it sounded as if it was almost directly over us, the engine stopped. A moment later we were all down on the floor between the seats and remained there in a heap for fifty palpitating seconds until there was the thud of an explosion down the line. Then rather shame-facedly we scrambled to our feet, dusted ourselves down, and returned to our respective corners. The train moved on slowly, stopping at every station, and as each passenger got out in turn he bade the others a courteous 'Good evening' as if nothing unusual had occurred.

I had a more profitable experience during the buzz bomb period in the West End of London. I was walking down the east side of New Bond Street when the Alert sounded, traffic came to a standstill and people looked apprehensively at the sky. There was no air-raid shelter or convenient basement. Therefore I took temporary refuge under an archway which, when I had time to look around, I perceived to be the main entrance to Sotheby's. Inside the building an auction was in progress; the auctioneer must have been deaf or very brave.

I had, of course, no knowledge what kind of an auction it was. For all I knew he was selling old masters, antique furniture, Chinese porcelain, or jade elephants. I said to myself: '*Whatever he's selling, now's the moment to bid!*' So I hurried in and raised my hand. I was rewarded, for a song, with a charming pair of late eighteenth-century candlesticks, which have graced my dinner table in dire memory of the buzz bombs for twenty-five years.

'A touch of nature makes the whole world kin' and in a great city like London, faced as we all were by a common danger, that undoubtedly was true. Some of my experiences, even in the worst times, are amusing to look back on. For example, there was that night during a heavy raid when I and my neigh-bours in Canonbury Place decided to leave our comfortable bedrooms for the comparative safety of the public air-raid shelter over the road. We left the front doors of our houses ajar so that, if the houses were hit by fire bombs, the fire watchers on duty would have no difficulty in getting inside. Three of the houses, Numbers 2, 3 and 4, are of identical Georgian design, and approached from the pavement by little winding flights of stone steps. The bombing went on intermittently hour after hour. A bottle of whisky, that I had taken into the shelter with me, was much appreciated; I must confess I had more than my fair share, which explains my decision in the early hours of the morning, fortified by Dutch rather than English courage, to go home to bed.

It was a pitch black night, and even if I had had a torch I should not have dared use it. With considerable difficulty I made my way across Canonbury Place and was thankful when I had a firm grasp of the iron handrail. A trifle unsteadily, I pushed the door open, groped my way along the hall, up the stairs and into my bedroom. To my surprise the black-out curtains were not drawn and for some unknown reason Bridget, who had stayed behind in the shelter with the others, had not made my bed. It further appeared—if in utter darkness 'appear' is the correct word—that the pillows were at the bottom end and my pyjamas missing. More than a little vexed, I lowered myself on to the bed with most of my clothes on and quickly fell asleep . . . I was awakened just after sunrise, with a bad headache, by the drone of the sirens sounding the All Clear. My surroundings were unfamiliar. I was not only in the wrong room, *but in the wrong house.*

If one side of the coin was gay, the other was grim. During the first week of the V1 bombardment the office of the Northampton Estates Society at Highbury Corner, of which I was chairman, received a direct hit. Two girls had gone down to the basement to have their lunch and were unhurt. Poor Hallett, secretary of the society, had elected to remain at his desk. He died at it.

After that tragedy I moved the whole staff of the estate office into the basement. It was on ground level at the back and access to it was across the garden. We built a blast-wall in front of the entrance, barricaded the windows and shored up the ceiling of the strong room. Having sent Bridget to stay with my mother in the country, I found myself alone—as was my next-door neighbour, Edward Barran. For company as well as for safety, he and I shared a bedroom which we had contrived in a vault under the lawn. It was entered from an area, and no doubt the eighteenth-century architect had intended it for coals. We whitewashed the walls, spread matting on the flagstones, installed some bunks and stools, and made an escape hatch at the far end. We were thus able to offer hospitality for the night to any visitor, irrespective of sex, caught napping by the sirens. But that was always on the understanding that neither he, nor she, complained about our other lodgers—one of whom was a friendly toad.

After taking all the precautions we could in this old house, we carried on and hoped for the best, and in the event the only damage caused by enemy action in Canonbury Place was trifling. I wonder whether the present lessee of Number 1 realizes that the house he occupies once had the distinction of being known locally as 'Fort Watson'.

No V2 weapon fell on either of the Northampton estates, and that was something to be thankful for. Like the V1s, more of the V2s fell in South than in North London. In Southwark, near to my juvenile court, a V2 hit a factory, causing appalling casualties among a staff consisting mainly of young girls. We had a V1 in Canonbury just off the Essex Road. Essex Road was the estate boundary, and although the bomb fell on the other side of the road it did us a lot of damage. Our worst experience was the one that demolished a row of old Georgian houses in Clerkenwell and severely damaged many others by blast. They were all tenanted by working-class families and the 'incident' occurred in the middle of the night. I think it was early the following morning that I received at Canonbury an unexpected visit from Arthur Villiers. Although he was a partner in Barings, he had never been concerned with the Northampton Settlement and I don't think he had ever been on the estate before. He told me he gathered that the tenants had been having a pretty rough time, and as none of the other partners was available he had come up as 'the landlord' to have a look round. It was typical of the man.

Looking back over those years, I realize that there was nothing out of the ordinary in any of my war-time experiences. I shared them with countless others, and much of what happened is now obscured by time. Yet, as one writes, the memories crowd back—of good things as well as bad things, and sometimes of dreadful things. 'Calling shapes and beckoning shadows' seen only dimly to begin with, reveal themselves in substance before they vanish once more into the mist. Here is a summing up.

Good things. The essential kindliness of people, not least the young. The effectiveness of most in their efforts to help. Courage. The patience and forbearance of the tenantry. Good news of the war. My splendid staff in the estate office. Work of the Heavy Rescue. The long clear note of the sirens sounding the All Clear. Cockney humour. Pear and apple blossom in spring-time in the gardens of ruined houses. Ripe mulberries. The delicious flavour of an off-the-ration joint. Mrs. Mops' morning bomb-story: 'Come clean between the chimney pots it did, saw it wiv me own eyes. Made all me 'air stand stright up on me 'ead; I was just saying to me old man . . .'

Bad things. The ineffectiveness of a minority and their glib excuse: 'Don't you know there's a *war* on?' Bad news of the war. Casualty lists. The miseries of the blackout. Queues. Filling in forms. Clothing coupons. The lingering smell of burned wood. Broken glass. Tin hats. Gas masks. Fire hoses all over the road. The wail of the sirens sounding the Alert. Fear. Bereavement. Bombed-out families. Sodden bedding and smashed furniture, piled pathetically on the pavements . . .

Dreadful things. Fire. Smoke. Blood. Stench. After effects of a buzz bomb. Terrified humanity surging towards the supposed safety of a tube-railway station. Man sprawling in the forecourt of a pub—might be drunk until you noticed his neck was broken. Arrival at a public building to find it bombed in the night—

air-raid shelter beneath and seventy dead. Corpses dug out of rubble. Stiffened body of a small boy, still clad in his pyjamas, being wrapped for removal in a rubber sheet . . . And so one could go on.

The post-war story of the Marquess of Northampton's estates in North London can be told shortly. It was a sad one for me and I would hazard even sadder for most of his tenants.

Some people appeared to be under the impression that once an armistice had been signed, the lights had gone up and the bombs had stopped falling, everything would quickly return to normal. Anyone who believed that was gravely mistaken. The frustrations we had endured in the war years did not fade away with the smoke of the victory bonfires. Food remained restricted and for a long time nearly all consumer goods were scarce. To begin with, very rightly, no building work was allowed except for the urgent repair of war damage. Then followed a long period during which all building had to be licensed, and there were severe penalties for anyone who exceeded the permitted expenditure. Here and there a few houses were built, but mainly with a priority for agricultural workers. And in the meantime, under Part VI of the Labour Government's Town and County Planning Act 1947, all development values were to be expropriated to the State on the payment of compensation to landowners which, had Part VI come into force, would undoubtedly have been considered inadequate.[1]

When the war ended there were many more empty properties in Canonbury than in Clerkenwell. Both estates were repopulated by degrees. In Canonbury, where there were a lot of attractive early nineteenth-century detached houses, and in Canonbury

---

[1] 'Development value' was the difference between the value of land and buildings for their existing use and their estimated value if put to a more profitable use. A global sum of £300 millions was to be provided to compensate the owners. Thereafter any increase in the value of land arising from its develpoment was to accrue to the State. Part VI of the Act was later repealed.

Square, where Colonel Story had converted a number of terrace houses into flats, I was able to pick and choose the new tenants. Canonbury Tower was a focal point. With the approval of the trustees, I lowered the high brick wall, that had surrounded what was once the priory close, and laid out the land as an attractive garden. With the willing co-operation of my building surveyors I made other improvements. The superb oak panelling and chimney pieces were brought back from the country, cleaned and stripped of their varnish on the expert advice of the late Mr. Ralph Edwards, Keeper of Woodwork in the Victoria and Albert Museum, and reinstated in the Tower. A few of the pre-war tenants were still living on the estate. Ronald Carton of *The Times*, who leased the most elegant of the 'elegant new villas' in Canonbury Place, had never left it. Hugh Popham, Keeper of the Print Room in the British Museum, who had been evacuated with his prints to the fastnesses of Wales, made haste to return. Sir Philip Hendy, newly appointed Director of the National Gallery, took a lease of a charming house in Canonbury Square.

Canonbury, although inconveniently situated in relation to the West End of London, is easily accessible from the City and Fleet Street. The new residents told their friends about it, and the friends came to look for themselves and made inquiries at the estate office. Gradually the district became known. Many of the early post-war lettings of the larger houses were to not-so-prosperous business men and journalists, with a sprinkling of artists, who might have preferred Chelsea but could not afford it and were attracted to Canonbury by the low level of the controlled rents.

On both estates it was quite different with the small weekly houses. Most of their occupants had remained throughout the war, spending the nights, when bombing was bad, in private or public air-raid shelters or deep down on the platforms of the tube-railway stations. Those who had been evacuated hurried back to London, thankful to find their old homes still standing. In this class of property there were *no* vacancies. On the contrary, we had long waiting lists, which in Canonbury were swollen by the tenants found in the big houses which were now reverting in batches on the expiry of the ground leases. Many of these big houses were grossly overcrowded and the tenants had to be thinned out.

These were the houses that I described earlier. Nearly all the ground leases were for 99 years or thereabouts. It was clear that the intention of the Second Marquess, when he granted them, was that when they expired his descendant would be able to redevelop the estate as a single entity. But in the meantime, as I explained, the neighbourhood had 'gone down'. Many of the lessees, in anticipation of the leases ending and their consequent liability for dilapidations, had conveniently disappeared; and some before their disappearance, had assigned the tail-ends of their leases to unsuspecting and impecunious tenants and thus shifted the liability on to them. Of the ground lessees who remained and faced up to their responsibilities, a number were men of straw. Nearly all the houses had been allowed to fall into bad condition, and works of repair, mainly at the trustees' expense were restricted by law to a bare minimum. For all these reasons it was not surprising that so many of the tenants, whom we took over, had long-standing grievances against landlords as a class.

There were other obstacles in the way of redevelopment by landowners. Rumours were rife about impending compulsory acquisitions—for municipal housing, public open spaces, new schools, ring roads. The metropolitan boroughs of Finsbury and Islington were Labour strongholds, and Clerkenwell and Canonbury, belonging as they did to capitalist landlords, appeared especially vulnerable. As early as 1943 I had been led to understand that if the trustees wanted to keep their estate intact and redevelop it themselves, the sooner they made some positive plan the better.

The late Mr. Louis de Soissons, R.A., the distinguished architect who was largely responsible for Welwyn Garden City,
had been brought into consultation. He was an old friend of mine,
full of ideas and a delightful person to work with. De Soissons
devised a comprehensive scheme for the redevelopment of
Canonbury over a period of years as an inner residential suburb.
Plans and elevations, expensively mounted and framed, were
exhibited hopefully in Islington Town Hall. They got us nowhere.
The most we were permitted to build after the war, a few
hundred yards east of Canonbury Tower, were thirty-two small
neo-Georgian houses each bearing a statutory price tag equivalent
to £1,500 freehold.

Rent restrictions of necessity remained in force, but the selling
prices of houses, either freehold or on long lease, except of
newly-built houses, were not controlled. In consequence there
was a strong inducement to the owner of any house, that might
possibly be saleable, to obtain vacant possession by hook or by
crook. By 'hook' I mean a cash offer, often inadequate, to a
sitting tenant who was not wise enough to take professional
advice. By 'crook' I mean the threat of applying for an eviction
order on grounds that no county court judge would have
accepted if the owner's bluff had been called. To obtain possession
by either of these methods would have been anathema to Lord
Northampton or the trustees. As a business proposition, the
sale of individual properties would have made it impossible
to do what they had been aiming at all through the war—
redevelop their estates as a whole. As a moral proposition, they
felt responsible for the welfare of their tenants.

When I accepted the agency in 1940 I was convinced that
when the war ended, whenever that might be, Lord Northampton's estates offered great possibilities. I never changed that
opinion. Canonbury in particular, so near the centre of London,
was potentially an extremely interesting residential mixed bag.
I am bound to admit that in the early post-war period, for the

reasons I have given, the short-term outlook was depressing. But the long-term outlook was full of promise and I had confidence in the future—particularly at Canonbury. I had lived in Canonbury for several years and knew the estate intimately. I was in touch with and to an extent had the confidence of the local authorities. I was witnessing week by week an ever-increasing demand for houses and flats, and I foresaw, when building restrictions were lifted, a corresponding demand for residential, commercial and industrial sites. Both these demands in an inflationary world would create an unprecedented rise in values—and so it turned out. Between 1949 and 1973 the market value of undeveloped commercial and industrial land in Clerkenwell has increased three times. In Canonbury the market value of residential sites has increased *ten times*, and one of the neo-Georgian houses I mentioned earlier, with a statutory price tag of £1,500, now makes £15,000 if sold freehold.

Towards the end of 1948 Lord Northampton told me he had decided to put the whole of his Clerkenwell estate into the market with the exception of some vacant sites and a few ground rents. His reasons were those I have indicated, and there were other reasons that were no concern of mine. Barings announced the same decision in regard to their Canonbury estate a few months later. So it was that except for the Clerkenwell sites and ground rents, Canonbury Tower, and a few houses near to the Tower which occupy the site of the monastic pleasaunce, everything was sold to commercial property companies. I was retired and the estate-office staff were disbanded, the senior members being pensioned off; I need not add that we were treated generously.

To say I was disappointed would be an understatement. It was the second time that my efforts to do something constructive in the field of private-enterprise housing had been stultified—and in much the same way. My first reaction to the news of the impending disaster, which was how I regarded it, was emotional. I had a genuine affection for the Northampton estates and had lived long enough in Canonbury to feel in a queer way that I formed part of it. The working-class tenants would suffer most. Here were families who had lived for generations 'on his lordship's estate'. They had been consistently looked after and well treated, perhaps a little spoiled. In return they had developed—especially some of the older people—a personal loyalty to their landlord that today is more prevalent in the country than in towns. Suddenly they were to be disinherited and this relationship was to go by the board. Henceforward, under the pressures of sales and resales in a pretty ruthless business world, who would exploit them and to what extent? It was a depressing outlook, and cold comfort to reflect that what happened to them in the future was no responsibility of mine.

My other reaction, I think, would have been the reaction of any professional man in the circumstances. I had been thirty-six years of age when appointed, and I was forty-six when I was retired. I felt that I had wasted what were probably the most important ten years of my professional life. They had been difficult years, frustrating years, tragic years, but all through them I had been looking forward, buoyed up by the prospect of the exciting things I had been led to believe were waiting to be done when the time came. It was unthinkable that almost over-night the entire prospect should have vanished and that there was nothing I could do about it except try to be philosophic. 'There is no good arguing with the inevitable. The only argument available with an east wind is to put on your overcoat.' I did just that.

In the last chapter I offered some advice to the younger of my professional readers. I warned them to think carefully before accepting a whole-time estate agency unless it was in the service of a permanently established corporate landowner. The wisdom of that advice, if I may presume to say so, is underlined by my experience in North London. Mercifully, by resisting all pressures to seduce me from an independent professional practice, small as it was, I had kept a foot in the door. That is how I survived.

But whole-time country land agents still exist in considerable numbers and, though they are less common, whole-time agents for estates in towns. Hypothetically a young surveyor, with a bent towards the human and absorbing occupation of estate management, is about to apply for an important agency. Hypothetically he pays me the compliment of seeking my grandfatherly advice. Let me end this chapter with a few of the things, based on my experience, that I should tell him—be it a country or a town agency, residential or non-residential, whole or part-time.

Before you apply for the job, my dear young Sir, find out all you can about your prospective employer; then, should you get it, you will know what is expected of you. At one extreme, is he concerned to obtain as large an income from the estate as possible, regardless of nearly everything else? Or, at the other, is he so charitable or so rich that he will encourage you to be generous and plough most of the income back? Or, somewhere between these extremes, does he want as much income as possible consistent with maintaining an old-fashioned, patriarchal landlord-tenant relationship?

Inquire also into the intended relationship between the prospective employer and his agent, and the extent of the agent's responsibilities. Will your employer concern himself with the day-to-day problems of management? At one extreme, will he give you a free hand subject to the production of audited accounts and to your writing, say, an annual report? At the other, will he drop into the estate office most weeks?

What outside professional help will you be able to rely on? For example, will you be permitted to consult or bring in specialists in connection with such matters as rating, town planning, the assessment and negotiation of dilapidations? If the staff in the estate office are paid by the owner, who engages them and what are their duties, qualifications and experience?

144

Once you have been appointed, come what may, be absolutely loyal to the man who employs you. Convey to everyone that he is an incarnation of the Archangel Gabriel—whatever your private thoughts may be. In conversation and in correspondence with him be frank. Stick to your guns and, should it become necessary, remind him tactfully that his reputation (much more valuable to him than the estate) is in *your* hands. Remember, however, that most of the honest differences of opinion that are bound to occur can be resolved by compromise. If your conscience tells you that no compromise is possible, then you must resign—but never, *never* threaten to do so unless you mean it.

Be just and kind in your dealings on the estate, and helpful in your attitude to adjoining owners and local authorities. Be friendly with the tenants, but avoid becoming intimate lest you be accused of favouritism. Listen patiently to a tenant's grievances, however petty they may sound; also to his requests, however unreasonable. Having done so, do not shilly-shally. 'Yes' and 'No' are the most potent words in an estate agent's vocabulary; but if you have to say 'No', whenever possible explain why.

Eventually, when the time comes for retirement, you will treasure something more than your pension: the knowledge that the estate in general, and in particular the relations between the owner and his tenants, are the happier for your having served them.

IX

God-bless-you Jobs

'God-bless-you job' defined – Central Housing Advisory
Committee, 1936-1947 – membership – Robertson Scott on
Pisgah – sub-committee's reports – battleships, Papists and
bed bugs – raising an army with B. of B. – Conservative
Housing Sub-committee, 1943–1945.

'God-bless-you jobs': I think I may claim to have had my share
of them. Some have been inevitable; most, but not all of them,
enjoyable; a few may even have been useful. What *is* a God-
bless-you job? The description was invented by the late 'Uncle'
Field-Richards, a much loved member of the Carlton Club, who
in his lifetime cheerfully undertook more God-bless-you jobs
than anyone else I have known. It is a job that you probably
don't want and have not asked for; have been persuaded to
accept; are not paid for; may well be blamed for and are not
always thanked for; are rarely praised for—but you hope you
may be blessed for, if the Almighty in His wisdom thinks fit.

The first[1] of my God-bless-you jobs arose from section 24 of
the Housing Act 1935, which had empowered the Minister of
Health (in those days the minister responsible for housing) to set
up a Central Housing Advisory Committee. Its functions were
to advise on the temporary relaxation of the anti-overcrowding
standards which the Act imposed, and on any other matters
connected with housing that the Minister referred to it. Sir
Kingsley Wood, Minister of Health in the National Government,

---

[1] Not counting God-bless-you jobs in connection with prisons and borstals
or service as a magistrate. These were in the Other Chap's department. See
Introduction.

appointed his Advisory Committee in 1936. He was its chairman and presided at all the meetings, as did his successors in office. I was one of the original twenty-five members and remained a member until 1947.

It was right and proper, even if we had not had a National Government, for a committee of this nature to be politically and occupationally a mixed bag. It included two Conservative peers, the wife of a Conservative peer and the wife of a Labour peer (both appointed on their own merits), one Conservative and one Labour Member of Parliament, two London County Councillors, the architect to a provincial city, the chairman of a building society, the chairman of a firm of builders, one or two other industrialists, and a distinguished author.[1]

The Earl of Dudley, formerly M.P. for Hornsey, was president of the British Iron and Steel Corporation. The Advisory Committee delegated most of its work to sub-committees, and Lord Dudley was chairman of the Design of Dwellings Sub-committee which reported in 1944. I served on that sub-committee and was responsible in a small measure for the standards of municipal houses it laid down. A three-bedroomed house containing 'two good rooms on the ground floor, one for meals and the second for other activities . . . a separate place for laundry or other dirty household work that should not be done in a room in which meals are eaten, and a bathroom and W.C. in separate compartments upstairs', the whole having a minimum over-all floor area of 900 square feet, became known to local authorities throughout the country as a 'Dudley house'.

Lord Balfour of Burleigh ('B. of B.') was a Scottish representative peer. Basically he was a banker, but between the wars he was chairman of the Kensington Housing Trust, which was a progressive and enlightened housing association, besides being

---

[1] Some of the people mentioned in this and the ensuing chapters were subsequently honoured. Unless the fact is recorded, the phrase 'as he [or she] then was' is to be understood.

chairman of the Housing Committee of the Kensington Borough Council; after the war he became chairman of Lloyds Bank. I got to know him well and shall have more to tell about him presently.

Sir Francis Fremantle, Conservative M.P. for St. Albans, and sometime medical officer of health for Hertfordshire, was highly intelligent, gay, inclined to be talkative and known to his friends as 'Gas Mantle'. Lewis Silkin was Labour M.P. for the Peckham Division of Camberwell and destined to become Minister of Town and Country Planning; he too was highly intelligent, but in contrast to Fremantle a rather dour man who said little. Megan Lloyd-George was another gay person and I liked her a lot. Lady Sanderson was the wife of the Labour peer who died in 1939. The Countess of Limerick, the only surviving member of the original team besides me, if she will permit me to say so, is an attractive and extremely wise woman, and was later to become chairman of the Standing Commission of the International Red Cross. Lancelot Keay was city architect and director of housing in Liverpool. Sir Harold Bellman was chairman of the Abbey National Building Society. Sir Felix Pole was chairman of Associated Electrical Industries and had formerly been general manager of the Great Western Railway. Sir George Burt was chairman of Mowlems, the building and engineering contractors. Richard Coppock, later to become chairman of the L.C.C., was general secretary of the National Federation of Building Trades operatives.

Others were appointed from time to time, and a member who merits a paragraph to himself was John Robertson Scott. We disagreed on many things, but got on very well in spite of it. He was a Socialist, a Quaker and as such a pacifist, an author, a journalist and editor of that delightful magazine, *The Countryman*, an opponent of 'blood sports', and a member of the Vegetarian, Cremation and Voluntary Euthanasia Societies. He lived at Idstock, a lovely village in Oxfordshire, and one of his nicest gestures was if you happened to die. He would then write to your widow: 'I am not sending flowers to your husband's funeral. Instead, I have today planted a flowering tree (genus and species stated) on the village green.' Alas, he has died before me, so I cannot hope to be commemorated in Idstock by *magnolia soulangeana*. Shortly after the end of the Second World War Robertson Scott went on a trip to the Far East and on his return spent a night with me in Canonbury. Next morning I took him to the top of Canonbury Tower and he exclaimed at the superb view of London. A few days later he sent me a book of Japanese prints with my name on the flyleaf 'in memory of the day we stood together on Pisgah'.[1]

I have quoted from the report of the Dudley Sub-committee on the Design of Dwellings. I served on several other sub-committees. One was the Sub-committee on Private Enterprise Housing, under the chairmanship of Sir Felix Pole, which reported in 1944. We said: 'Given favourable conditions, the housing needs of a large section of the people of this country can be met without assistance from public funds. The conditions required include cheap money, a plentiful supply of labour and materials, building costs in close correspondence with the cost of living, and stability of values.' Because those conditions did not obtain we recommended that in the short term, to enable private enterprise to play its part, a subsidy was called for, and that when private enterprise was meeting the same needs as a local authority it should be the same subsidy for both. But we added that this must be subject to some measure of control in regard to such matters as rents and selling prices and standards of size and construction. We recommended further that there was need for a voluntary scheme with official backing, on the lines of the National House Builders' Registration Council, for

[1] 'Get thee up into the top of Pisgah, and lift up thine eyes westward, and northward, and southward, and eastward, and behold it with thine eyes . . .' *Deuteronomy*, 3, 37.

securing the maintenance of good standards of building. A report of a panel appointed to devise the necessary machinery was annexed to the main document.

In 1946 Lewis Silkin presided over a sub-committee to examine the scope for, and the difficulties in the way of, the conversion and adaptation of existing houses that had been requisitioned or suffered war damage. We recommended that in general the full conversion of an obsolete or obsolescent house was preferable to mere adaptation. We listed what we deemed minimum standards of conversion and advised that where possible the work should be done by the owner with State assistance, or alternatively by a local authority having powers of compulsory purchase. Typical plans and analyses of actual costs of conversion were attached.

Lord Balfour of Burleigh was chairman of the House Management and Housing Associations Sub-committee. We produced three reports over the years. One was on the work of housing associations (1939) and the other two on a subject in which I was particularly interested—housing management. The first report on management was pre-war: *The Management of Municipal Housing Estates* was published in 1938. The second, in 1945 and bearing the same title, was made in response to a request by the Advisory Committee to consider whether any further advice on management ought to be given to local authorities in the light of the special conditions likely to obtain in the immediate post-war period.

In both reports we ranged over a wide field. In the 1938 report we began by considering the meaning and implications of good housing management, which I discussed at length in an earlier chapter.[1] After reviewing the evidence of the Society of Woman Housing Managers, the Institute of Housing and other professional bodies,[2] we reached the conclusion that for a local authority devising a system of management for any particular

[1] See *ante*, pp. 90 et seq.
[2] The Society of Women Housing Managers and the Institute of Housing amalgamated in 1965 to form the Institute of Housing Managers.

estate there could be no hard and fast rules. We went on to plan a syllabus, partly practical and partly sociological, for the instruction of women employed in this work. In the 1945 report we considered post-war problems and brought our earlier recommendations up to date.

I think these reports may also have been of value to ratepayers, because they gave some idea of the variety of operations good housing management entails. An important and often highly controversial part of municipal management is the allocation of new houses, involving as it does an assessment of the needs of each individual applicant. The housing of old people presents special problems, as does the treatment of 'difficult' tenants. And when it comes to slum clearance there are all sorts of problems; not the least is to persuade a family to face the prospect of moving from a squalid street or court, with its busy social life, to the strangeness of an outlying estate where they are only too likely to be lonely.

Disinfestation is another important operation in connection with slum clearance. In this context it is primarily from bed bugs. As every housing manager knows, bugs are extraordinarily difficult to get rid of once they are in possession. One piece of evidence, not recorded in the sub-committee's report, concerned the German battle fleet which was scuttled at Scapa in 1919. When the ships were refloated, half a generation later, the eggs of bugs that had been dormant in the air-locked forecastles hatched out in a matter of days.

Then there was the mystery of the connection between bed bugs and the Roman Catholic Church. We were told that in Liverpool there was an inflexible rule that, before a slum tenant was rehoused, every single thing he owned must pass through the gas chamber. The disinfesting process did the property no harm, but the tenants considered it an indignity. In spite of a rigid enforcement of the rule, a number of the new houses and flats became infested, and it was discovered that the great majority were occupied by Roman Catholics. There was a simple explanation. Nearly every Roman Catholic family possessed at least one portrait of the Pope and several of the Holy Saints. Often they were framed in decaying plush or backed with thick wads of ancient newspaper. Bugs or no bugs, it was unthinkable that these sacred objects should be desecrated. When their owners saw the officials coming, they snatched them off the walls, hid them under their clothing and smuggled them through. Later, when the bugs were comfortably established in their new quarters, they lined up and marched out.

So much for the Central Housing Advisory Committee. The reader may be wondering how I came to be appointed. I was nominated by the president of the Chartered Surveyors' Institution and I am glad he chose me. I enjoyed myself immensely and my colleagues were very kind. They were also very patient— seeing that for eleven years I generally talked too much.

In 1943, while still a member of the Advisory Committee, wisely or unwisely I accepted another God-bless-you job in the same field. It had all begun during the winter 1939-40 when my friend, Elizabeth Munro, asked me whether I would care to join a group who were meeting for supper once a month in a flat in Wynnstay Gardens, Kensington, to discuss—informally but not in their opinion prematurely—problems of post-war reconstruction. Our host was David Maxwell-Fyfe, subsequently the Earl of Kilmuir and Lord Chancellor. The others included R. A. ('Rab') Butler, now Lord Butler of Saffron Walden, Geoffrey Crowther, the economist and subsequently Lord Crowther, and Geoffrey Faber, the distinguished publisher and Fellow of All Souls. They were nearly all older than I and much more intelligent. During some of our discussions, especially when they involved economics, I was often out of my depth.

That is how I came to know David Kilmuir and Rab Butler. Two years later they were jointly responsible for setting up the

Central Committee on Post-War Reconstruction of the Conservative and Unionist Party Organization. The function of the Central Committee was 'to survey and report on the many new political social and economic problems created by the war'. A number of sub-committees were appointed, consisting mainly of people who had specialized in the subjects referred to them. Their reports, in a series called *Looking Ahead*, were presented to the Leader of the Party and published later by Central Office. One of the sub-committees was to consider Housing, and Rab Butler asked me to become its chairman.

I was hesitant about accepting. Though a life-long Conservative, I have never been deemed 'true-blue'. On the contrary, I am often described as 'pink', which I regard as a compliment well knowing that that is not the intention. I asked Rab whether he thought it would be in the interests of the Party as a whole if I took on such a responsibility. Rab said:

'When we enter this world from heaven, or wherever we come from, people who think like you and me fall fortuitously on one or other side of the party-political fence. Either we fall on the 'left' side in chokers and dungarees, or on the 'right' side wearing white collars and black jackets. It doesn't really make all that difference. You and I happen to have fallen on the white-collar and black-jacket side. Please accept the job.'

He gave me a high-powered team. It included Lord Dudley, my colleague on the Central Housing Committee, whom I have mentioned. Also Balfour of Burleigh, whom by this time I had come to know well. Towards the end of 1939, only a few weeks after war had broken out, B. of B. and I had been in a strange partnership. He had asked me to help him form the British contingent of an International Force to go voluntarily to Finland to aid the Finns in the defence of their country against the Russian invasion. Although I had had no experience of raising an army, I agreed. Our recruiting office was in Caxton Hall, Westminster, where we signed on an assortment of belligerent gentlemen, who were longing to get to grips with somebody and were finding the opening months of the war with Germany too pacific for their taste. We provided them with uniforms, some of which had been surplus to the requirements of an earlier British contingent that had gone to Spain during the Civil War—presumably under the auspices of the League of Nations. Conveniently, the bronze buttons on the tunics were inscribed NI for 'Non-Intervention'. With the buttons sewn on upside-down, IN stood for 'International Force'. Unfortunately, or perhaps fortunately, only a small part of the Balfour-Watson Division of the British contingent reached its destination before the Finns concluded an unsatisfactory peace.

I saw quite a lot of B. of B. during the war in one way or another, and more than once he came to stay in Canonbury. His practice was to travel down from Scotland on the night train and arrive in time for breakfast. He stayed the night and returned by sleeper the night after. He was always charming to Bridget, and one morning I thought we should get no breakfast because he insisted on telling her the history of his ancestor, Robert the Bruce, including the story of the spider, before getting up. B. of B. was a simple man with simple tastes, some too simple for Bridget's liking. She confided to me that in the early morning, on his arrival on our doorstep from King's Cross, his lordship had his pyjamas over his arm and his toothbrush sticking out of his pocket. In her opinion *not at all* the way a lord should behave.

The other members of the Conservative and Unionist Housing Sub-committee were John Laing, the builder and engineering contractor, Sir Harry Selley, M.P., a past-chairman of the Housing Committee of the L.C.C., Louis de Soissons, the architect, Sybil Eccles, the wife of David (now Viscount) Eccles, Mrs. M. K. F. Fleming, a member of the Society of Women Housing Managers, and A. H. B. Talbot-Ponsonby, land agent to the Duke of Norfolk.

The sub-committee produced two reports. *Foundation for Housing* was published by Central Office in March, 1944, and *A Policy for Housing in England and Wales* in January 1945.

In *Foundation for Housing* we began by identifying the two factors which, before all others, have a long-term effect on the housing of the nation. First, population trends, which in 1944, following the pattern of the immediate pre-war years, appeared to be on the decline. We defined the second as 'our urgent need for a thriving industrial economy, which must include agriculture and of which the essence is efficient production'. Then we discussed housing standards, and perhaps the following paragraph is worth quoting:

> 'For every family that requires it we desire to see a separate dwelling soundly constructed and self-contained. It should be near enough to the occupant's place of work, but within reasonable distance of the open country. The church, the shops, the local centre of entertainment—whether super-cinema or village hall—should be close at hand . . . [The house] must be large enough to accommodate them without overcrowding. Its cost, whether expressed in rent or terms for purchase, must fall within the occupant's means. It should be a thing of beauty, domestic in scale and in feeling. It should be of simple, unaffected design and possess a personal quality . . that will endear it to its occupants and help them make it a home; but externally it should be well-mannered enough to agree with its neighbours. . . . Above all, wherever possible, it should consist of a private house with a garden.'

We acknowledged a need for flats, but said we thought that for a family with children a flat must always be a poor substitute for a house. There was an almost universal public preference for houses or bungalows, and we recorded that in Birmingham it had emerged from 7,000 interviews that 96.7 per cent of the applicants wanted a house as opposed to a flat, and 92.4 per cent had asked specifically for a garden.

Then we gave some figures. In 1939 the total number of

houses in England and Wales had been approximately 11,400,000. Of these, 7,295,000 had been old houses built by private enterprise before 1919. The remaining 4,105,000 had been built during the inter-war period, 1,137,000 by local authorities and 2,968,000 by private enterprise without the aid of subsidies. As the total number of families in England and Wales in 1939 had been 11,350,000—slightly less than the total number of houses—were we well on the way to solving our housing problem when war broke out? We made haste to reply that we were not.

For one thing, a margin of 5 per cent of empty houses is needed in order that the population shall be mobile; its provision would require over half-a-million more. For another, a certain proportion of the 7,295,000 old houses were uncleared slums, a much larger proportion would become slums sooner or later and all would have to be replaced. Nor, we said, did the picture provided by the 4,000,000 houses built between the wars bear critical examination. We conceded that most of them were reasonably well built and let at moderate rents, but regretted that so many had been built in the wrong places. We deplored the nation's failure in that respect and pointed to the haphazard growths of badly sited building estates distending our cities into the countryside; to the ribbon development strung across the landscape from town to town; to the accretions of cafés at national beauty spots; to the bungaloid development that defaced the hillside; to the agglomerations of huts and chalets that disfigured the coast; not least to the loss, with scant discrimination, of thousands of acres of good agricultural land.

We likewise deplored the economic consequences of uncontrolled suburban growth, and pointed to a consequent soaring of land values in central positions. We said: 'The larger the city the greater the demand, and the greater the demand the higher the land values at the centre become . . . The effects of these high land values are far-reaching. High rents increase overheads and thus indirectly place a burden on industry, and high land costs preclude the making of necessary public improvements except at vast expense.'

We went on to discuss planning. We regretted the parochial outlook of the last of the pre-war planning Acts, the Town and Country Planning Act 1932, which had allowed local authorities to plan their areas in local rather than in regional or national interests. We drew attention to a tendency by some authorities, fearful of incurring claims for compensation, 'to zone their land according to what seemed to them the most likely demand and to pursue the purely negative policy of planning, not for what should be, but for a continuance of what was there already'. If, for example, there was a demand for houses or flats, almost automatically they zoned accordingly. An investigation in 1939 had revealed that, in draft planning schemes throughout England and Wales, enough land had been zoned for residential development to house more than six times the entire population!

Finally we came to industry, 'the key to housing', and the location of industry, which determines where houses should be built. We strongly supported the findings of the Royal Commission on the Distribution of the Industrial Population (commonly called the Barlow Commission) which had reported in 1939. They had said that the lack of any central planning of industry, and the consequent pre-war drift of population southward to London and the Home Counties, constituted a social, economic and strategic problem. The commission had recommended the following objectives of national action:

(a) Continued and further redevelopment of congested urban areas, where necessary;
(b) Decentralization or dispersal, both of industries and population, from such areas;
(c) Encouragement of a reasonable balance of industrial development, so far as possible, throughout the various divisions or regions of Great Britain, coupled with appropriate diversi-

fication of industry in each division or region throughout the country.

In pursuit of these objectives the Barlow Commission had recommended the creation of a central planning authority, national in scope and character, one of whose first duties would be to consider in what areas decentralization was desirable and to what extent it could be achieved by building satellite towns, garden suburbs, trading estates, and by enlarging existing towns. Besides supporting the Barlow proposals, we made some suggestions for the development of towns and—a matter we regarded as of supreme importance—the preservation of the countryside.

We replied briefly to an objection that was commonly made to any proposal to influence the location of industry—namely, that this could only be achieved by controls that would operate as a 'dead hand' on enterprise. We conceded that if the controls were excessive there was weight to the objection, but we emphasized that at the other extreme, if there were no controls, the unrestricted growth of our existing towns would be equally disastrous to the industrial economy. *Foundation for Housing* ended as follows: 'In the absence of a single comprehensive policy on the issues of the location of industry and the protection of agricultural land, we see no alternative to the continued promiscuous growth of our cities and the drift of our people from the countryside, and to an aggravation of all the evils that must inevitably result.'

The sub-committee's second report, *A Policy for Housing in England and Wales*, was longer and more detailed. Having laid the foundations, we ventured to design the superstructure. This is not a text book on housing, and for that reason, as well as lack of space, I will summarize briefly.

We said the solution of the post-war housing programme should comprise three stages—Emergency, Intermediate and Long-term.

159

Stage 1: *Emergency Programme*
The first objective must be to provide adequate shelter for everyone within two years of the end of the war in Europe. This would necessitate the building of 750,000 new houses. The greater part of the shortage should be made good by the extended use of new forms of permanent construction rather than by temporary construction. There should be an early release from the Forces of architects, town-planners, surveyors, engineers and building craftsmen. Building materials should be rationed and the prices controlled. Where temporary housing was inevitable, it should be subject to a limited life fixed at the outset.

Stage 2: *Intermediate Programme*
A national survey should be made of the housing shortage related to forecasts of future population, and the twin-evils of slums and overcrowding should be our first concern. We recorded that when war broke out the balance of houses in the slum clearance programme, not yet dealt with, had totalled approximately 105,000. Except for the slum houses that had been destroyed by enemy action, that balance remained, plus all those other houses that during the war had deteriorated into the slum category. The same with overcrowding. War-time shifts of population plus the normal increase in population had increased the number of overcrowded houses. We estimated that a further 150,000 new houses would be needed.

Stage 3: *Long-term Programme*
The resources of private enterprise and of the local authorities should be employed to the full, and, as long as there remained a gap between the cost of building and the rent-paying capacity of the prospective occupants, subsidies should be available to both. We said, however, that there were two solid grounds for thinking that the gap would steadily close. On the one hand, methods of construction were continually being simplified and

made cheaper; on the other, the country was united in its determination to achieve a high and stable level of employment which, we hoped, would bring with it a considerably higher level of earnings than was general before the war. But 'our objective must be to end the need for subsidies at the earliest possible moment'.

Having recognized the need for subsidies, at any rate for a period, we discussed the form that they should take. The existing position was governed by the Housing (Financial Provisions) Act 1938, as extended by the Housing (Temporary Provisions) Act 1944. Under those Acts the subsidies available were payable by annual amounts over forty years. We recommended that from the points of view of all parties a 'lump sum' subsidy was the simplest and most satisfactory if care was taken not to subsidize inefficiency or extravagance. In our considered opinion the amount of the subsidy—payable to a local authority, a housing association or private enterprise—should be half the difference between the pre-war and post-war costs of building, subject to annual review; and when building costs fell, the whole of the saving should be applied to reducing the subsidy. We added that, as long as subsidies remained, a system of controlling the rents and selling prices of subsidized houses must remain also.

Other of our long-term recommendations were that there must be enough houses in all areas, not only for renting, but for people to buy them if they so desired and could afford to do so; that the reconditioning and conversion of obsolescent houses should form an essential part of the programme, and that the Rent Acts should be amended to make it possible to gain possession of houses suitable for that purpose; that grants for reconditioning under the Housing (Rural Workers) Acts should be increased, and that the responsibility for the administration of those Acts should be transferred from the county councils to the rural district councils; that there should be periodical reviews of bye-laws in the light of new materials and new methods of construction. We ended by stressing the importance of good housing management and pointing to the need for more facilities for community services and recreation.

The report, published in January 1945, was well received by the press. *Punch* had a whole-page cartoon by E. H. Shepard. John Bull, a builder's labourer, is standing in an English landscape, his hod piled high with 750,000 houses—*The houses that Jack ought to build*. The national dailies contained summaries of the document and most of them reviewed it. *The Times* called it 'notable' and gave us a 'first leader' entitled *Housing Prospect*: 'It is good that this expert committee should pitch the housing target so high during the emergency years', even if its writer would have liked us to provide more evidence how in so short a period the demand could be met. He was distrustful of our financial proposals ('Finance needs second thoughts') but described the report as 'a document which contains many valuable ideas'.

It remains to add that within a few months of the publication of *A Policy for Housing*, the Labour Party were returned to power at the first post-war general election. Inevitably, but I trust decently and respectfully, the fruits of our labours were buried; and there is no evidence of their later disinterment. As chairman of the sub-committee, the most I can hope for is that we contributed to the pool of ideas that crystallized eventually as the housing policy of the Conservative Party—to which I am proud to belong.

THE HOUSES THAT JACK OUGHT TO BUILD

E. H. Shepard in Punch, *January 16, 1946*

X

God-bless-you again

New Towns Committee, 1945-1946 – membership – a
painful broadcast – committee's reports – Lord Reith fully
stretched – and 'ejected' – ships that pass . . . – Regent's Park
and the Gorell Committee, 1945-1947 – committee's report –
lugubrious survey – whitewash in high places – Regency
regenerated.

In the autumn of 1945 I received a letter from Louis de Soissons.
He said he had seen in the press my appointment to a very
important committee and wanted to congratulate me; he added:
'I hope you will enjoy having Jehovah as your chairman.' The
committee was the New Towns Committee, appointed jointly
by the Minister of Town and Country Planning and the Secretary
of State for Scotland[1] under the chairmanship of Lord Reith.
These were its terms of reference:

> 'To consider the general questions of the establishment, develop-
> ment, organization and administration that will arise in the pro-
> motion of New Towns in furtherance of a policy of planned
> decentralization from congested urban areas; and in accordance
> therewith to suggest guiding principles on which such towns
> should be established and developed as self-contained and balanced
> communities for work and living'.

In the event I got on well with 'Jehovah' and shall have more
to say presently about that remarkable man.

The most outstanding of the other members, who contributed
enormously to our deliberations, was F. J. (later Sir Frederic)

---

[1] The Right Hon. Lewis Silkin M.P. and the Right Hon. Joseph Westwood
M.P. respectively.

Osborn. He was co-founder and first manager of Welwyn Garden City and later edited that admirable journal, *Town and Country Planning*. A dedicated follower of Sir Ebenezer Howard,[1] Osborn has devoted his life to the interests of good planning, and some of us other members of the New Towns Committee soon came to realize that he had forgotten more about the subject than we had ever learned. I had known him for some years and was delighted to find he was a fellow member. An earlier occasion when he and I collaborated had been agonizing —for him more than for me. In March, 1942, we had been commissioned to undertake a joint broadcast in the Home Service entitled *Who shall own the land?* Osborn, a Socialist, favoured extensive public ownership; I, a Conservative, disagreed but conceded that in some cases public ownership was inevitable. In war-time every broadcast discussion had to be scripted in advance and 'passed for security'. It was then rehearsed and on the night, when the red light came on, you read your part like a play, making it sound as spontaneous as possible. To everyone's dismay, less than five minutes before we were due on the air, Osborn, who had not been looking well, became doubled up with pain and fell to the floor. The producer hurried to help him, got him a glass of water and, because he was shivering, put a rug round his shoulders; he said he would send for the B.B.C. doctor. But the patient would not hear of seeing a doctor until after the broadcast. He had come to tell the listeners who *should* own the land and, pain or no pain, was going through with it. The producer, obviously worried, had no alternative but to let him do so, but he drew me aside and told me in a whisper that he would come into the studio with us and stand behind Osborn. Should he break down or faint, on no account must any indication of what had happened be given to the listeners. In that event I could rely on the producer to grab the script, continue reading Osborn's part from the

[1] 1850 to 1928, author of *Garden Cities of Tomorrow*.

point where he had stopped, and we must hope that the listeners would not detect a change of voice. I gathered that in the meantime the unhappy Osborn would remain unconscious under the table. At that moment the red light began winking and we were hushed into silence. For fifteen minutes I read my part with one eye on my opposite number and the other on the script. Osborn, hunched over the table and looking like death, read his part superbly. He showed great courage, and fortunately the consequences were not so serious as we had feared; I think the doctor found he had passed a stone. Whatever the trouble was, it must have been excruciatingly painful, and for me, in those days not a very experienced broadcaster, it was a nerve-racking experience. But to return to New Towns.

Lawrence Cadbury, another member, besides being managing director of the chocolate firm, was chairman of the Bournville Village Trust and a recognized authority on population. Sir Malcolm Stewart had been Commissioner for Special Areas before the war and was head of a number of brick and cement companies. W. H. Gaunt had been concerned with the development of the Trafford Park Estates, also of Letchworth Garden City, where he lived. Sir Henry Bunbury was a retired civil servant. Sir Percy Thomas, an eminent architect, was a past-president of the R.I.B.A. and chairman of the Welsh Board for Industry. W. H. Morgan was county engineer for Middlesex. Ivor Brown, the prolific author and journalist, was at that time on *The Observer*. Captain J. P. Younger (now Sir James), later Lord Lieutenant of Clackmannan, and Sinclair Shaw K.C., later chairman of the Scottish Council of the Labour Party, represented Scotland. The youngest member of the committee and the only woman was Mrs. Monica Felton. She was a Labour member of the L.C.C. from 1937 to 1946, an attractive red-head but sadly crippled, brave, tempestuous, indiscreet, politically as far left as was possible without falling over the edge, and a most entertaining companion.

Reith worked us hard and we had frequent meetings in the Old Treasury building overlooking the Horse Guards Parade. We decided we ought to see what the Swedes had been doing during and since the war, and spent an extremely interesting fortnight in Stockholm and other Swedish towns. By the summer of 1946 we had produced three reports, and it was greatly to our chairman's credit that they were all unanimous. For lack of space I can do no more than summarize them.

In the First Interim Report[1] of the New Towns Committee (March, 1946) we were mainly concerned with the question of 'agency'—i.e. the body of persons charged with responsibility for developing the land and its subsequent management. We said that one possibility was a public corporation, sponsored and financed by interested local authorities. Another was an 'authorized association' within section 35 of the Town and Country Planning Act 1934—that is to say 'any society or body of persons appointed by the Minister whose objects include the promotion, formation or management of garden cities . . . and which does not trade for profit'. We rejected a housing association as being unsuitable, and by and large came down in favour of a government-sponsored corporation financed by the Exchequer. Although we ruled out private enterprise, we recommended that the agency, whatever it was, should have freedom of action comparable to that of an ordinary commercial undertaking, subject to governmental direction on major policies. An important section of the First Report concerned finance. We recommended that funds for the government-sponsored corporation, first in our order of preference, should be advanced by the Public Works Loans Board or the Exchequer, and that payments of interest should be deferred in the early years if that became necessary. We further recommended that the agency should be placed on the same footing as a local authority for the receipt of subsidies and grants.

On our appointment, in 1945, we had been told that the Labour

[1] Cmd. 6759

Government's New Towns Bill would not be introduced until the autumn of 1946. Therefore we had planned to present our Final Report in May, 1946, which would have been in plenty of time. In the early spring, however, we were told that an unexpected opportunity had arisen to introduce the Bill sooner, necessitating the speedy completion of a Second Interim Report[1] (April, 1946) dealing with matters that needed to be considered in advance of legislation. They included methods of compulsory acquisition, entry, site ownership, land policy, advice to be given to industrialists, the need for a variety of employment, and the importance of keeping the agency in close touch with national industrial development.

The Final Report[2] of the New Towns Committee (July, 1946) was the longest; 'We deal not only with the physical tasks involved and the devising of machinery for them, but also with the more complex and delicate problem of founding the social structure of a new town and fostering its corporate life.' Here are some of the headings: types of new town, entirely new or extension; size; selection of site; social structure; layout, design and standards of construction; byelaws and building regulations; landscape treatment; public services; transport; industrial development; residential development; policy in regard to shops; parks; health; facilities for education; social life and recreation.

I have yet to describe our chairman, whom Louis de Soissons had referred to as 'Jehovah', but before I do so the following facts may be of interest. The New Towns Act was passed in the autumn of 1946 and embodied most of our recommendations. The first of the New Towns, an enlargement of the old town of Stevenage in Hertfordshire, was established in the same year. At December 31, 1972, there were 27 New Towns in England and Wales, six in Scotland and four in Northern Ireland. In the first 27 of these New Towns, at the same date, there were 261,700 new houses and flats, 3,487 new shops and 2,060 new

[1] Cmd. 6794   [2] Cmd. 6876

167

factories. Their total population was 763,400, of whom 350,000 were employed in the factories.

And now about our chairman. I admired him; I was sorry for him; I liked him. John Reith was born in 1889, the fifth son of the Very Reverend George Reith, Doctor of Divinity of Aberdeen and Glasgow. Of course I admired Reith! How could anyone fail to admire this offspring of a Scottish manse, trained as an engineer, who before the First World War joined the Territorial Army in a spirit of adventure and a fervour of enthusiasm; in 1914 was sent to France; was badly wounded and declared unfit; was sent to America to supervise the supply of armaments to Great Britain; came back; was employed in the Admiralty and the Ministry of Munitions; returned to civilian life; applied for the post of general manager of the newly-formed British Broadcasting Company; got it; directed a skeleton staff from a general manager's office six feet square—and from that small beginning, by virtue of drive, imagination, hard work, and what appeared an almost incredible self-confidence, created in the short span of fifteen years the greatest broadcasting organization in Europe, if not in the world?

I was sorry for Reith because of what had happened to him in his early fifties when, as a minister of the Crown, he was concerned with matters of great importance to surveyors in connection with works and planning; I must lead up to it by continuing the story from where I have left off. I never knew Reith intimately, but during the deliberations of the New Towns Committee I enjoyed a close association with him. Most of what I shall relate is told by him in much more detail in his book, *Into the Wind*.

Sir John Reith (as he then was) resigned his post as director-general of the B.B.C. in 1938. It was against the advice of nearly all his friends and despite the entreaties of the B.B.C. governors. He had been restive for some time and was feeling more than ordinarily frustrated. Basically one may think, from reading his book, that the reason for his going was a conviction that his work for the B.B.C. was finished. A second war was in the offing. He had a longing to be 'fully stretched' (one of his favourite expressions) and had arrived at a crossroads. A lesser man might have paused, looked back, contemplated with satisfaction the extent of his achievement and relaxed. Not so Reith. He might decide to change direction, but as long as a road lay ahead it was not in his nature to look back; to contemplate would have been waste of time; to relax would have been anathema to him. Always he must go on, press on, drive on . . . 'A man's reach should exceed his grasp, or what's a heaven for?'

The Prime Minister (Neville Chamberlain) wanted him to accept the chairmanship of Imperial Airways in succession to Sir Eric Geddes, who had died. Reith was not enthusiastic and did so with reluctance. He went, and what he found shocked him. He was critical of the managing director, contemptuous of the way the company was organized, and revolted by its offices 'in an old furniture warehouse behind Victoria Station'. His first duty as chairman was to approve the expenditure of £238 on passengers' lavatories at Croydon: 'From Broadcasting House to this!'

Inevitably under Reith's chairmanship the company was revitalized, reorganized, expanded. Within a week of his first appearance in the furniture depository, he announced his intention to effect an amalgamation of the two great commercial air lines, Imperial Airways and British Airways, and seek the establishment of a public corporation. He got his way. Imperial Airways later became the British Overseas Airways Corporation.

War was now imminent. Reith learned that he had been tipped for the war-time post of Minister of Information, but it was some little time before he got it. He held it for four months until, under the Coalition Government, he was moved to Transport. Four months later Churchill offered him the Ministry of Works, which was about to be formed. Hitherto Reith had been

M.P. for Southampton, a seat that had been found for him, but Churchill proposed to move him to the Lords. Reith would have preferred one of the Service ministries, but accepted the offer.

The new Ministry of Works was superimposed on the old Office of Works and given much greater responsibilities. Its creation was a necessary part of the mobilization of the country's resources, which was the chief objective of the Coalition. Hitherto there had been little co-operation between departments in regard to their works programmes and there was a struggle for priorities; in 1940 it was obvious that the total of the works programmes was in excess of capacity. The first task of the Minister was to sort things out. Order had to be instilled into the chaos that existed in connection with the building of munition factories, storage depots, hostels, camps, training centres, landing grounds and so forth; to say nothing of Reith's ultimate responsibility for the repair of widespread war damage, which Churchill insisted was his. He was an engineer and a born organizer, and he did the job well. But there were moments of exasperation, as for instance on the morning after the great air-raid on Coventry when Kingsley Wood, the Chancellor of the Exchequer, sent him a 'personal and urgent' message complaining that the clocks at Number 11 Downing Street were all telling different times!

Having been given the job, Reith was not long in seeing a need to look beyond the immediate problems to the inevitable post-war problems that could only be solved by imaginative planning. That led to the first of a series of wrangles with the Ministry of Health, which on this occasion culminated when Attlee (then Lord Privy Seal) was deputed to effect a compromise. When the terms of reference were eventually agreed Reith was still dissatisfied on the ground that they were vague, but he derived some consolation from the final paragraph which Attlee had written:

'It is clear that the reconstruction of town and country after the war raises great problems and gives a great opportunity. The

Minister of Works has, therefore, been charged by the Government with the responsibility for consulting the departments and organisations concerned with a view to reporting to the Cabinet the appropriate methods and machinery for dealing with the issues involved.'

Reith wasted no time, and by the end of November had consulted all the relevant departments and made his report. His main recommendation, based on those of the Barlow Commission on the Distribution of the Industrial Population, was that the basic objectives should include the controlled development of all areas, economic land use, and a curb on the indiscriminate growth of towns. He stressed the need for a central planning authority to lay down the principles of good town and country planning and take responsibility for the execution of a national plan; and, in urging an investigation into the practicability of controlling and acquiring development rights, he made an oblique reference to the vexed problem of compensation and betterment.[1] The Prime Minister wrote that he had read the report 'with great interest' and was in general agreement with its author's proposals.

So far so good, but troubles lay ahead. The first was a directive from Number 10 which looked like having the effect of entrusting the responsibility for post-war planning to Arthur Greenwood, who was now Minister without Portfolio. That did not suit Reith. A meeting to discuss his report to the Cabinet was indecisive, except to the extent that he was authorized to set up a committee on compensation and betterment. He did so at once, and the Uthwatt Committee consisted of two eminent

[1] When land in private ownership is acquired for public works, and the dispossessed owner suffers financial loss, he is entitled to be paid compensation. Conversely it may happen that the operation results in the dispossessed owner, in respect of other land, or some other owner who is not dispossessed, deriving financial benefit; in that case it is argued that the person benefited should have to pay betterment. In theory the amounts of compensation and betterment should be equated. For many years successive governments, by a variety of legislative expedients, have been trying to resolve this equation without appreciable success.

chartered surveyors, Mr. James Barr and Mr. Gerald Eve, with Lord Justice Uthwatt (as he later became) as chairman.

Eventually, after protracted negotiations between Reith and Greenwood, another compromise was arrived at. Within the framework of the study of post-war problems, to be undertaken by Greenwood, Reith was given a special responsibility in the physical sphere. He was authorized to tell the Lords that planning had been accepted as national policy, that a central authority was required, and that the authority when constituted would devise policies for such matters as agriculture, industrial development and transport. But what was the projected central authority to consist of? A council of ministers, with Reith as chairman, was appointed to make recommendations. To make a long story short, the council eventually recommended that the authority should comprise two parts—an executive council for policy and a new ministry for planning.

The constitution of a central authority on these lines was discussed by the Cabinet on February 9, 1942, but objections were raised to the proposal to create a new ministry. Instead it was decided that the planning responsibilities hitherto belonging to the Minister of Health should be transferred to Reith; that it should be Reith's ministry which the local authorities would have to consult on planning questions; and that Reith's ministry should exercise the powers of central government under the Town and Country Planning Acts and lay down general principles to which town and country planning must conform. In future the Minister's title was to be Minister of Works and Planning. 'So', he wrote, 'the nation had a planning policy for the first time.' Reith was never slow in patting himself on the back, and if he was ever justified in performing that contortionate exercise it was now. . . .

At that moment the blow fell. Totally unexpected, almost inconceivable, it was delivered from a clear sky. More literally it was delivered by a motor-cycle despatch rider from Number 10

Downing Street. The Prime Minister wrote: 'I am very sorry to tell you that the reconstruction of the Government which events have rendered necessary makes me wish to have your office at my disposal . . . I am very much obliged to you for the work which you have done and also for your unfailing courtesy and kindness to me.' The note ended with an apology for Churchill's inability to see him personally because of the press of affairs.

To an ordinary politician in Reith's situation, with Reith's fine record of achievement, an intimation of this nature coming at such a time would have been a bitter disappointment, and few would have blamed him had he shown it. But a politician, said Baldwin, must acquire the hide of a hippopotamus. Setbacks, which may or may not be transient, are bound to occur. He must expect them, watch out for them, brace himself against them, always be ready to repel the 'slings and arrows of outrageous fortune' with the shield of a clear conscience and the buckler of restraint. But Reith was not an ordinary politician. Except fortuitously, he was not a politician at all. He had never mounted the hustings, sparred with hecklers, or been mortified by defeat at an election; he had never observed the plaudits of the crowd change swiftly to recrimination; he was not inured to hard knocks. The subject of this curt rebuff was not equipped to cope with it.

I am sure he did his best to do so, but it was altogether too much for him. For several weeks he scarcely spoke to anyone except his friend and admirer Sir John Anderson, who was then Home Secretary, and that other loyal old friend B. of B. They counselled patience. Reith wrote later: 'Both were absolutely sure, as were most of those who wrote to me, that some other important work would soon come.' He never ceased hoping. More than four years afterwards we were together in Stockholm, and I remember one evening his coming into my bedroom. On this particular evening he was unusually silent and stood for a long time with his back to me, gazing out of the window.

Suddenly he turned. 'What do *you* think? [*me* of all people!] Will they *ever* give me another decent job?' I have said I liked him. Is it a wonder that I was sorry for him?

After receiving the intimation from Churchill, he was distraught. How should he answer hundreds of letters? How explain things to his children? What to do? Churchill offered to make him Lord High Commissioner of the Assembly of the Church of Scotland, which Reith acknowledged to be one of the most outstanding honours that can come to a Scot. But he was not in the mood, and declined it because he said the post demanded a background of status and achievement: 'Status now I had none; any achievements had been obliterated . . . A man should not move from the ignominy of dismissal to receive the keys of the City of Edinburgh . . .' so on and so forth. Clearly he had the whole business tragically out of proportion.

Then he proceeded to hold an inquest. What was the *reason* for his summary ejection ('ejection' was Reith's word). A criticism that he had not always been co-operative was fiercely resented. He wrote: 'Probably I had shown a disinclination to co-operate in procrastination and muddle.' Some years later Churchill, who in the meantime had himself been ejected, replied not unkindly to a moving letter which Reith, now that Churchill was no longer Prime Minister, had written him. 'Several times since then [February, 1942] I have considered you for various jobs, but I have always encountered considerable opposition from one quarter or another on the ground that you were difficult to work with.' But Reith preferred another explanation: a 'Gladstonian-Liberal' was the victim of a Tory plot!

Reith's most fervent admirers could scarcely deny that at times he *was* difficult to work with. He was a disciplinarian (and one wishes there were more of them in these ill-disciplined days). He did not suffer fools gladly. He was determined and opinionated, could be stern and unbending, and in pursuit of an objective would ride roughshod. Such a man is bound to make enemies. But there was another side to his character and I am indebted to the writer of his obituary for the following: 'Well over 6 feet 6 inches in height, and with strongly marked features accentuated by beetling eyebrows and a conspicuous scar, he was a formidable figure . . . Yet his quiet, deep voice belied these externals and on occasion his face would light up with a smile of great beauty and warmth.'[1] He also made many friends, including those who worked for him. When they came to understand him they loved him, laughed at his foibles (need I say secretly?) and gave him that unswerving loyalty which is a condition of service.

The New Towns Committee could not have had a better chairman. He became deeply interested in the matters referred to us and had views, sometimes strong, on most of them. But he held himself in, encouraged each of us to have his say and showed exemplary patience which (*vide* his own assessment of his character) was foreign to him. He even remained patient when the mischievous Monica Felton, irked by his almost Calvinistic sense of the proprieties, sought to provoke him.

Obviously he had failings. We all have. But I think Reith's most obvious failing was more an affliction than a fault. Gradually, as I got to know him, I came to suspect that this formidable man, apparently sustained by a tremendous fund of self-confidence, in fact suffered from a lack of it. That there were moments, though he would not have dreamed of admitting it, when he was by no means sure of himself. That, if true, would have accounted for his hankering after approbation, commendation and the reassurance that stems from praise. It would have accounted too for his extraordinary sensitivity, his resentment of criticism, his impatience when crossed. Again, it would have explained the tendency, verging on the childish, to imagine slights where there were no slights and take offence when none was intended.

[1] *The Times*, June 17, 1971.

A typical instance of the last was on the arrival of the New Towns Committee by air in Stockholm. A dreadful thing happened. *We were met at the airport by the wrong man!* Our plane taxied to the apron, and before we began to leave it an agreeable young Englishman came on board. He introduced himself as a representative of the British Minister and said he had come to welcome us. We made polite remarks, as one does on these occasions, and he shook hands all round. I noticed Reith said nothing and that his handshake was perfunctory. When we emerged into the sunshine, no doubt because we were the first British mission to visit Sweden since the war, it was clear we were going to be given a VIP reception. There was a group of Swedish officials, a larger group of reporters hoping for interviews, and a battery of whirring cameras. Reith greeted the officials courteously. Then, looking neither to right nor left, he strode across the tarmac and into the first of the waiting cars. I knew the signs and realized something was wrong.

It was evidently still wrong when we arrived at our hotel. I feared that one of us had unwittingly committed a gaffe and hoped devoutly it had not been me. So, as soon as there was an opportunity, I got alongside him and said something to that effect.

'Of course not,' said Reith, 'but you must have seen what happened. *It was that man!*'

'Which man?'

'Do you seriously mean to tell me you don't know? Why, that man who came to meet us.'

Much relieved, I was foolish enough to say he had struck me as a nice man, and (worse still) went on to say how polite I thought it of the Minister to have sent him . . .' That was *too* much!

'Nice man! *Nice* man! What matter if he was a nice man? Disgracefully bad manners! A studied insult! Here we are, a highly important government committee with me as its chairman. *The British Minister should have come to meet us himself.*'

176

Lord Reith
1889–1971

And that was not the end of it. Reith assembled us and said he knew we deplored what had happened as much as he did. He went on to say he was sure we would agree that we had no alternative but to decline to attend a banquet to which the British Minister had invited us. It took Younger and me all that evening, reinforced by Osborn, to calm him down. Happily next morning the storm had passed and we attended the banquet after all.

There are other 'Reith stories' in the same vein; but it would be a thousand pities if his faults, which were venial if at times exasperating, were allowed to tarnish his memory. He lived another quarter of a century, but to my regret we drifted apart when the business of the New Towns Committee was finished. He *did* get other important work but, mercifully perhaps, not as a politician. From 1947 to 1950 he was chairman of Hemel Hempstead New Town, and from 1946 to 1950 chairman of the Commonwealth Communications Board 'bringing his mind to bear on the engineering and administrative problems of a world-wide network of communications'.[1] From 1965 to 1968 he was Lord Rector of Glasgow University, and in 1967 (despite his earlier 'ignominy') he became Lord High Commissioner of the Assembly of the Church of Scotland and was created a Knight of the Thistle. He died in 1971 at the age of 81.

John Reith was among the truly great men of his time; he had able and distinguished contemporaries, but metaphorically as well as literally he towered above most of them. He was a fearless and an upright man, although at times extremely petulant. All in all he was a good man, who always strove to observe those high principles laid down for him by his father for the living of a Christian life. I am grateful for my near view of him. Ships that pass in the night . . .

The first of my God-bless-you jobs in the capacity of a chartered surveyor, the Central Housing Advisory Committee, was

[1] *Ibid.*

concerned with houses throughout England and Wales. So was the Conservative Party's Housing Sub-committee. The recommendations of the New Towns Committee affected Scotland as well. The fourth job in the series was my appointment to a committee concerned with only 374 houses in what at that time was the metropolitan borough of St. Marylebone in North-West London. But the houses were, and are, part of the architectural heritage of the nation.

The Prime Minister's Committee on the Regent's Park Terraces was appointed on January 12, 1946, with these terms of reference: 'To consider the future of the terraces adjoining Regent's Park from all aspects, architectural, town-planning and financial, and to make recommendations as to their future adaptation or replacement to meet modern requirements.' The committee consisted of Lord Gorell, the educationist, as chairman, and six other members: Mrs. I. M. (Douglas) Bolton, chairman of the Town Planning Committee, L.C.C.; Sir Edward Forber, deputy keeper, Department of Architecture and Sculpture in the Victoria and Albert Museum; J. H. Forshaw, chief architect, Ministry of Health; Sir Eric Maclagan, past chairman of the Board of Inland Revenue; Sir Drummond Shiels, sometime Labour M.P. and a junior minister in the pre-war National Government—and me.

We interpreted 'terraces' in our terms of reference as all the terraces of houses, built between 1812 and 1827, which surround Regent's Park (404 acres) and form a superb background. They belong to the Crown and are commonly called the 'Nash terraces' because John Nash,[1] favourite architect of the Prince

---

[1] John Nash, 1752–1835, was a prolific architect. His other buildings in London included Carlton House, residence of the Prince Regent (demolished); the east wing of Carlton House Terrace; Regent Street (since almost entirely rebuilt); All Souls' Church, Langham Place (the view of which is now ruined by the hideous flank wall of Broadcasting House behind it); the Haymarket Theatre; the United Services and Royal Aero Club; and Marble Arch, which was originally a gateway to Nash's Buckingham Palace. In the provinces he designed or remodelled a number of country houses and made extensive alterations to the Royal Pavilion at Brighton.

Regent, was responsible for them. Nash, however, confined himself to the lay-out, a splendid piece of town planning, and the elevations. The sites were let to speculative builders, who built the houses to their own or other architects' interior designs. Nash's Office provided detail to half-size of all external work, and the sculptor, John Bubb, was brought in to design some of the pediments. All the houses were faced with stucco, which in those days was not highly thought of. Hence a satirical jingle dating from 1826:

> Augustus at Rome was for building renown'd,
> For marble he left what of stone he had found;
> But is not our Nash, too, a very great master?
> He found us all brick and he left us all plaster.

The original leases, under the terms of which the lessees were fully responsible for the maintenance of their properties, were for 99 years; they expired shortly before, during, or soon after the First World War, 1914 to 1918. The Commissioners of Crown Lands, who administered the Regent's Park Estate, then re-let the houses for a further 21 years and occasionally for longer. During the Second World War the terraces suffered extensive damage by enemy action, and by the end of 1942 the leases of 128 houses had been disclaimed, 83 more had expired, been surrendered, or forfeited, and a number of houses that had come into hand later had been abandoned. At the time of our appointment most of the estate was in a semi-derelict condition and a very depressing sight.

At the first meeting of the committee we were given information which, regrettably, had not been given to Gorell when he was invited to become chairman. Whether the Prime Minister himself knew the facts is doubtful. By prior agreement between the Crown Commissioners and the Minister of Works over 200 houses were to be requisitioned and occupied 'temporarily' (whatever that might mean) as government offices. Although the elevations were not to be interfered with, considerable works were to be done to the interiors to fit them for that purpose. This meant that, instead of our being concerned with the years immediately ahead, we were concerned only with the ultimate future.

Gorell was angry, and with the concurrence of the committee wrote a strong letter to Attlee. He said it was clear that our inquiry was arousing wide public interest. Whether or not the conversion of more than half the houses into offices was a good move or a bad one, he said he must make it clear that his committee could not accept responsibility for a decision taken before their appointment. He went on to tell the Prime Minister that we were dismayed by the state of many of the bombed houses, which were still open to the ravages of wind and weather. He added that unless essential repairs were done quickly 'it is obvious that, in a few years' time, the problem will not be whether the terraces are to be retained, but only what should replace them.'

Attlee's reply was not very satisfactory. He made no attempt to explain the agreement made prior to our appointment, but regretted that 'there has been this difficulty'. He enclosed the draft of a press notice, making it clear that the responsibility for the projected requisitioning and conversion of the 200 houses into government offices had nothing to do with us. He said that repairs would be put in hand immediately, and a month later wrote again to say that the work would cover all the houses and not only the requisitioned houses.

The Prime Minister's undertaking in connection with repairs was never fully complied with, and our report (January, 1947)[1] contained the following passage:

'We feel impelled to state that even today the repair of the requisitioned houses is a hope and a promise, not a performance; a number of these houses are still subject to the same progressive deterioration. It is not too much to say that . . . apart from those houses which

[1] Cmd. 7094

180

are now being scaffolded without and busily repaired and altered within by the Ministry of Works for subsequent use as government offices—[there is] not a single terrace, with the partial exception of Hanover Terrace (where a number of houses have recently been relet to private owners who are effecting what repairs and renovations they can) which does not give the impression of hopeless dereliction; there are, in fact, few more lugubrious experiences in London than that to be obtained from a general survey of the Nash Terraces in Regent's Park Elsewhere in London there is activity, energy and planning . . .'

This severe censure was unanimous, and we made it after hearing the evidence of all concerned and listening attentively to their explanations and excuses. The failure to carry out even temporary repairs to the bomb damage was bad enough. The dilapidation caused, or likely to be caused, by the resultant condition of dry rot was worse.

I doubt if any member of the committee was more shocked by what we found in Regent's Park than I was. I was a practising surveyor and estate manager, and in Canonbury I had a number of badly bombed houses that did not begin to compare architecturally to these Nash houses. Unlike the Crown Commissioners, I had had no labour except that of small local builders and no materials except what we could scrounge. Nor did I have the backing of the Prime Minister. If, twenty months after the last bomb fell on London, any of my houses capable of restoration had been in that condition I should have been ashamed.

Before the Gorell Committee was appointed it had become clear that three possible courses were open: (1) to repair and continue to pursue the pre-war policy of letting the houses as single dwellings; (2) to reconstruct in line with modern requirements behind the existing façades as flats, maisonettes and in the case of some of the smaller houses as single dwellings; (3) to demolish everything and redevelop the estate subject to a unified architectural control.

In 1943 the Crown Commissioners, who at that time appear to

181

have been more inclined to take positive steps to preserve the terraces for residential occupation than they were three years later, had instructed Louis de Soissons to produce plans in accordance with Course (2). A sample of 18 houses in York Terrace was selected for the purpose, which was to convert them into 24 self-contained units of modernized accommodation behind the façades. The work was to include complete repair and restoration, the preservation as far as possible of the spaciousness of the Regency interiors, the installation of lifts and the renewal of all services.

Louis de Soissons was assisted by Sydney Paine, F.S.I., an eminent quantity surveyor, and by R. T. James, a consulting engineer. The scheme that they produced was ingenious, but there were three major difficulties to contend with. The first was the high cost (estimate for 18 houses at 1946 prices £202,542; therefore for 374 houses say £4,200,000); the second was the life of the reconstructed buildings, which de Soissons would not put at more than 50 years; the third was the problem of estate management of a kind which the Office of the Commissioners of Crown Lands was not geared to, and the fact that when the outgoings were taken into account the accommodation provided would be out of reach of all except the well-to-do. But in spite of these difficulties the de Soissons scheme was very helpful.

The evidence that we were given in 1946 was conflicting. It came from local authorities, learned and professional societies, and private persons more or less skilled in this particular field.

The London County Council favoured Course (1). They considered that 'the Regent's Park Terraces both individually and collectively are of such architectural importance' that all except Cambridge Gate (a Victorian block without architectural merit) ought to be preserved. They envisaged the adaptation of the interiors as flats and maisonettes, but admitted that they had not gone deeply into the question of cost. The council made it clear that, whatever the cost, they were not prepared to contribute.

The St. Marylebone Borough Council expressed a different view. They had decided, with reluctance, that the best plan would be to demolish all the terraces and replace them by multi-storey blocks of flats of a mixed character, a proportion of hotels, and a few modern houses for single-family occupation. The St. Marylebone Labour Party thought that Nash's architecture was not worth preserving, having regard to the housing needs of working-class people in the neighbourhood. The St. Pancras Borough Council propounded a scheme for preserving the terraces on the east side of Regent's Park and converting them into a centre for national hospitality.

There was an even smaller measure of agreement between the institutional and professional witnesses. The Chartered Surveyors' Institution said that any adaptation of the existing buildings would be 'an expensive and unsatisfactory compromise' and recommended large-scale residential redevelopment, provided that two or three of the Nash terraces were retained and 'suitably modernized'. The Auctioneers' and Estate Agents' Institute said the same without the proviso. At the other extreme, the Georgian Group were for preserving all the terraces whatever the cost of doing so might be. They challenged the evidence of expert witnesses who had cast doubts on the stability of the structures and said it was 'irresponsible'. As to dry rot, they maintained that 'what would be a serious defect in a single house becomes negligible when the house affected is only one out of many sound ones'. As, however, the Georgian Group had to admit that they had inspected—and that superficially—only ten per cent of the houses, their evidence was not of great value.

Our report was unanimous and the following is a brief summary of our recommendations.

The Nash terraces were of national interest and importance

and should be preserved, as far as that was practicable, without regard to the economics of 'prudent' estate management. For that purpose a combination of the repair and reconditioning of the houses in their existing form (Course (1)), with their conversion on the lines proposed by Louis de Soissons (Course (2)), was perfectly feasible. In the opinion of the committee there was a minimum of seven terraces that ought to be restored and preserved at all costs, namely: Hanover Terrace (20 houses), Sussex Place (26 houses), Cornwall Terrace (19 houses), York Gate (10 houses), Park Crescent (27 houses), Chester Terrace (42 houses), Cumberland Terrace (33 houses). The committee realized that York Terrace (58 houses) was not of quite the same architectural merit, but nevertheless felt that it too should be preserved. This was a total of 235 houses out of the 374 houses that comprised the estate. But, we said, it was impossible to devise any scheme until the problem could be looked at as a whole, and that depended on the date the Commissioners could regain possession of the 200 houses to be used for government offices: 'We would indeed be sanguine if we considered that this use would come to an end in seven years.' Some rebuilding would be needed, but it should be in accordance with a master plan and the existing building line should be permanently adhered to.

Then about use. We recommended that with minor exceptions the use should be residential. One exception was the provision of a hostel for students at London University, and another the provision of a music centre to replace the Queen's Hall, which had been destroyed in the blitz. Offices and hotels to be barred, and occupations by professional people, such as doctors, restricted.

The final section of the report contained our criticisms of the Commissioners of Crown Lands—in particular for their failure to effect even temporary repairs within a reasonable time of the damage caused by bombing, about which the chairman had complained earlier to the Prime Minister. But this time the committee went further and expressed a doubt on more general grounds as to the 'fitness of the Office of the Commissioners of Crown Lands *as at present organized* [my italics] to carry out whatever policy may be finally agreed'.

I doubt if any of us were wholly satisfied with the report, but in the adverse circumstances it was the best that we could do. The last straw was when the report was published. A 'Statement by His Majesty's Government' preceded the text and the following was its concluding paragraph:

> 'The Government cannot agree that blame rests on the Commissioners or on the Ministry of Works in respect of the action taken during and since the war years to preserve and repair the terraces. The repair of these houses, important though they are from the aesthetic point of view, is expensive in labour and materials, in relation to the accommodation rendered habitable, and, at a time of severe shortage and widespread damage, when much building work was urgently necessary, for many purposes essential to the life of the community, it would have been wholly unjustifiable to accord the terraces a high priority.'

But the members of Lord Gorell's committee were not unpractical aesthetes. They had heard all the evidence available and had weighed it. Who, more than an *ad hoc* committee that included in its membership a past chairman of the Board of Inland Revenue, the chief architect of the ministry concerned with housing generally, and an ex Labour M.P. who had been a minister in the previous government, could have been better qualified to determine on the evidence the vexed question of priorities? Obviously we had taken into account all the factors pleaded in the apologia. The 'Statement by His Majesty's Government' was a lamentable piece of official whitewashing.

More than a quarter of a century has passed, and, such is the national importance of the Regent's Park Terraces, that a sequel is called for to relate what has happened since. It is a satisfactory story, and it may be thought appropriate that one of the surviving members of the Gorell Committee, who were censorious, should tell it.

We were not alone in being critical of the way in which the Office of Crown Lands was organized, but eight years passed before any positive action was taken. Then, in 1954, a second Prime Minister's Committee was appointed 'to examine the organization for the administration of Crown Lands generally' with Sir Malcolm Trustram Eve (now Lord Silsoe) as chairman. I can summarize the report by saying that the committee considered that the management of a great estate was in the nature of a *business* and should be conducted on business lines; they accordingly recommended a basic change that would give the organization the semblance of a board of directors rather than of a government department. Hitherto there had been three commissioners—the Minister of Agriculture and Fisheries and the Secretary of State for Scotland with the 'Permanent Commissioner', a high-ranking civil servant, as chief executive. The Eve Committee recommended that they should be replaced by a selected team of part-time, salaried commissioners, each an expert in his particular field; that the First Commissioner, part-time, should be chairman; that the Second Commissioner, a whole-time civil servant, should be secretary.

These recommendations were accepted, and the Crown Estate Act 1956 changed the name 'Crown Lands' to 'Crown Estate' and provided for the appointment by the Queen of up to eight persons to be 'Crown Estate Commissioners' with a duty to manage the estate and report annually. The First Commissioner and chairman was Lord Silsoe himself. The other members of the team were the former Permanent Commissioner of Crown Lands (as Second Commissioner and secretary), the President of the Central Landowners' Association, a Labour peer, two bankers (one a Scot) and two past-presidents of the Royal Institution of Chartered Surveyors.

One of the most urgent problems the Commissioners were faced with on their appointment was the future of the Regent's Park Terraces, and during the next few years they made three public statements on policy and progress. The first was in 1957, when the position was as follows: 150 houses were still occupied as temporary government offices (fulfilling the Gorell Committee's forecast that 'temporary' would exceed seven years); 157 were let as private residences; 48 were empty; 19 had been demolished in consequence of war damage.

'Having regard to the unique character of the estate' the Commissioners were clear on three things. First, the terraces could not be left in their existing condition, 'doomed to decay.' Second, there was no point in demolishing the Nash houses merely to build replicas. Third, it would not be economically practicable to restore all of them at a cost to the Exchequer of between £8 million and £10 million, the equivalent of the Gorell Committee's estimate obtained in 1946.

Methods (1) and (2) were thus ruled out, but there was a possible alternative to Method (3). The Commissioners had already been approached by developers seeking an opportunity to explore the economics of reconstructing one or more of the terraces for residential occupation as a commercial proposition. They were attracted by the suggestion, but felt that as a first step they ought to obtain up-to-date and practical experience by reconstructing a large sample themselves. The sample they chose was Cumberland Terrace, one of the most beautiful of the Nash terraces. which had the advantage of being nearly empty. Louis de Soissons' firm were employed as the Commissioners' architects, and the work was put in hand. The plans provided for the retention of the north block as six single houses. The centre and south blocks, which originally contained 21 houses, were completely rebuilt as 44 flats, everything behind the Nash façades and within the end-walls being new. In addition, three recessed pairs of houses were restored and two modern blocks of flats were built on the sites of unwanted structures behind the terrace and unseen from the park. The job was finished in the autumn of 1961 and is universally recognized as an outstanding achievement in the face of many unforeseen difficulties.

The economics of the Cumberland Terrace reconstruction turned out better than the Commissioners had expected, and the effect was to whet the appetites of a number of development companies, advised by architects of the highest standing. Negotiations proceeded on the basis that in general the leases should be for 99 years, subject to the developers complying with two conditions. The first was that the reconstructed accommodation overlooking the park should be residential, but with certain exceptions, of which Sussex Place, now the London Graduate School of Business Studies, is one. The second condition was that wherever possible the original façade and end-elevations were to be retained, and where it was agreed that that was not possible they were to be replaced by replicas.

Since 1957 there has been steady progress. The whole of Park Crescent, originally 27 houses, has been demolished and rebuilt, one by the Commissioners and the other 26 by the lessees. The new façades are identical with the originals and impossible to distinguish from them, but the opportunity was taken to remove (i.e. by not reinstating) a miscellany of ugly structures that over the years had been allowed to project above the roof line. Park Crescent now houses a number of institutional tenants, including the International Students' House, the Royal Institute of Public Administration, the University Grants Committee and two county courts.

It will be remembered that the Gorell Committee's minimum requirement for retention comprised eight terraces. Of these, Sussex Place, York Gate, Park Crescent, Chester, Cumberland and York Terraces have now been restored. The restoration of Cornwall Terrace is due to begin in 1973 or 1974, but the houses in Hanover Terrace, which were in better condition than most,

Cumberland Terrace,
Regent's Park

are leased until 1983. Nearly all the other terraces have either been restored or plans for doing so are far advanced, and by the time this book is published little will remain to be done.

The Ministry of Works have been co-operative ever since the work was started, by occupying the houses and keeping them in structural repair until the Commissioners, terrace by terrace, were ready to deal with them. It would have been impracticable to restore all the terraces simultaneously. By agreement between the Commissioners and the Ministry the process was so phased that the houses, when restored, could be fed back gradually into the market.

In 1946 the Gorell Committee recorded sadly that there were few more lugubrious experiences in London than that to be obtained from a general survey of the Nash terraces in Regent's Park, and I can testify to the truth of that observation. But all has changed now, and for those who care for lovely buildings such a survey is exalting. If the reader is not a Londoner, or is a Londoner who does not know his London, I advise him to go and look. Here is a guide.

Preferably, go in spring. Go early, when the dew is on the grass and the air is filled with bird song, and discern the symmetry of these splendid houses dark against the dawn sky. Or go at noon and enjoy the daffodils and tulips, lilacs, laburnums, cherries, before a backcloth of gleaming white façades. Or go at dusk when the shadows are lengthening and walk south from Hanover Gate. The park is on your left with its wide expanse of turf; trim hedges; formal flower beds; boats on the lake, their sails glimpsed between the trees. On your right are the terraces, panoramic tribute to a pride of royal dukes. Hanover Terrace with its classic porticos raised on a loggia of segmental arches, its fluted columns and delicate ironwork. The gracious curve of Sussex Place: pointed cupolas with slender finials, Corinthian columns and recessed balconies. Cornwall Terrace, which vies with both. Now to the east, past York Terrace and the slightly self-conscious 'Doric Villa'. Park Crescent, in the distance, with its uncorrupted roof. Go north now, past Albert, Cambridge and Chester Terraces, golden in the evening sunlight—and so to Cumberland Terrace, restored to its glory. Leave, entranced, by Gloucester Gate.

'One generation passeth away, and another generation cometh.' It is pleasant, having had cause to blame an older generation, to accord a younger unstinted praise.

XI

President, Royal Institution of Chartered Surveyors

A new partnership – on making enemies – 'how much
for Watson?' – the Archbishop calls me monstrous – 'how
old were all the other presidents?' – *The Spirit of a Profession* –
Lord Jowitt – Whiligh oaks – after-dinner speaking.

In 1947, before the sale of the Northampton estates was mooted,
I had dissolved my partnership in Ferris and Puckridge and become an associate partner in Alfred Savill and Sons, who in
those days had their head office in Lincoln's Inn Fields. Bill
Gillett and I were sad at parting, but happily there were no
recriminations and no bitterness and we were close friends until
his death.

For some time we had both seen the parting coming. After the
bombing of our City office in 1940, Gillett had continued his
practice from a branch office in Ealing. But as it was the kind of
practice that was badly hit by the war, he left a junior partner
to hold together what was left and accepted a temporary commission as a valuer in the War Office Lands Department.

For my part, I had become increasingly involved during the
1930s with Claude Leigh and his companies, mainly in connection with rating and taxation. Their headquarters were in
West London and it suited me to conduct my end of the Ferris
and Puckridge practice, which was in a different category from
Gillett's, at a branch office in Hanover Square. Bill and I met
only occasionally. Then came the war, and although I continued
in Hanover Square and remained for two years a director of

Leigh's management company, from 1940 onward I devoted nearly all my time to the Northampton agencies.

Soon after the war ended the Earl of Jersey, a personal friend, asked me if I could help him. The agent for his estate at Briton Ferry in South Wales, which was mainly industrial, had died suddenly and the agent for the Osterley Park Estate in Middlesex was gravely ill. Lord Jersey asked me whether I was in a position to take over the management of Briton Ferry at once, and of Osterley if and when his then agent retired. He asked me to recommend someone else if I was unable to do so.

It was an attractive proposition and had it not been for the Northampton agency, which at that time I had no reason to suppose was other than for life, I should have been interested. As things were, it was out of the question. So I wrote to Gillett, who was still in the army, suggesting that he should apply for demobilization and take on these important jobs. To my disappointment he refused. He said that for one thing he would have more than enough to do rebuilding his old practice when he returned to civilian life; for another, which was probably true, Ferris and Puckridge were not geared to take on two such big agencies at short notice.

My second choice fell on Fred Ragg. He was a partner in Alfred Savill and Sons, a much bigger firm than we were, which had several other partners and a highly qualified staff. He accepted both agencies and, because I was a friend of Jersey's, paid me the compliment of consulting me informally from time to time. That was the beginning of a long association with Ragg, which became closer as time passed. When problems arose on the Northampton estates it was Ragg I brought in, and when other important jobs came my way I tended more and more to pass them to his office. I needed a big organization behind me, and Alfred Savill and Sons could provide it.

Bill Gillett died suddenly in 1953. Thereafter his son Alan Gillett, who is my godson, joined his father's old firm and Ferris and Puckridge amalgamated with Charles P. Whiteley and Son, a City firm whose offices in the same block as ours had been destroyed by fire bombs on the same night. Then C.C.O. Whiteley died and there was a further amalgamation with Kemsleys. Today the head office of Kemsley, Whiteley and Ferris is in Poultry, which, as every Londoner knows, has nothing to do with cocks and hens and is part of ancient Cheapside.

Throughout my life I have been fortunate in my partners and colleagues; they have also been my friends. In general I like people and flatter myself that in general they like me. Of course there are exceptions and I have my enemies. It works both ways; it is idle to suppose that if I dislike a man he will reciprocate by liking me—or the other way round. Years ago, when comparatively young, I became aware for the first time that I had enemies, who had been saying unkind things behind my back. The discovery worried me so much that I confided in two friends, both considerably older than I; one was that wise man Julian Marks and the other B. of B. Julian wrote to me:

'No one can accomplish anything without making a certain number of enemies . . . I know I have made many and I have little enough idea how I made most of them. You can take it as a general proposition that a man who is so colourless that he makes no enemies is also so colourless that he makes no friends.'

B. of B. contented himself with citing an old Scots maxim, and counselled me to repeat it under my breath when the need arose: 'They say . . . What say they? . . . *Let 'em say!*'

I mentioned earlier the advice given me by Ernest Hall. He had had a lawsuit with a partner, and although he had got the best of it he remarked ruefully that it was much more difficult to get rid of a partner than a wife. As mercifully I have never wanted to rid myself of either, I am not qualified to judge. But, having observed from an independent standpoint, I am inclined to think—except about what shall happen afterwards—that the wording of a partnership contract, like the wording of a marriage contract, matters little when it comes to the crunch. Should the continuance of an association result in misery to the parties, no amount of lawyer's jargon ('*Whereas*' . . . '*Now this deed witnesseth*' . . . '*Provided always that*' . . .) will hold it together.

But every well regulated firm *must* have a deed of partnership. How else would lawyers live? So in a friendly way we got down to it—Fred Ragg and his partners on one side, and I on the other. For reasons that the reader will appreciate I was not interested in a full partnership, which would have required me to devote the whole of my time to the firm's business. Solicitors and accountants were brought in. Watson would have his name on the firm's notepaper; Watson must be diligent in attending the office; Watson must behave; Watson or the partners could bring the whole thing to an end at six month's notice if either side got fed up. The burning question was: '*What should Watson be paid?*'

Simple enough, one might think, but only at first sight. Suppose Watson found a client and did the job himself, two-thirds of the fee to Watson. If he passed it to his partners, only one-third to Watson. Conversely, if the partners found the client and Watson did the job, only one-third to the partners. But what would happen if the partners found the client and Watson did the job assisted by the staff the partners paid? And supposing Watson's client, whose job he passed to the partners (one-third to Watson), produced another client who went straight to the partners, whose client was this? And if the client in the second degree belonged to the partners, and the job was done by Watson (a) aided by the partners' staff, (b) unaided by the partners' staff, what then? And suppose the client in the second degree found yet *another* client, to whom did the clients in the second and third degrees belong? There was no end to it. 'Great fleas have little fleas upon their backs to bite 'em, and little fleas have lesser fleas and so *ad infinitum*.' The combinations and permutations would have made it difficult for the accountants, though happily in those days we had no computers to make it impossible.

One morning Fred Ragg came into my room. My partnership agreement had been under negotiation for several months and I gathered that he had been in consultation with two of his senior partners, A. W. (Conky) Turner and Jim Eve. Fred was a quiet, shy man who sometimes took so long in coming to the point that there was a danger of your forming quite a wrong idea about what he was thinking. I could see from his expression that something was troubling him; so I asked my secretary, to whom I was dictating letters, to go away and close the door.

'John,' he began . . .

'Yes, Fred?'

'About this wretched deed of partnership; it seems to be taking an awfully long time. [I agreed that it was] I suppose . . . I suppose . . . (*do* say frankly if you don't like the idea) I suppose you wouldn't like to leave it to us?'

'Leave what to you?'

He flushed and began to explain, but before he had got very far I tumbled to what he was after:

'You mean—leave my remuneration to you?'

'Well, yes . . .'

I was greatly relieved. That seemed to me the only way out, and I accepted with alacrity. So the lawyers got busy and a deed was signed under which I was entitled only to the fees for jobs for my own clients that I did myself. My partners were not required to pay me anything for my other work, except what was 'agreed' between us from time to time.

It remains to add that it was a happy partnership and lasted nine years. There was never a cross word in the whole of that period, except an annual disagreement during the second half of January when the partners ignored my protests that they were paying me too much.

In my younger days I had taken an active part in the affairs of the Chartered Surveyors' Institution. The Institution had been founded in 1868 and for years had had a number of provincial branches; in the 1920s there were nearly 40. They catered mainly for the senior members and the Junior Meetings, as they were then called, were centred on London. Very properly, the Junior Meetings were extended until in 1930 every provincial branch, with two or three exceptions, had a junior branch attached to it. So it was that the Junior Meetings became the Junior Organization. I was honorary secretary of the Junior Organization from 1928 to 1933, and in 1933-34 its chairman. From 1929 to 1933 I had a seat on the council of the Institution, representing the professional-associate class of membership. In 1946, having in the meantime become a fellow, I was brought back on to the council and in the same year was elected a vice-president.

In 1946 I was aged 43, which was young for this distinction; I had a suspicion, which I am sure was well-founded, that my election as a vice-president had little to do with my being a surveyor. Circumstances had arisen in which my professional and non-professional lives overlapped. I had been appointed a magistrate in 1934, and since 1935 had sat a day a week as chairman of a juvenile court in South London. In the autumn of 1944 I unexpectedly found myself a national figure. It was the result of a splendid row that I and Basil Henriques, chairman of the East London Juvenile Court, had with the London County Council.

It was all about a girls' remand home in Hammersmith called Marlesford Lodge, which belonged to the council. The London juvenile court magistrates had complained frequently about its mismanagement. But the L.C.C. had ignored our complaints and the Children's Branch of the Home Office, who ought to have intervened but were frightened of the council, sat on the fence. During the same week I and the other members of my bench in South London, and Basil Henriques in East London, blew up. Our public statements, a grave indictment of the L.C.C., were reported verbatim in every daily newspaper and were later debated in County Hall and in both Houses of Parliament.

Eventually Herbert Morrison, the Home Secretary, ordered an inquiry; but, whereas we had asked for a *public* inquiry, Morrison, disregarding strong protests in the House of Commons, insisted that it should be *in secret*. He appointed as his inquirers Mr. Godfrey Russell Vick, K.C., and Miss Myra Curtis, their terms of reference being to investigate and report, not merely on Marlesford Lodge, but on the administration of L.C.C. remand homes generally. And during the twelve-day hearing at the Law Courts, as happens when you dredge a dirty pond, unsuspected and unsavoury things came to the surface. Why did the inquiry have to be *in secret*? The party in office at County Hall, who were responsible for the administration of children's remand homes, was the Labour Party. It may or may not be significant that Herbert Morrison, before he became Home Secretary, was himself a Labour member of the L.C.C.

The magistrates were supported by members of all three political parties; it is difficult to conceive of anything that should be further removed from the political arena than a children's home. Both Russell Vick and Myra Curtis are dead, and I will say no more than that the way in which Russell Vick conducted the proceedings astonished the lawyers (including Simon, the Lord Chancellor) who got to know about it. One unsavoury matter brought to the surface cast a reflection on the Church of England; the authorities in the Diocese of London had manifestly failed in their duty to be aware of, approve, and keep an eye on the clergy who became officially attached to children's institutions. That led to a stormy encounter between Basil and me on one side, and the Archbishop of Canterbury (Fisher) and the Bishop of Kensington (Montgomery Campbell) on the other. The Archbishop, unwisely, took the offensive; he had formerly been a schoolmaster and he behaved like a schoolmaster. He took the line that we should never have brought this unfortunate matter to light. How dared we do so? He went as far as to tell me I had been monstrous. Basil, who had no fear of bishops, arch or sub-arch, hastened to my aid. He replied 'with deep respect' that if the word 'monstrous' was appropriate at all, it might be thought to apply to their neglect. So we were quits.

In the committee's report, in February, 1945, all three parties were slapped. Basil Henriques and I, also my two fellow magistrates, were rebuked for our 'lack of moderation of statement' and for 'deliberately securing the co-operation of the press'. [Why not?] The *officers* of the L.C.C. were censured for 'remoteness of interest and sluggishness of operation', but the *members* were exonerated from any responsibility. [How lucky for Morrison!] The Children's Branch of the Home Office were blamed for not discharging their statutory duty of supervision. But the press, who continued to co-operate, came down solidly on our side, and I have a collection of congratulatory cuttings. Even *Punch* was provoked into a whole-page cartoon by E. H. Shepard, which must have annoyed the L.C.C. The original drawing hangs on the wall of my study. The figure of Mercy is sheltering a little waif beneath her cloak; in the background looms his pursuer, the sinister figure of Bumble. She cries: 'I thought that ghost was laid for ever!' And here is a passage from the *Daily Telegraph:*

> '[The committee of inquiry] have made every possible effort to whitewash the London County Council and the Home Office, but they are unable to avoid finding both guilty of blunders and slackness. At great length . . . they exhibit some inaccuracy in the statement of Mr. John Watson who first drew attention to the treatment of children in Marlesford Lodge. As the committee themselves pronounce the conditions there undesirable, they should have added that Mr. Watson performed a public service.'. .

The committee, despite their strictures on Basil and me, endorsed nearly all the recommendations that we and our witnesses had made for the improved administration of remand homes generally. We were rewarded by seeing them applied by local authorities all over the country. Eventually, however, the time came when in the interests of London children the magistrates and the L.C.C. decided it was time to bury the hatchet. Basil and I were entertained to a sumptuous tea at County Hall by the Leader of the Council, Lord Latham. Herbert Morrison remarked to me good-humouredly that, what with me and the 'cleft-chin' murderer[1] during the same winter, it was more than any Home Secretary could be expected to stand. Even the Archbishop detached himself from a group of cabinet ministers at a reception and shook me warmly by the hand. And I was further rewarded—much to my surprise, but even more to that of Sir John Oakley—by being elected a vice-president of the Royal Institution of Chartered Surveyors. A vice-president, unless he blots his copy book, normally succeeds to the highest office. I managed not to blot mine and in June, 1949, became its president.

Now the most important person in any professional society—much more important than the president, who changes every year—is the secretary. His job is in the background, but it is no exaggeration to say that nearly everything depends on what he says and does, and in times of difficulty on the line he takes. In 1949 the secretary of the R.I.C.S. was Brigadier Killick, later to become Sir Alexander Killick and now retired. Killick began life as a regular soldier. He came out of the army in 1932 to become our secretary on the understanding that if by chance there was a war the army would want him back. There *was* a war. Shortly after it broke out he became secretary of the Standing Committee on Army Administration, which created the permanent executive and secretarial machinery for the Army Council—of which in 1941 he became joint (military) secretary. Need I say he is a brilliant organizer? He was also a delightful person to work with.

[1] The 'cleft-chin' murderer was a notorious criminal who had been a lot of trouble to the Home Office. I forget the details.

It was not long before the secretary discovered, as the outcome of his researches, that at 45 I was the youngest president in the Institution's history. When he told me I was pleased, but a little doubtful when he went on to say he intended to make full use of it. He said it was a piece of interesting information that ought to be passed discreetly, via their secretaries, to presidents of kindred societies and others, who would be expected to mention me in after-dinner speeches and would be wondering beforehand what on earth they could find to say. So Alec had his way and the 'interesting information' was made use of—*but only once*.

If you are a man, to look more than your age has advantages. I have always appeared *much* older. I was bald by the time I was thirty, and a year before I became president, with my wife's approval, I had grown a small beard. Unhappily, owing to some misunderstanding, it turned out white instead of, as I had hoped, auburn.

One evening, early in my year of office, the president of the society in whose company I had been dining made a beautiful speech, and said a lot of things about me that would have been gratifying if they had been accurate. But at least he was truthful in his peroration. 'Finally, Gentlemen, I think you should know that our distinguished guest, Mr. John Watson, is the youngest president in the 80 years' history of the Royal Institution of Chartered Surveyors.' The revelation was well received and it was quite a time before the applause subsided. They had scarcely done so when the thick voice of a well-dined guest was heard to exclaim: 'Good God! How old were all the *other* presidents?'

The heaviest responsibility of a president is his inaugural address. Mine had to be delivered in November, which was the first meeting of the new session. Therefore, as the presidential election was in the previous June, I had several months to prepare my address and to get a lot of help from my friends. The first step was to choose a theme.

November, 1948, was one of the dying months of the Labour Government that had been returned to power in 1945. During the intervening years there had been an unprecedented volume of legislation—most of it valuable—affecting land. There had been the Agriculture Act, which my predecessor, Richard Trumper, had described in his presidential address as 'a charter for agriculture'. There had been the Coal Industry National-ization Act. I have already mentioned the New Towns Act. The Local Government Act, as I recorded earlier, had transferred to a central authority the responsibility for making assessments for local taxation, which since the Statute of Elizabeth had belonged to local authorities. The most recent Labour measure had been the Town and Country Act 1947, which had given wide powers to the planning authorities and, as we have seen, had sought to solve the compensation-betterment problem by providing that all development values in land should be com-pulsorily acquired.

Much of this legislation had been controversial, especially the last. Suggestions had been made within the Institution that a professional society concerned with land, land values and land use, should enter the lists and make pronouncements in the hope of influencing the course of events. The council, however, had very properly declined to do so, on the ground that it was the duty of a profession to remain politically impartial. But some of the members were dissatisfied, and that explains my decision to devote the greater part of my address to a discussion of the attitude a corporate professional society ought to adopt towards political issues. I gave my address a title. *The Spirit of a Profession*, delivered in Great George Street more than a quarter of a century ago, has long been forgotten except perhaps by a handful of my contemporaries.

A chartered surveyor, I said, like any other subject of the Crown, is entitled to his own opinion of what is right and just. But in matters of public policy 'right' and 'just' are relative terms; what one man considers right and just another, no less honest, considers wrong and inequitable. I instanced the controversial provisions of the Act I have just referred to. Some people, I said, had an unshakable conviction that when a private person was dispossessed of his property by the State, he should be fully compensated for his loss. But there were others, no less worthy, who shared the view expressed by the Government in a memorandum 'that owners who lose development value as a result of the passing of the [Town and Country Planning] Bill are not on that account entitled to compensation'.

I quoted Bismarck: 'Politics are not an exact science.' I said that among surveyors it was not surprising, and in no way regrettable, to find a divergence of political thought; but that it was sometimes difficult to divorce political convictions from professional considerations. Was it likely, I asked, for the agent for a great landed estate belonging to some ancient family to be an ardent advocate of land nationalization? Or for the surveyor to a progressive local authority to believe that the interests of his authority ought to be subservient to those of private land-owners? But, I said, these *might* be their opinions and the holding of them as individuals should not prevent the effective discharge of their duties as professional men.

I went on to say that a professional man, as an individual, was not only entitled to hold views on controversial political issues; he was entitled to express them with the freedom that Milton ranked 'above all liberties'. He could do so from the platform of the Fabian Society or of the Primrose League—both honourable bodies—according to his way of thinking. But he must not expect his professional society, comprising thousands of members of all shades of political opinion, to take sides. I warned my hearers that if we did so we should imperil the structure of public confidence we had built up over the years. We should no longer, as acknowledged partisans, command the respect and retain the ear of successive governments; and no longer could we expect, as we had come to expect, service on our council and committees by every class of member by whomsoever employed.

For these reasons I concluded that the policy of the Institution must always be to remain aloof from the political arena. That, however, was not to say that it should refrain from giving advice, based on the technical knowledge and experience of its members, on what the consequences of any legislative proposal might be. But the advice should be objective and available to all persons irrespective of their political affiliations. Were we to go further and assert that this or that consequence was for or against the public interest, we should exceed that duty. I returned to the Town and Country Planning Act. If, I said, it was the opinion of the profession based on evidence that the provisions of the Act would deter private development, it was not only our right but our duty to say so—at every opportunity and with all the force we could command. But were we to say that to deter the private development of land was a *good* thing or a *bad* thing, we should exceed our proper function and benefit ultimately neither the public, nor the Institution, not its individual members.

The war had ended only four years earlier, and in the last few minutes I widened my theme and addressed the younger generation:

'*Ich dien*. The finest tradition of any calling is a readiness to serve. The spirit of a great profession is the spirit of service. It is a spirit that must govern our approach to every question, for it is active in all sections of our membership, in all branches, and at all ages. Witness the devotion, during nearly seven years of war, of the thousands of our members who offered their lives in the righteous cause for which we fought it. Nor was it absent among the others. It was in the darkest days, you may remember, when most of them were understaffed and overworked . . . it was then that the council appealed to members, in their evenings and at weekends, to staff the Poor Man's Valuer Associations. The response was instant and uncomplaining. It is the same unselfish spirit in which

203

so often a senior member will help a junior member over some awkward stile in the path of his practice. It is a spirit that derives, I suggest, from an interest not in things but in people—which alone begets understanding. And the gift of understanding, you will remember, was first among all the gifts which that great architect, King Solomon, prayed for.

'I say to you most earnestly—the younger members of the profession—maintain that tradition. At junior meetings, in your daily work, in your leisure, seek at every turn to gain a knowledge of people—of what they think and why they think it. As an older member, I speak in all humility to those who, in the Forces of the Crown, found and grasped so great an opportunity of doing so. For if anything good was engendered by the war, was it not that communion with human nature, in all its strength and in all its weakness, that is born of comradeship in arms? You know that better than I. "One learns", wrote Donald Hankey during an earlier war, "to trust each other and to look for the essential qualities rather than for the accidental graces. One learns to love men for their great hearts, their pluck, their indomitable spirits, their irrepressible humour, their readiness to shoulder a weaker brother's burden in addition to their own. One sees men as God sees them, apart from externals such as manner and intonation . . . When the war is over, and the men of the citizen army return to their homes and civil occupations, will they, I wonder, remember the things that they have learnt? If so, there will be a new and better England . . ."

Another war has taught the same lesson to a younger generation, who have proved once more the power that lies in men and women who can repress their selfish desires and ambitions and work in harmony for a cause far greater than themselves. It is a power to work miracles, a power "to build Jerusalem in England's green and pleasant land"—a Jerusalem that is builded as a city at unity in itself. In the presence of visible and immediate danger, this nation has never failed to achieve that harmony and brotherhood that are conditions of its deliverance. Moving now into an era where danger is less visible and less immediate, but perhaps for that very reason even more insidious, can we preserve the unity we achieved in the presence of the enemy, "fitly joined together and compacted by that which every joint supplieth" in the lithe and powerful metaphor of St. Paul? That is the challenge to post-war England. It is for us of the surveying profession to contribute our "joint" towards compacting the unity of a great nation. Let no man think it is a little thing because we deal ostensibly with men's and women's material environment. Our work will be finally judged, and we hope justified, not by fertility of fields or by stability of houses, but by the quality of living that these things promote.'

I have mentioned the dinners a president of the Institution has to attend in his year of office. Their number is legion. Nearly all the Institution's branches have an annual meeting followed by a dinner, and members are disappointed if their president does not come to it. Then there are the Quantity Surveyors' dinner and the Junior Organization dinner, and a dinner of his own council after every ordinary general meeting. Other professional bodies, who make a practice of inviting the president of the Royal Institution of Chartered Surveyors to their dinner, include the Law Society, the Architects, the Town Planning Institute and the Rating Surveyors' Association. No one should accept the presidency of a professional society unless he has a good digestion, a strong head and (in my day) a plentiful supply of boiled shirts.

The annual dinner of the Chartered Surveyors is held in London in March—the most important function of the year except the presidential address. Even in my time, when the profession was much smaller, several hundred members and their guests attended. In addition there are always a number of official guests. The practice is to invite a minister of the Crown as chief guest and principal speaker and seat him on the president's right. On the president's left, to mark our political neutrality, is a distinguished member of the Opposition. In my year the Lord Chancellor in the Labour Government, Viscount (later Earl) Jowitt, was invited as chief guest and his opposite number was Lord Woolton.

Jowitt was a highly intelligent man, but a curious and unpredictable character. In his younger days he had been unpopular with his contemporaries, mainly because of his vacillations in politics. In 1922 he entered Parliament as Liberal member for the Hartlepools, but lost that seat at the next General Election. In 1929 he had just been returned as Liberal member for Preston when Ramsay MacDonald, in process of forming a government, found himself short of forensic talent and asked Jowitt if he would consider becoming his Attorney General. Jowitt accepted with alacrity, and changed from Liberal to Labour apparently without any hesitation. His subsequent political career has been described as a 'see-saw of alternating allegiances'. Possibly he lacked any profound convictions and it has been suggested that, being primarily an advocate, he failed to realize what a bad impression his inconsistencies made.

Both may be true, but it is fair to record that in connection with juvenile courts I found him sincere and refreshingly unpompous. I received a message that, if I could spare the time, the Lord Chancellor would be grateful if I would call to see him in his room in the House of Lords one afternoon the following week. As I knew him only slightly I made discreet inquiries, and gathered it had to do with a Criminal Justice Bill then in Parliament. To a lay justice, the lowest form of judicial life, who was not even a lawyer, such an invitation was a command. Naturally I went, imagining I was to be present at some sort of informal conference. Not at all. Tea was brought in, the door closed, and we were alone. He put me completely at my ease, and the lay justice quickly forgot it was the Lord Chancellor he was talking to. Then he began to question me, and did so almost humbly. 'Watson,' he said, 'I am worried about the possible consequences of one or two clauses in this Bill that affect young people. Here they are. Please read them and tell me off the record what *you* think.' I cannot remember the drift of the conversation between the president of the Royal Institution of Chartered Surveyors and the Lord Chancellor at our 1950 dinner, but probably it was more about child delinquency than anything else.

Another of our guests was that dear old man, Lord Courthope, who had been an honorary member of the Institution for many years. I suppose that in his period he was the supreme authority on British forestry, and there can be few bodies concerned with forestry over which George Courthope did not preside at one time or another. He was chairman of the British Forestry Association, 1916–1921, president of the Royal English Arboricultural Society, 1918–1920, chairman of the Consultative Committee under the Forestry Acts, 1919 to 1927, and a Forestry Commissioner, 1923–1948.

Courthope came of an ancient Sussex family who had had estates at Whiligh near Wadhurst for centuries, and in that connection there is a Courthope story worth retelling. In A.D. 1394 the oak for the great beams and rafters for the roof of Westminster Hall were bought by King Richard II from Courthope of Wadhurst. More than 500 years later, when the same roof needed repair, Lord Courthope, his direct descendant, supplied the oak for that purpose *from trees that had been standing at the time the original oaks were felled for Richard II.*

> 'There is no antidote to the Opiate of time,
> which temporally considereth all things . . .
> Generations pass while some trees stand, and
> old families last not three oakes.'

What a negation of those words by Sir Thomas Browne is the great English family of Courthope, a family coeval with its forests!

When one's principal guest is a man as brilliant and as eloquent as Lord Jowitt, one expects a good after-dinner speech— and we certainly had one. But there are *other* kinds of after-dinner speech, and it occurs to me I might profitably end this chapter with a few notes about after-dinner speeches in general.

The president of a professional society has to make a lot of such speeches in his year of office, but has to listen to far more. Looking back over my life, I can recall a few after-dinner speeches that were really brilliant, many that were good, more that were adequate, and a residue that were unutterably dull.

It is not easy to make a good after-dinner speech. Nor is it easy to appear to enjoy listening to a bad one. But in courtesy one must try, and the likelihood of its being a bad speech generally emerges in the first few sentences. Then I suggest one should replenish one's glass, if the decanter is within reach, and observe four rules. *Rule 1*: Make an effort to follow what the speaker is talking about and cry 'Here, here!' at appropriate moments; one such moment is when he loses his place in his notes. *Rule 2*: Laugh loudly at his jokes, whether or not one has seen the point. *Rule 3* (for use only when the speech is exceptionally tedious): Cultivate the art of closing the eyes while sitting upright, conveying an impression of intense concentration when in fact one is asleep. *Rule 4*: When eventually the speaker sits down, applaud vigorously and refrain from explaining in the hearing of one's neighbour, who is probably his wife, 'Thank God for that.'

Now about *making* after-dinner speeches. 'I am no orator as Brutus is' and not qualified to instruct. But I have learned what little I know the hard way, and I hope I shall not be thought presumptuous if I pass on to the younger and less experienced of my readers a few of the things I have had to find out for myself.

It is safe to say that the great majority of after-dinner speakers are too long, but a minority make up for it. They are the brilliant people who, apparently without effort, can make their hearers rock with laughter until they are in danger of falling off their chairs. Such speakers can continue almost indefinitely. Time does not signify, nor the risk of missing the last bus.

But should you not be in that class, for goodness' sake be short. You can hardly be *too* short. You may not be acclaimed an orator if you speak for only three minutes, but (which some may think preferable) you will be deemed a decent, considerate chap. Your hearers will say to one another 'Wish we had a few more after-dinner speakers like him,' as they help themselves to brandy and resume their conversations where they left off. Here for the inexperienced speaker is a guide to length. Five minutes, *ample*; six or seven minutes, *permissible*; eight to ten minutes, *regrettable*; over ten minutes, *insufferable*.

The crucial parts of a speech are the beginning and the end. If you hope to hold the attention of an audience, you must first capture it—hence the importance of your first sentence. The middle of a speech, assuming you know your subject, should look after itself. Your last sentence—short, crisp and delivered pat—should be the most telling.

If you are in constant demand as a speaker, in the same role and on the same theme, be warned. Resist the temptation to have only a single speech. For one thing, it is lazy; for another, it is disappointing, when you think you have held your audience spellbound by your novel ideas, to be told afterwards: 'We *so much* enjoyed hearing again all the interesting things you said at the Ratcatchers' annual dinner last week.' Instead I recommend a framework, neatly padded at the ends but hollow in the middle; you can vary the stuffing according to taste. In fact what you need is 'manna in the wilderness', and should the reader fail to see the connection between manna and public speaking the reference is to Oscar Wilde. In *The Importance of being Earnest*, Act II, the Reverend Canon Chasuble has offered to refer in his sermon on the following Sunday to the tragic death 'in Paris of a severe chill' of the mythical Ernest. The Canon continues:

'My sermon on the meaning of the manna in the wilderness can be adapted to almost any occasion, joyful, or, as in the present case, distressing. I have preached it at harvest celebrations, christenings, confirmations, on days of humiliation and on festal days. The last time I delivered it was in the Cathedral as a charity sermon on behalf of the Society for the Prevention of Discontent among the Upper Orders. The Bishop, who was present, was much *struck* by some of the analogies I drew.'

As the main purpose of an after-dinner speaker is to entertain the diners, adherence to truth is no more important than in the Andy-Pandy Show on television. My maternal grandmother used to say that anyone who heard a good story and passed it on without adding to it was *mean*. How right the old lady was! I have always followed her precept. Always connect a good story with yourself or your family if it is possible to do so. Do *not* begin: 'That reminds me of a tale I once heard about a man who fell down a manhole . . .' ('Reminds' is a lie anyway; you were not reminded; you have been rehearsing it for days.) Begin like this: 'When my Uncle Timothy fell down that manhole, he was heard to say . . .' The fact that you have no Uncle Timothy and never had an Uncle Timothy, or indeed any relative who had the misfortune to fall down a manhole, is of no consequence.

Now I come to a delicate subject. Perhaps I should say 'return' to it, for I discussed it at some length in my earlier book, *Nothing but the Truth*. I refer to the speaking of good English and, of great importance to the public speaker, its correct pronunciation. If the reader is confident that he has nothing to learn on this subject—he may be right—he is advised to skip. I offer no apology for making yet another attempt within my limited sphere, conscious as I am of my own imperfections, to repel the dastardly assaults that are made almost daily on our beautiful language. 'The English', wrote Bernard Shaw, 'have no respect for their language, and will not teach their children to speak it. They spell it so abominably that no man can teach himself what it sounds like. It is impossible for an Englishman to open his mouth without making some other Englishman hate or despise him.'[1]

Happily there are exceptions. Without doubt there are highly educated people, whose mastery of their language is such that they

[1] *Pygmalion*: preface.

can be relied on never to make a grammatical error or pronounce a word wrongly. Alas, I am not one of them. I know my limitations, and claim no more than that in speaking and in writing English I am a little more flexible than when I was younger. And I admit that I still sometimes hear a word pronounced differently from the way in which I pronounce it, make inquiry, and discover to my shame that I have been pronouncing that word incorrectly all my life.

A mispronunciation is a solecism, and 'solecism' is defined in *The Concise Oxford Dictionary* as 'offence against grammar or idiom, blunder in the manner of speaking or writing; piece of ill breeding or incorrect behaviour'. It is because of the last definition that our friends, when we offend in this way, are reluctant to tell us. Most of us are like a bishop who would rather be told he was 'not a Christian' than 'not a gentleman'. Our friends are fearful lest they should be taken as implying that they consider themselves better bred or better educated than we are. So, left in ignorance of the offence, we go on committing it. Certainly it is not the sort of criticism that should be made publicly, and there is a pleasant story of the kindly consideration once shown a young barrister by the Court of Appeal.

The barrister was not only young and inexperienced, but palpably nervous. Even so, he ought to have known better. In his opening he was guilty of the enormity of pronouncing *sub judice* to rhyme with *dicey*. The court was seen to wince, and to wince more noticeably when the false quantity made another appearance a few sentences later. What were their lordships to do? To correct his pronunciation in public would have mortified the young man and have thrown him into confusion. To pronounce the Latin tag correctly would have drawn attention to his error, almost certainly with the same result. By common consent, without any need for consultation, the judges set an example in good manners. Everyone in court said *sub judicey* throughout the case.

Today by far the largest purveyors of the spoken word are radio and television. Some excellent English is broadcast daily, a lot of indifferent English, and a residue so atrocious that it does not merit being called English at all. The tragedy is that the last, with its welter of mispronunciations, clichés, genteelisms and redundancies, is quickly adopted by so many of the listening public. The following are a few of the more common mispronunciations.

Contrōversy (the second syllable to rhyme with *stove*) is our oldest enemy and heads the list. *Formīdable* is now so frequent that I shall soon find myself saying it. *Lamēntable, sedēntary* and, on this side of the Atlantic, *primārily* are in the same vein. I have been told about memōrable, but cannot have heard it or I should have memōrised the occasion. Among my particular dislikes are *exquīsite* with the accent on *quis*, and *hospītable* with it on *spit*. The other evening a television announcer praised Mr. Percy Thrower's *clemātis* (to rhyme with *'taties*), and in the programme that followed a Conservative Minister of State deplored the *harāssment* of the Israelis by the Egyptians, or vice versa: I forget at that moment which were *harāssing* (to rhyme with *massing*) which.

To the younger and therefore less experienced of my readers, and to those who are older but not too proud to learn, I recommend a practice I mentioned earlier. It is based on the advice given me more than fifty years ago by my maternal grandfather. Buy two copies of a good dictionary that gives pronunciations as well as meanings. *The Concise Oxford*[1] is of a handy size and I know of none better. Keep one copy permanently in your office and the other at home. Whenever you hear someone pronounce a word in an unfamiliar way, make a written note and at the first opportunity consult your dictionary and find out who is right.

In speaking English, as in writing English, obey the golden rule. Use short words. Never use a long word if there is a shorter one that will do the job as well. Why *donate* when there is *give*? Why *purchase* when there is *buy*? Why *inform* when there is *tell*? Why *residence* when there is *house* or *flat*? The courteous shopkeeper,

---

[1] 5th Edition, 1964: Oxford University Press.

out of stock of the thing you want, will '*endeavour Sir, to obtain it*'. You may be sure he does not talk like that at home. Had he been better educated, and were he in consequence less anxious to impress, he would '*try to get it*'.

Another book that every speaker, as well as every writer, should possess is Fowler's *Modern English Usage*.[1] *Fowler* is much more than a reference book; it is fascinating to browse in. The countless articles in its 725 pages are concerned first with usage—defined as grammar, syntax and choice of words; secondly with the formation of words, their spelling and inflexions; thirdly with pronunciation; fourthly with punctuation and typography.

Lesson succeeds lesson: about faulty constructions and common illiteracies; tautology; fused participles; careless repetition and its self-conscious counterpart, 'elegant variation'; the correct use of capitals, inverted commas, hyphens and stops. We are taught the differences between *compared to* and *compared with*; *due to* and *owing to*; *mendacity* and *mendicity*; *laudatory* and *laudable*; *prescribe* and *proscribe*; *perspicuous* and *perspicacious*. And we learn why it is inconceivable for an individual to have more than *one* idiosyncrasy.

He is merciless in his condemnations. Of clichés (*tender mercies/in durance vile/leave no stone unturned*); of vogue words (*image/viable/confrontation*); of misquotations ('*A little knowledge is a dangerous thing*'); of redundancies (*true facts/grateful thanks*); of genteelisms (*perspiration/perfume/toilet*); of outworn humour (*sky pilot/trick cyclist*); of stock pathos (*all that was mortal of/departed this life/in her great sorrow*); of the misuse of *while* (*Mary recited while her sister sang*); of what he calls 'officialese' (*Appropriate weekly rate means, in relation to any benefit, the weekly rate of personal benefit by way of benefit of that description which is appropriate in the case of the person in relation to whom the provision containing that expression is applied. . . .*) O dear!

Fowler is also a splendid debunker not least of some of the pedagogic nonsense that was inculcated into us at school. It is

[1] Second edition, 1965, revised by Sir Ernest Gowers: Oxford University Press.

satisfactory to discover that the theory that *different* must always be followed by *from*, never by *to*, is a mere fetish; that it is permissible, should the sense require it, to split an infinitive; that a preposition is a part of speech that we may properly end a sentence with; that *under the circumstances* is as correct as *in the circumstances*; and that to expect a man to write flexible English, yet forbid him to use *whose* as a relative pronoun of an inanimate object (necessitating one of those clumsy *of which* clauses), 'is like sending a soldier on active service and insisting that his tunic collar shall be tight and high'. . . . But it is time we got back to that after-dinner speech.

I made the point—did I not?—that the primary purpose of an after-dinner speech is to entertain. But it may also have some noble purpose. You have been entrusted with responsibility for proposing a toast: 'The Chairman'; or 'The Corporation of the City of Barchester, coupled with the name of His Worship the Mayor'; or merely, on behalf of the guests, to thank the Mayor and Corporation for the munificent hospitality you have enjoyed at their hands. Whatever duty has been assigned to you, be sure to discharge it. That advice may appear unnecessary, but I have known after-dinner speakers so carried away in the flood of their own oratory, so convulsed with laughter at their own jokes, that they have sunk back into their chairs and relighted their cigars without having proposed anything or mentioned anybody. If there is any danger of your forgetting to do what you have set out to do, my advice is to begin with it. Once you have got the Mayor and Corporation off your chest (figuratively of course) you can afford to turn to lighter topics. One further point. Should your toast be 'The Guests', confine yourself to the Mayor, the Mayoress and the Town Clerk. To identify each guest in turn, cataloguing his or her distinctions, can be as boring to the diners as reading aloud from *Who's Who*.

The most important toast is 'The Loyal Toast'. It always falls to the president or chairman to propose it, and it is important that he should do so correctly. Relate the Sovereign to the assembled company by citing after the royal designation any office she may hold that is relevant. The fact that the Queen is Patron of the Royal Institution of Chartered Surveyors should always be mentioned when proposing her health at a chartered surveyors' dinner. She is Colonel of certain regiments and it is always mentioned. In the County Palatine she is always described as the Duke of Lancaster. Subject to that, as in nearly everything, be short. Do *not* say: 'I now invite you to charge your glasses [why not *fill* them?], be upstanding [why not stand?] and join with me in drinking the health of Her Most Gracious Majesty, Queen Elizabeth.' That rigmarole, in the mouth of a scarlet-coated toastmaster, may be etiquette at a Lord Mayor's banquet, but personally I think it pompous. The simple formula is much more impressive: BANG on the table; the chairman rises; a moment's silence. Then: 'Ladies and Gentlemen, "The Queen".'

Final piece of advice to a chairman. When the Loyal Toast has been honoured, and later in the evening, when the chandeliers are vibrating to the applause so richly merited by your brilliant speech, do *not* resume your seat. Just sit down.

XII

Via Stevenage to Lands Tribunal

Silkin and Silkingrad – Stevenage New Town – Lands
Tribunal: constitution, jurisdiction and practice – *Letchworth*:
piggeries, Magna Carta and varicose veins – strange coincidence – bribery and corruption – postscript from a
wheeled chair.

The sale of Lord Northampton's estate in Clerkenwell was
completed in 1950 and that of Canonbury early in 1951. The
trustees were good enough to offer me a lease of my house, Number 2, Canonbury Place, at a moderate rent, but I declined
it. I felt that this particular job was finished as far as I was concerned and I ought to make a clean break. So my wife and I
and our two young children went to live in North Essex, in
the village of Ashdon near Saffron Walden, and I joined the
army of commuters to London.

My professional headquarters were now in Lincoln's Inn
Fields and I returned to private practice as a partner in Alfred
Savill and Sons. The next five years were uneventful, but my
membership of the development corporation of the New Town
of Stevenage deserves a mention; besides relieving the monotony
of private practice, which was never really my line, it enabled
me to observe the practical application of the principles we had
preached on the Reith Committee.

When I saw my management of the Northampton estates
coming to an end I had put out feelers, through Alec Killick,
with a view to joining the development corporation of one or
other of the New Towns that were springing up like mush-
rooms around London. The appointments were by Silkin, who

was still Minister of Town and Country Planning, and as I had served on his New Towns Committee I did not expect to encounter any difficulty. But I was wrong. For some reason Silkin declined to appoint me and I could not fathom what it was. Eventually I took the bull by the horns and inquired. I got the answer off the record; it was Marlesford Lodge again! This time it was a liability, not an asset.

The reader may not see the link between the administration of children's remand homes and the building of New Towns. According to my informant, it was Silkin himself. He had been a prominent member of the L.C.C., and members of the L.C.C. in that period were unduly sensitive to criticism. As a result of the Marlesford Lodge row I knew I had made enemies, and I was given to understand that Silkin was one of them. If that was the reason for my non-appointment, the dates are revealing. The Marlesford Lodge trouble blew up in November, 1944. The Vick Committee on remand homes reported in February, 1945. I was appointed by Silkin to the New Towns Committee in October, 1945—more than six months later. If the Minister appointed me to the New Towns Committee when the Marlesford Lodge affair was still a matter for public comment, why did he refuses to appoint me to the development corporation of a New Town several years later, when nearly everyone, except some members of the L.C.C., had forgotten all about it? Had it anything to do with the fact that whereas membership of the New Towns Committee was a God-bless-you job and I had *not* asked for it, membership of a development corporation was a paid job and I *had* asked for it?[1] In the event I had to wait until 1950, when Silkin became a lord. His successor in the Ministry of Town and Country planning, Hugh Dalton, made no difficulties and offered to appoint me to Stevenage the following

[1] In case the reader should assume that the membership of the development corporation of a New Town was a lucrative appointment, the remuneration at that time was £400 a year.

year. I took up my duties on January 1, 1952, and remained a member of Stevenage Development Corporation for four years.

I have already mentioned that Stevenage was the first of the New Towns, having been 'designated' in 1946. Previously it had been an attractive market town in Hertfordshire with a population of about 6,500. It is 32 miles from London on the main line from the north, and at that time (i.e. before the bypass had been constructed) the Great North Road ran through the middle of it. As the prototype of a New Town, I think it was a good choice. The plan was to enlarge it, surround it by an agricultural belt to prevent satellite development by speculators cashing in on the enhanced values, and increase the population to 60,000 over the years.

Some of the inhabitants of the old Stevenage, including many shopkeepers, welcomed the proposal; it was attractive from a business point of view. But many of the middle-class residents in Stevenage and in villages near by were bitterly opposed to it. That too was understandable. They enjoyed, and wanted to be allowed to continue to enjoy, life in or near an old-fashioned English country town; the last thing they wanted was to find themselves in what they described as a 'Socialist conurbation'. A protection society was formed and there were vehement protests. Silkin, very properly, went down from London to attend a mass meeting in the hope of appeasing at least some of the protesters, and it was not to their credit that while he was in the hall they deflated the tyres of the ministerial car. But everyone laughed when a humorist invaded the railway station and repainted the name boards. When the first commuters arrived next morning, they found that the name of their town had changed from STEVENAGE to SILKINGRAD in the night.

The New Town of Stevenage had been going for six years before I got there, and in the meantime the corporation had had several chairmen. Between them they had brought in a number of pet architects and some of the results were bizarre, if that is the appropriate word. A block of flats towering in one of the residential neighbourhoods was so hideous from the approach road that I concluded the 'front' must be the back—until I saw the back. A drawback to Stevenage, which may have righted itself by now, was that so much of the terrain was devoid of trees.

A major problem for the development corporation of any New Town is to synchronize three events: the completion of the new factories for the imported industries, which are the life-blood of the town; the completion of enough new houses and flats to accommodate the people imported to work in those factories; the provision of adequate social services—churches, schools, youth centres, clubs, public houses and recreation grounds—to serve the needs of the workers. It is extraordinarily difficult to get all these things off the conveyor belts in proper proportions at the same time.

Another problem in Stevenage, and I expect in most New Towns, was to produce what had been described in the terms of reference to the Reith Committee as 'self-contained and balanced communities for work and living'. It was accepted that 'balanced' meant socially as well as economically balanced. Basically the English are snobs, and there was a danger of creating one-class towns. In Stevenage we tried to prevent that happening by providing groups of larger houses for occupation by the executives in the imported industries, but in my time it was not a success. There was little demand for them. Every weekend the business executives, accompanied by their wives and in their Jaguar cars, toured the countryside for miles around in search of old cottages containing 'a wealth of old oak' that were recommended as 'suitable for conversion' by the local estate agents.

I cannot claim to have made any substantial contribution to the development of Stevenage. The corporation met only once a month, and four years is not long. But the progress of the work was stimulating, my colleagues delightful, and the staff of the corporation extremely efficient. I wanted more than this part-time job and longed (Reith's phrase) to be 'fully stretched'. That is why during the winter 1955–1956 I came to consider seriously a proposition which, should it mature, would enable me to become so. I considered the Lands Tribunal.

The Lands Tribunal Act 1949—for which Lord Jowitt was responsible—had been passed in my presidential year. The purpose of the Lands Tribunal was to take over the work of the official arbitrators, but in a wider jurisdiction and with greater responsibilities. It consists of as many members as the Lord Chancellor sees fit to appoint. The president of the tribunal has to be a barrister who has held judicial office or is of at least seven years' standing. The other members are barristers or solicitors, or persons experienced in the valuation of land and buildings. They are commonly referred to as the 'lawyer members' and the 'valuer members' respectively. Membership of the tribunal is a whole-time office under the Crown, the members being a part of the judiciary and not civil servants. At the time of writing there are three lawyer members of whom the senior, Sir Michael Rowe, Q.C., is president. There are six valuer members.

The first president of the tribunal, in 1950, was Sir William Fitzgerald, Q.C., known to his friends as 'Fitz'. He retired in 1965. An Irishman, he was born and bred in County Tipperary, and educated at Blackrock and Trinity College, Dublin. Called to the bar in 1922, he entered the Nigerian Administrative Service. In 1933 he went to Rhodesia, where he took silk and became Attorney General. He held the same office in Palestine from 1937 to 1943. He was Chief Justice of Palestine from 1944 to 1948. The acknowledged eminence of the Lands Tribunal and the high regard in which it is held are almost entirely due to the influence of the first president during its formative years. He brought to the task a rare combination of human qualities— imagination, tact, charm, a ready wit and a fund of good sense.

Under section 2(2) of the 1949 Act, before appointing a valuer member, the Lord Chancellor must consult the president of the Royal Institution of Chartered Surveyors. That is how it fell to me to make the first batch of recommendations. One of the valuer members, appointed on my advice, was my old friend John P. C. Done, previously an official arbitrator.

I had scarcely vacated the presidential chair before I was approached by Alec Killick and my successor, H. P. Hobbs. Would I like my own name put forward as a member of the tribunal? It was a compliment, but I refused and persisted in my refusal for five years. I was rising fifty, which is not old but the time in a man's life when one is conscious of the sap beginning to run back. I no longer possessed the self-confidence—perhaps I ought to say conceit—that I had had in my younger days. A series of R.I.C.S. presidents, spurred on by Alec, tried to make me change my mind. I was much attracted by the idea, but went on refusing because I did not feel I filled the bill of what a member of the Lands Tribunal should be—a surveyor who has spent a life-time in general practice. What with M.H.C. estates, the Northampton estates, my God-bless-you jobs and the Other Chap's chairmanship of a juvenile court, I felt I had strayed too often and too far from the main road. Then pressure was brought to bear from other sources, including the tribunal itself. John Done did all he could to persuade me and introduced me to Sir William Fitzgerald, who appeared as keen for me to join the tribunal as Done was. Early in 1956 I began to waver. I told Bill Brackett, president of the R.I.C.S., that if he really had confidence in me he might put my name forward—and a week later wished I had not done so. I wrote John Done a letter running into hundreds of words, containing the story of my life. I listed my deficiencies, asked him to show what I had written to Fitzgerald, and if Fitzgerald accepted it—as I was sure he must—never to mention the matter again. John replied briefly. He had seen the president of the tribunal, who had said: 'If I had any doubts *before* Watson's letter he has completely disposed of them.'

Sir William Fitzgerald

But I made a condition to the Lord Chancellor, who at that time was David Kilmuir. The condition was that if I became a member of the Lands Tribunal the Other Chap would be allowed to continue presiding in his juvenile court. The Clerk of the Crown, Sir George Coldstream, asked me to go and see him. My recollection is that we talked very little about the Lands Tribunal, but a lot about juvenile courts (Other Chap again!), and a day or two later he wrote on behalf of the Chancellor offering me the job. He added:

'The Lord Chancellor [has] considered carefully the point you yourself made, that is to say, that you should be allowed to continue your work as a juvenile court magistrate. The Lord Chancellor is obliged to point out that any assurance which he gives you in this behalf cannot bind his successors on the Woolsack. But so far as he is concerned, he willingly agrees to your continuing as a magistrate on the footing that you will continue to take your share of the work in the juvenile courts.'

I accepted. A few days before Christmas, 1956, I said a sad farewell to my friends and partners in Lincoln's Inn Fields, and they gave me a beautiful piece of Georgian silver as a keepsake. On January 1, 1957, I became a salaried public servant for the first time.

The jurisdiction of the Lands Tribunal extends to England and Wales and includes the following. Any question that before 1949 fell to be decided by the Panel of Referees under Part I of the Finance Act 1910, e.g. the value of land and buildings for death duties. It is 'the authority' under the Law of Property Acts for hearing applications for the modification and discharge of restrictive covenants. It is the court of appeal from decisions of the local valuation courts on rating, a jurisdiction formerly exercised by the rating appeals committees of the courts of quarter sessions. The 1949 Act permits the tribunal to 'act as an arbitrator under a reference by consent'. And since my retirement it has been given responsibility for hearing appeals against levies by the extinct Land Commission and for determining disputed payments by tenants for the enfranchisement of leaseholds.

There is little doubt that Parliament envisaged that the lawyer members should try the cases involving law, and the valuer members those involving valuation. To an extent that is what happens. If the parties certify in advance that there is a point of law, the case goes to one of the lawyer members. But not infrequently, when there is no certificate, the issue is a mixture of law and fact. That can result in a valuer member's becoming bogged down in law, or a lawyer member's becoming bogged down in valuations. Soon after my appointment I spent a morning arguing with counsel about the implications of a judgment of the Court of Appeal so complicated that, at the adjournment, my mind was in a whirl. After lunch, by a piece of luck, one of the lawyer members, an eminent Q.C., came into my room. I said: 'I have had a dreadful morning; have you heard of *The King v Blennerhassett?*' 'Oh yes!' he replied, 'that's a nasty one, but if you sort it out the point is really quite simple . . .' and he went on to explain it.

I replied: 'I can't thank you enough; now I can go back into court and not appear so stupid.' He went away and I heard his footsteps receding down the passage. But he was back a moment later and popped his head round my door: 'Tell me, John, how would *you* value Southend Pier?'

The Lands Tribunal in all its jurisdictions is final on fact, but there is an appeal by way of 'case stated' to the Court of Appeal on a point of law. Mr. Spencer Rodgers in his book *The Lands Tribunal, Procedure and Practice* discusses at considerable length the status of the tribunal. He writes: 'It is quite clear that it was the intention of Parliament that the tribunal, in its own specialized sphere, should have a standing not far short of that of the High Court.' He goes on to debate whether, having regard to its constitution, it is technically a tribunal or a court; if it is the former, he comments that it is 'a most extraordinary tribunal'.

A most extraordinary tribunal . . . Perhaps it is, but it appears to have given satisfaction for nearly twenty-five years. It is one of those anomalies which, because of the confidence of the inconsistent English in their own dispositions, is beloved by them. In the Lands Tribunal, possibly because the lawyer members suspect that they know almost as much about these specialized forms of valuation as the valuer members, and the valuer members that they know almost as much about these specialized branches of the law as the lawyer members, it works.

In 1971 the Lands Tribunal, established under the Act of 1949, came of age. To mark the occasion, on January 18, 1971, the members, and the retired members including Sir William Fitzgerald, gave a dinner in Gray's Inn. There were twenty-two of us in all, with Sir Michael Rowe in the chair.

Our guests were the Lord Chancellor (Lord Hailsham of St. Marylebone), the Master of the Rolls (Lord Denning), and Lord Justice Widgery who shortly afterwards became Lord Chief Justice of England; also four High Court judges who had practised regularly in the Lands Tribunal when at the bar—Mr. Justice Lyell, Mr. Justice Browne, Mr. Justice Willis and Mr. Justice Bridge; also Sir Denis Dobson, Clerk of the Crown, and Mr. E. J. Battersby, President of the Royal Institute of Chartered Surveyors. It was a delightful evening, which none of those present is likely to forget. The Lord Chancellor proposed the health of the Lands Tribunal, and the Master of the Rolls replied for the guests. Both made complimentary and witty speeches, but about what they said, as it was a private dinner party, my lips are sealed.

Where is the Land Tribunal? Number 3 Hanover Square is a dismal building in what the estate agents call 'the heart of the West End'. The heart of the West End of London, as anyone who has lived or worked there knows, is an expensive area served by buses which stand endlessly in traffic blocks, and a tube railway which carries its human freight no longer packed like sardines but compressed like potted shrimps; an area where the pavements are crowded with shoppers and window-gazers; where the air is polluted by petrol fumes; and where taxis with their flags up, in the rush hour when you most need them, have long ceased to exist.

There is no forecourt to Number 3 Hanover Square. Leave your car outside for one minute and a traffic warden, male or female, black or white, is waiting to pounce. Should you be lucky and secure a meter, note the limit of two hours; even simple cases in the tribunal last four. Hanover Square is so far from the Temple that counsel are unable to get back in the lunch hour, and the haunts of solicitors are farther still. No member of the tribunal, unless he can afford Claridges (which he can't), dares lunch out. In a lesser eating house he risks being jostled at the bar by the vexatious litigant who was half-way through his evidence when the court rose.

Now venture inside. You ascend three steps from the pavement and put your shoulder against a front door, which is made of wrought iron with glass panels and has the heaviest spring in London. You find yourself in a small box-like compartment at the foot of the lift shaft, its walls hung with notices. Should one of the notices tell you that the lift is out of order, have a look round. If your opponent, with his lawyers and expert witnesses, is also imprisoned in the box-like compartment, you would be well advised to re-open negotiations and settle the case. If that is not possible, you must climb the stairs. Upstairs are three courts. The plaster enrichments of the walls in Court 1 confirm your suspicions that it was formerly a dressmaker's salon. Courts 1 and 2 overlook the square. They have double-glazed windows, thus ensuring that the court will be noisy in summer when they are open, and stuffy in winter when they are closed. There are no public waiting rooms. The clerks' offices, typists' department, filing department and members' retiring rooms are scattered indiscriminately about the rest of the building.

Now about the arrangements for the hearings. It is the responsibility of the president to allocate the cases and decide whether the tribunal shall consist of more than one member. In the early days, when the tribunal was not so busy as it is now, we occasionally sat a bench of three. Today there are scarcely ever more than two members on a case, and generally only one. The member is attended by his clerk, who calls on the case, swears the witnesses, sits below the bench and is responsible for seeing that everything is in order.

Only some of the hearings are in Hanover Square, but all the cases from London and the Home Counties are brought there. Nearly all the provincial cases are heard by a member or members on circuit. The tribunal only sits during the law terms, but the intention is not to give the members a pleasant holiday several times a year. The Act requires a written decision in every case, and at the end of a busy term members are likely to find themselves in arrears; the law vacation enables them to catch up.

How are the circuits arranged? The system is agreeably informal. At least once in every term the tribunal meets in the president's room, each member having been provided in advance with a list of the cases ready for hearing. Once a member has accepted a case, it belongs to him alone and he is responsible for it up to the moment when he gives his decision. Members often consult each other, but no member—not even the president who is *primus inter pares*—may interfere with the decision of any other member.

In the allocation of cases certain conventions have emerged. Naturally the president has first choice. In winter the south of England tends to be more popular than the north, and I remember keen competition for a case in the Scilly Isles in early spring. Any member, who is young enough to have a son or daughter at a boarding school or university, takes the adjacent circuit from time to time. One member, a prominent freemason who has now retired from the tribunal, used to gravitate to a city where it is rumoured that the local freemasons perform unique and intriguing rites. Another retired member, a Yorkshireman, knew a farm where they specialized in producing a delectable Blue-Wensleydale cheese, and his brethren always encouraged him to go that circuit just before Christmas. There are only two rules. Unless there is some special reason, no one goes the same circuit twice running, the intention being that every member shall go all the circuits over a period of years. The other rule, the reason for which is obvious, is that no member sits near his home.

The date of a hearing, and the choice of place where the tribunal sits, is for the member or members concerned. The tribunal has regard to the convenience of the parties, but is dependent on the availability of courts. It is usual for the clerk to go a day ahead to make the necessary arrangements.

The trial of a case normally involves three stages: the hearing, the inspection (in legal language the 'view'), and the writing and the delivery in open court of the tribunal's decision. One difficulty—it exists in most jurisdictions—is in estimating how long a case will take. If it looks like being complicated, the registrar will ask the parties how long they think it will last; and in my experience, and I think in that of other members, the tendency by the parties is to *under*-estimate. Their legal advisers should guard against it. A case that seriously over-runs the time allotted can be a great nuisance, and the parties run the risk that the tribunal, having finished the evidence, will hear counsels' submissions at some later date in London. It is unfair to other litigants to be kept waiting day after day for their cases to come on. In general it is better to *over*-estimate than to *under*-estimate, for if a hearing ends sooner than was expected or, as sometimes happens, is settled out of court at the last minute, the matter is not of grave consequence. If the next case in the list is not ready, you may be sure that the member has brought his notes on earlier cases and has enough home-work to keep him busy in the meantime.

But the over-running of a case is not always the fault of the parties or of their professional advisers. I speak only for myself when I say that some members of the Lands Tribunal, like some judges and some magistrates, are tempted to talk too much. A valuer member in particular, because his technical knowledge enables him to foresee what is coming, is tempted to try to hurry things by inviting an expert witness to take a short cut. More often, the invitation has the converse effect. It is infuriating for counsel, examining in chief, who wants to take his witness through his evidence stage by stage. It can be even more so for counsel who is cross-examining, if the tribunal asks prematurely the key question he is leading up to and suggests a plausible answer. A newly appointed valuer member has many things to learn. One is that if he will wait patiently until the examination-in-chief, cross-examination and re-examination are finished, nearly every question he had intended to ask at the end of the evidence will have been answered. Bacon's essay, *Of Judicature*, is full of wise precepts for judges, although he himself did not always observe them: 'Patience and gravity of hearing is an essential part of justice; and an over-speaking judge is no well-tuned cymbal. It is no grace to a judge first to find that which he might have heard in due time from the bar; or to show quickness of conceit in cutting off evidence or counsel too short, or to prevent information by questions, though pertinent.'

A member of the Lands Tribunal, like a judge, takes a note of the evidence and generally does so in longhand. Provided, however, the witnesses address the bench (not the wall above counsel's head) and go reasonably slowly, the proceedings are not unduly delayed. Much more difficult than recording evidence is to follow, and simultaneously record in your notebook, an argument by counsel on a point of law. It is easy to lose the thread, and there is no quicker way of doing so than to try to write as he goes along. You find yourself concentrating on what you are writing, which is a record of what counsel said *a minute ago*, instead of on what he is saying *now*. Better, I suggest, to push aside your notebook and give all your attention to the argument. If you still lose the thread, then of course you *must* interrupt; counsel are paid to make themselves clear. But inevitably a duologue with counsel slows things up.

In an important case, especially if it is likely to go to the Court of Appeal, it is common practice for the parties to arrange for a verbatim record by a firm of specialist shorthand writers. The typed transcript that is available to the court each morning, containing every word spoken the day before, can be immensely helpful to the judge. Again, I speak only for myself when I add that it can also be humiliating. A point that one found obscure, when one studies counsel's patient efforts to explain it, is now seen to have been as plain as a pike-staff from the beginning. One wonders how one could have been so dense. And I recall an occasion when I was reading a transcript at home. My wife asked: 'Why do you keep groaning?' I replied, 'O dear, it's because, every time I turn the page, *here I am talking again*!'

The longest case I heard during my membership of the tribunal was *First Garden City Limited v Letchworth Garden City Corporation*. It was a reference, under a special Act of Parliament, of the amount of compensation payable for the compulsory acquisition of Letchworth Garden City, which had been classified as a New Town. I sat with Mr. Erskine Simes Q.C., who presided. The claim by the owners was about £3,600,000 and the offer by the compensating authority £2,100,000. The hearing, in London, occupied 77 working days and the first draft of our decision, which was my responsibility as the junior member of the bench, kept me at home for a further two months. In all, *Letchworth* occupied two members of a seven-member tribunal nearly a year and created problems for the other five.

There were three Queen's Counsel in the case, with their respective juniors. One Q.C. was made a High Court judge about two-thirds of the way through, and the others became judges soon after it finished. The expert witnesses were all leading members of their professions, and we were told that the costs were running at several thousand pounds a day. Had Erskine or I died during the hearing, it would have had to begin again. Because of this danger, which always exists when a case is prolonged, our lives were insured for a prodigious sum. I hasten to add that the premiums were not paid by us.

However, we stayed the course. Mercifully, an attack of chicken pox, to which I succumbed about the fiftieth day and which delayed everything for several weeks, did not prove fatal. At last we were ready to give our decision, and because of its length (some 30,000 words) we took turns in reading it. When I record that our award of compensation was about half-way between the amount of the claim and that of the offer, let no one smile or sneer. A common complaint about arbitrators has always been that they tend to 'split the difference'—i.e. add the two amounts together and halve the total. I understand that the same criticism is sometimes made of the Lands Tribunal. But, as I have written elsewhere, if the opposing expert witnesses are equally experienced, equally skilled and equally honest, and if there is no fundamental difference in the assumptions on which they have based their valuations, is it not possible—nay probable —that the answer is about midway between their opinions?

Counsel and solicitors do not robe in the Lands Tribunal, as in the High Court and in the county courts. When the tribunal was formed in 1950, a majority were against their robing. I understand it was not because the valuer members had no legal robes; some suitable costume could have been designed for us. The reason, a sound one, was that there are many cases in the tribunal where litigants appearing in person are simple people, who might be scared by wigs and gowns. But I am bound to say that in *Letchworth* it would have been a relief if counsel *had* robed. As week followed week I got to know all their suits in turn. I wondered why Mr. Abraham Haphazard had not worn his grey pin-stripe for so long (perhaps it had gone to the cleaners?) and found myself speculating which of his collection of ties he would be wearing next morning.

One of the attractions of the Lands Tribunal to its members is the variety of the cases that are brought to it. I cannot remember what I heard immediately after *Letchworth*. It may well have been an appeal by a ratepayer, contending that his bungalow was over-assessed having regard to the smell of piggeries nearby. A litigant who appears in person is apt to be long-winded and has to be handled with care. He has probably sat up all night preparing his case and arrives in court with a bundle of foolscap covered with small handwriting, all of which he is bent on reading aloud. You are then in a quandary. If after ten minutes you tell him that nothing he has read so far is of the slightest relevance and look meaningly at the clock, he will sit down abruptly, cast aside his papers and reflect gloomily that there is little justice in the world anyway and none at all in the Lands Tribunal. If on the other hand you allow him to go on, he may continue all day and insist on reading passages from Magna Carta that have absolutely nothing to do with piggeries.

Litigants in person also tend to expostulate loudly if your decision is against them. On a hot summer afternoon Court 3, the smallest of the courts in Hanover Square, was crowded for the giving of decisions by a lawyer member. There were counsel and solicitors, expert witnesses, claimants and ratepayers in person, the press and members of the public; also Mrs. Snodbury, a portly lady in her late sixties who was well known in the tribunal as a vexatious litigant.

Mrs. Snodbury had come to hear the decision in her rating appeal, which had occupied a lot of the tribunal's time a few weeks earlier. She had an immense shopping bag, which she

232

opened on the table in front of her; it contained her notes, her correspondence, her deeds, copies of her conveyances and the remains of her lunch. The registrar's staff knew the lady, and from past experience scarcely expected her to receive what was going to be yet another adverse decision in silence. So they called her case first in the hope of getting Mrs. Snodbury 'out of the way' as quickly as possible.

But Mrs. Snodbury, when she had heard enough of the decision to realize it was against her, had different ideas. She made it plain that she was not going to be got out of the way unless several people carried her. Standing in her place, she thumped the table, hurled abuse at the member and declaimed as though to a public meeting about the wicked injustice that had to be suffered by a poor widow . . . so on, and so forth. Presently, as the Lands Tribunal is not a court of record with power to commit for contempt, the member withdrew. But the pandemonium continued. Then the clerk of the court remembered that on the last occasion, when Mrs. Snodbury had behaved in the same way, George, one of the ushers, was the only person who had been able to pacify her. George was sent for and came hurrying into court. 'Leave her to me' he said, and the next time Mrs. Snodbury paused for breath he whispered softly in her ear. The effect was magical. She allowed George to help her repack her bag and left contentedly in his company.

When everything was over, the decisions given, the member mollified and the court room cleared, the clerk asked George: 'What on earth did you say to Mrs. Snodbury that led her to go away so quickly, leaning on your arm?'

'Quite easy, really. I've known that old girl a long time and she's for ever telling me about her ailments. I just said: "I'd like to have a look at your varicose veins." '

Members of the tribunal, even the valuer members, do not regard themselves as appraisers. They are judges of law and fact, and a decision on fact must be based on evidence; the undoubted value of the technical knowledge of the valuer members is to help them follow it. They do not themselves make valuations. If one expert witness has said that the correct method of valuation is Method A and the value £5,000, and his opposite number has said that the correct method is Method B and the value £10,000, the tribunal will adopt Method A or Method B, or some combination of those methods; and the award will be £5,000 or £10,000, or an intermediate figure. At one time the authorities were conflicting, but the dictum of Lord Evershed M.R., in *Sheffield City Council v Meadow Dairy Company Ltd.* (1964) is one of the most recent: 'Although the members of the tribunal are men chosen for their experience as surveyors, still it is not competent for them to express their own superior wisdom as compared with the valuers on both sides.'

Admittedly there have been exceptions to the tribunal's present practice, particularly in the early days long before the judgment I have cited. The late Mr. James Milne F.R.I.C.S., one of the original members appointed in 1950 and a rating surveyor of wide experience, not infrequently rejected evidence both on method and value and propounded his own. He made no secret of the fact that he had done so in his decision. Today that is referred to in the Lands Tribunal as 'Milne's Law', and a member who obeys it is said to 'do a Jimmy Milne'.

A view of the subject property after the hearing—occasionally during the hearing—can be enlightening and sometimes revealing. A judicial view has been described as 'part of the evidence', and in a sense it is; but its primary purpose is to assist the tribunal in understanding and evaluating the oral evidence. The member goes alone or with his clerk, and if one of the parties or his representative wants to assist—generally by identifying something but *never* by giving further evidence—the tribunal will require the other party or his representative to attend also.

I had an extraordinary experience in Bristol, one of the comparatively rare instances of my jurisdiction and that of the

Other Chap overlapping. By permission of the Lord Chancellor, as I explained earlier, the Other Chap used to sit one day a week as chairman of the South London Juvenile Court; and to avoid interference with my work in the Lands Tribunal he sat there on Fridays. When I went on circuit I would sit in the provincial court from Monday to Thursday, returning to London on the Thursday evening. On a certain Wednesday I had been hearing a case about the value of a factory on the outskirts of the city, and when I rose at four o'clock told my clerk, John Denehan, that I proposed to go and have a look at it and asked him to come with me.

The factory was on an industrial estate, and when I had seen all I wanted I turned my car round and headed back towards my hotel in the city centre. We were still on the trading estate when the clocks struck five and the workpeople came pouring out of the factories. A bus had stopped just in front of us. As it moved from the curb and was gathering speed, two 'teen-aged boys emerged from a factory and ran across the pavement in an attempt to catch it. But the faster they ran the faster went the bus until eventually, exhausted and out of breath, they abandoned the chase. I was rather sorry for them, and as we had no one in the back of the car suggested to Denehan that we might be helpful. I slowed down, pulled alongside and called out 'Want a lift?' The taller of the two, a boy with dark hair, stopped in his tracks and looked at me with astonishment written all over his face. I supposed that in Bristol it was not 'done' to offer lifts and wondered why, but I repeated the invitation and Denehan, leaning across, opened the rear door. The boys climbed in, the one with dark hair seating himself behind me. I noticed that he looked hesitant as well as astonished, so I tried to put him at his ease by making conversation. The conversation went like this:

Me: 'What part of Bristol do you want to go to?'
Him: 'Don't reely know—'bout the middle.'

235

Me: 'About the middle? All right, I'll drop you in the big square. Do you live in the middle of Bristol?'

Him: 'Don't live in Bristol.'

Me: 'Then where are you going to now?'

Him: 'To me youth 'ostel.'

Me: 'A youth hostel—how interesting! But tell me, where is your home?'

Him: (apparently surprised): 'Off the Old Kent Road.'

Me: (my turn to be surprised): '*The Old Kent Road?* Why, that's in South London and I know it well!'

No answer.

Me: (to keep the conversation going): 'Do you like your hostel?'

Him: (emphatically): 'I 'ates it.'

Me: 'Oh dear.'

Another silence.

Me: 'Do you like the job you've got in that factory?'

Him: (emphatically): 'I 'ates that too!'

The conversation had taken such an odd turn that when we stopped at the next traffic block I looked over my shoulder. He was a nice looking boy, but with a rather sulky expression, and I had a feeling that I knew someone a bit like him:

Me: 'Well it's not my business; but if you don't mind my saying so, yours is an odd story! You live off the Old Kent Road in South London; you have come to Bristol to live in a youth hostel and you hate it; what's more, you hate your job. Why on earth did you leave South London? What did you come to Bristol *for?*'

Him: 'Why, Governor, yer sent me 'ere yerself last Friday week.'

Truly, a remarkable coincidence! I fear that the boy, whom I delivered safely to his hostel, thought that the only reason the magistrate had come to Bristol was to spy on him. The reader who is mathematically inclined can calculate the odds against my meeting that particular boy, at that particular place, at that particular time.

Now about bribery and the Lands Tribunal. Bribery and corruption in this country are no longer what they used to be. Moral standards have changed, and conduct by persons in authority which at one time was accepted, or at least tolerated, would be regarded to-day as disgraceful. Pepys, it will be recalled, was outspoken in his condemnation of contemporaries who took a rake-off, notably Sir William Batten, but was not averse to taking one himself if circumstances arose in which he considered he was entitled to it. If, for example, the Navy had been offered a consignment of masts for £4,000, and Pepys had got the price reduced to say £3,000, he argued that he had saved the King £1,000 and was justified in putting part of the saving into his pocket. Francis Bacon put the bribery of judges in three categories: 'There be three causes of bribery, charged or supposed in a judge: the first, of bargain or contract for reward to pervert justice; the second, where the judge conceives the cause to be at an end by the information of the party or otherwise and useth not such diligence as he ought to inquire of it; and the third, when the cause is really ended, and it is *sine fraude*, without relation to any precedent promise.'[1] At his trial in 1621 he admitted bribery in the second category, which he seems to have regarded as little worse than negligence. As regards the first category, he eventually conceded that there had been corruption and neglect 'for which I am heartily and penitently sorry'. But it is significant that in the cases of Aubrey, Egerton and Lady Wharton, who were his principal accusers, Bacon had decided *against* the party who had paid him and had given Lady Wharton a crushing sentence. No wonder they complained!

[1] From a memorandum he wrote in preparation for an interview he had with King James I, in April 1621, during his own trial.

To the best of my knowledge, with one exception, no member of the Lands Tribunal was bribed or corrupted during the twelve years I was a member. To my shame, the exception was me. I will relate the circumstances of my bribe and its dire consequences.

Everyone who knows Barchester will remember the wide road that runs from the east almost into the centre of the city. To the west of Orley Road, where the shops begin, are a row of Victorian houses with large gardens interspersed by a few bungalows which from the look of them were built soon after the turn of the century. Just east of the almshouses owned by Hiram's Charity, on the south of the road, is a bungalow of slightly eccentric appearance. Its owner, an elderly widower whom I will call Mr. Tolworthy, had lived there all his married life and had built the bungalow, when he was a young man, virtually with his own hands. Its slightly eccentric appearance was due to his having incorporated in the structure doors and windows removed from a big Georgian house that was being demolished nearby. Mr. Tolworthy was proud of his bungalow and even more proud of his garden. When, however, his rating assessment was increased he was very angry and appealed against it. The local valuation court upheld the assessment, so he appealed to the tribunal.

The case was due to be heard in Barchester County Court at half past ten in the morning, and I arrived ten minutes before. My clerk warned me that we were probably in for trouble. He said that Mr. Tolworthy was an old gentleman of great determination, who had a hatred of what he called 'officialdom' which amounted to an obsession. He was appearing in person and had already been very rude to the respondent valuation officer outside the court. At the moment he was occupying one of counsels' seats, glowering in all directions.

I went into court and the appeal was called on, and as Mr. Tolworthy was the appellant it fell to him to begin. He made a long speech from the witness box, which was largely irrelevant and mainly about the iniquities of officialdom in Barchester. He referred to the valuation officer as 'that man' and conducted a cross-examination designed to show me and everyone else what he thought of him. The valuation officer, a calm and courteous person, bore it all with exemplary patience. Shortly before one o'clock, having heard the evidence, I said I should like to have a look at the bungalow and if convenient to Mr. Tolworthy would be there at three. Mr. Tolworthy was delighted until I added that the valuation officer must come too.

I arrived in my car from one direction, and the valuation officer in his car from the other. Mr. Tolworthy, who had mellowed a little, was waiting at his gate. In single file (Mr. Tolworthy, then I, then the valuation officer) we went into every room and Mr. Tolworthy pointed out the alleged defects in his bungalow compared with a friend's house, assessed at a lower figure, down the road. Then he said we must go round the garden, and on the way I happened to remark on a splendid vine growing on a south wall. Mr. Tolworthy was obviously pleased that I had noticed his vine, and told me that it was a Black Hamburg producing beautiful grapes that he had planted himself nearly half a century earlier. He then asked me if I would kindly walk down the road and look at the outside of his friend's house.

When I returned Mr. Tolworthy was standing on the path leading to the front door, clasping in his arms an untidy parcel wrapped in newspaper with twigs protruding from one end. 'Sir,' he said, 'this seedling is a great-grandchild of the vine you admired, and I'm going to *give* it to you. Plant it against a south wall in a sheltered spot . . .' and he instructed me in viticulture at some length.

Naturally I demurred. I said I made it a rule never to accept presents from litigants. He insisted, and I demurred again. He went on insisting, said he had dug up the precious seedling especially for me and declined to take 'no' for an answer. It became clear that if I did not accept it the old man would be very upset—and in spite of his truculence I had come to like him. Suddenly I had an idea. The valuation officer was standing quietly in the background. 'If,' I said, 'you care to dig up another seedling and give it to the valuation officer to plant in *his* garden, and he sees no objection, I will accept this one.'

Needless to say, my condition did not please Mr. Tolworthy. The idea of giving one of his vine's great-grandchildren to 'that man' shocked him. However, he realized I was in earnest, put the parcel on the ground and disappeared behind the greenhouse muttering to himself. Three minutes later he returned with a second parcel wrapped in newspaper. We both thanked him, and he came out into the road to help us stow the parcels in the boots of our cars. Then we drove off.

On arriving home I handed my vine to our part-time gardener and told him what superb grapes it would yield if we looked after it properly. He examined the seedling, a little suspiciously I thought, but followed my instructions and planted it. Then I went indoors and wrote my decision, which, in Baconian tradition, was against Mr. Tolworthy, and ordered him to pay the valuation officer five guineas costs. I worded the decision as kindly as I could.

That was in October. A week before Christmas I received in Hanover Square an envelope with the Barchester post mark. It contained a letter from Mr. Tolworthy. He began by saying that he trusted he was not doing wrong in writing to me, but he could not resist the temptation to inquire how my vine was progressing. Had I put in it a really sunny position? Did it get enough water? What about manure? Only at the end of the letter did he refer to the tribunal's decision and regret that it had been against him. 'But, Sir, you described me as "an elderly gentleman of character and determination", having thus per-ceived in a few hours what the Mayor and Corporation and officials of this city have failed to discover in fifty years. They printed what you said on the front page of the *Barset Advertiser*. Clearly at five guineas he had thought it well worth it.'

That, however, is not the end of the story. Next spring the seedling produced a few leaves, but showed no inclination to climb the wall. I told my gardener to fix some wire behind it and he did so. The months went by. The following year it had more leaves, but showed no signs of producing any tendrils. I became seriously worried and consulted the gardener, but he was non-committal. One evening when I was in London I happened to be sitting at dinner next to my friend Sir Kenneth Atkinson, who at that time was chief valuer of the Inland Revenue. I told Kenneth the story of Mr. Tolworthy and he was much amused. He told me that the valuation officer in question had since moved to the Midlands, and said he hoped he had taken his vine with him. He undertook, as a joke, to send him an official chit from Somerset House, referring to *Tolworthy v Inland Revenue* and saying that the chief valuer wanted to know how his **vine** was getting on.

A week later he reported back. He had received an assurance from the valuation officer that the vine was doing well in spite of the move, and that it was about to produce its first bunch of grapes. I re-inspected my own vine. Alas, Mr. Tolworthy's gifts must have got mixed up. My 'vine' was also doing well *and about to produce its first crop of blackcurrants.*

Membership of the Lands Tribunal is pensionable and the normal age for retirement is 72. A member may go earlier, subject to his continuing in office until 65 unless prevented from doing so by ill-health.

I have suffered all my life from a rare complaint called muscular dystrophy. It progresses slowly and inexorably, but is benign in the sense that I get no pain and am assured I shall not die of it. Sir Farquhar Buzzard, the distinguished neurologist, diagnosed muscular dystrophy when I was in my early twenties, rejecting a provisional diagnosis of multiple sclerosis by an inexperienced doctor which had caused me grave anxiety. Sir Farquhar put my mind at rest, but told me that if I lived to be seventy, and no cure had been found in the meantime, my condition would cause me considerable inconvenience. He said his fee was five guineas and added, presumably by way of consolation for a young man, that my body would be interesting to dissect. Vastly relieved, I wrote a cheque, wrung him by the hand, waltzed down the hall and made off down Harley Street as fast as my legs (not yet affected) would carry me. At the corner of Wigmore Street, hearing the pad pad of running footsteps, I turned. The great neurologist was hatless and out of breath: 'Mr. Watson, if you will kindly *give* me the cheque you have kindly written for my fee, instead of taking it away in your pocket, it will save a lot of unnecessary correspondence.'

All that he forecast came true. When appointed to the tribunal in 1957, I was rising 53. I was lame and conscious that I was getting lamer. Would I last for twelve years? The Lord Chancellor's office, at the instance of the Treasury, said I must be medically examined. So I consulted Doctor Dudley Hart and the following is an extract from his report:

'I have today examined Mr. Watson at 152, Harley Street. He has all his life suffered from a condition of the muscles (muscular dystrophy), and the various odd movements in his ordinary activities are due to this disease. This is his only disability; he can do almost any activity except running, and though certain movements are weak, he can by using other muscle groups adapt himself satisfactorily . . . I consider that Mr. Watson is fit for active duties for a period longer than twelve years from now. His general health is excellent.'

In the Lands Tribunal there is normally no need to run, but slowly, as the years passed, my legs wore out. First I used a walking stick at times; then all the time; then I found I needed two sticks. I had an electric hoist fixed over my bath and a second handrail beside the staircase. I obtained, and studied surreptitiously, catalogues of wheel-chairs. Not infrequently I fell down. I fell off the bench at Bridgnorth and was picked up by counsel, and again outside Bath County Court, where I was picked up by John Denehan. My worst fall was in Cheltenham (not on the racecourse), where I broke a leg. Presently it became necessary to pick and choose my cases, and the registrar had to inquire of the parties what inspections the tribunal would be asked to make.

If any reader has lost faith, or is in danger of losing faith, in the innate goodness of most people, I offer him this advice. Buy two walking-sticks with rubber ends, or, better still, hire a wheel-chair. Limp or propel yourself into any public place. The kindness you will meet with will amaze and reassure you; nearly everyone is ready to help. 'Nearly everyone' includes a variety of public servants (especially policemen), hall porters, taxi drivers, shop-keepers, bus conductors, barmen. It also includes ordinary members of the public of both sexes, whom you do not know and are unlikely ever to see again—rich and poor, old and young, black and white, clerks as much as clergy, typists as much as nurses, schoolboys and schoolgirls, social workers, students, lay-abouts and hippies. It is a pity, perhaps, that the early twentieth-century poet, Sir Walter Raleigh ('I wish I loved the human race . . .'), did not become disabled. He might have fulfilled his wish, and the experience might have been good for his soul.

I became 65 on July 24, 1968, and soon afterwards told the Lord Chancellor, very sadly, that the time had come to retire from the Lands Tribunal. The Other Chap had already retired from the juvenile courts. I was as well as I had ever been, except for my legs, and the outlook was bleak. The Chancellor, Lord Gardiner, was considerate enough to give me leave to return to my old firm, now called Savills, in a part-time capacity on the understanding that I would not engage in any activities connected with the Lands

Tribunal. I have now been a 'consultant' to Savills for nearly five years and it forms an agreeable link with the past.

I found the work of the Lands Tribunal both interesting and rewarding, and I look back on those years as a very happy part of my life. But I have enjoyed nearly all my life and have much to be thankful for, and that is the note on which I should like to end this book. Winston Churchill, in a passage in *Thoughts and Adventures*, expresses largely what I feel and puts it far better than I can:

> 'Let us be content with what has happened to us and thankful for all we have been spared. Let us accept the natural order in which we move. Let us reconcile ourselves to the mysterious rhythm of our destinies, such as they must be in this world of space and time. Let us treasure our joys but not bewail our sorrows. The glory of light cannot exist without its shadows. Life is a whole, and good and ill must be accepted together. The journey has been enjoyable and well worth making—once.'

And here is a postscript from my wheel-chair. To my partners and all who have worked with me or for me; to those who have employed me; to my fellow members and the staff of the Lands Tribunal who have helped me; to the advocates and expert witnesses who have been so courteous to me; to my many friends who have been so kind to me; above all, to my dear wife who has been so patient with me—I am deeply grateful.

Bibliography

Modern Methods of Valuation of Land, Houses and Buildings by D. M. Lawrance, W. H. Rees and W. Britton, 6th edition, 1972. Estates Gazette.

Law of Copyholds★ by C. Elton and H. J. Mackay, 2nd edition, 1893. Wildy and Sons.

Goodin and Downing's Domestic Sanitation, 2nd edition, 1972, revised by A. L. Moseley and M. Curtis. Estates Gazette.

Clean and Decent (*The fascinating history of bathrooms and water closets*) by Lawrence Knight, 1st edition, 1960. Routledge and Kegan Paul.

Ryde on Rating by David Widdicombe QC, Hon. David Trustram Eve QC, and Anthony Anderson, 12th edition, 1968. Butterworth.

The Second World War by W. S. Churchill, 2nd edition, 1954 (6 volumes). Cassell.

New Towns: the British Experience, ed. Hazel Evans, 1st edition, 1972. Charles Knight.

Green-belt Cities by F. J. Osborn, 2nd edition, 1969. Adams and Dart.

Into the Wind★ by Lord Reith, 1st edition, 1949. Hodder and Stoughton.

John Nash★ by John Summerson, 2nd edition, 1950. George Allen and Unwin.

The Concise Oxford English Dictionary by H. W. and F. G. Fowler, revised by E. McIntosh, 5th edition, 1964. Oxford University Press.

A Dictionary of Modern English Usage by H. W. Fowler, revised by Ernest Gowers, 2nd edition, 1965. Oxford University Press.

What a Word!★ by A. P. Herbert, 1st edition, 1935. Methuen.

★ Out of print, November, 1973.

Index

247

248

EARLIER BOOKS BY THE SAME AUTHOR

Published June 1971: reprinted October 1971: The Estates Gazette Ltd.

NOTHING BUT THE TRUTH

EXPERT EVIDENCE IN PRINCIPLE AND PRACTICE
FOR SURVEYORS, VALUERS AND OTHERS

with a foreword by

THE RIGHT HONOURABLE LORD WIDGERY, PC, OBE, TD

Lord Chief Justice of England

'Should find an honoured place on the shelves of all surveyors and valuers . . . as full of wisdom and wit as it is mercifully devoid of footnotes.'—*The Chartered Surveyor.*

'This is an entrancing book . . . first-class reading for a leisure hour.' *Rating and Valuation Reporter.*

'Written in a style so easy and flowing that it can be read in a day. We would recommend the day before the hearing! . . . With this excellent book and diligent reading of the appropriate features in the Journal there is now no excuse for an expert witness not living up to his title.'—*Arbitration.*

'Mr. Watson knows the highways and by-ways that the expert witness has to tread. . . . It is gilt on the gingerbread that his own writing is such a pleasure to read.'—*Law Guardian.*

The author's royalties on the sale of the book have been given to the Royal Institution of Chartered Surveyors' Benevolent Fund

Price £1·50 *post free from*

THE ESTATES GAZETTE
151 Wardour Street, London W1V 4BN

Published 1969: George Allen & Unwin Ltd.

WHICH IS THE JUSTICE?

The reflections of a London juvenile court magistrate of long standing. The author draws on a wealth of experience in the courts, but more especially on his personal contacts outside them, and the result is a narrative that is sometimes amusing, occasionally critical, but always human in its approach. The leading characters are always boys and girls in trouble; John Watson discusses the temptations that assail them in modern society, and the mistakes and injustices of which they are the main victims.

'A heart-warming and oddly reassuring book.'—*New Statesman.*

'This kaleidoscope of experience.'—*Daily Telegraph.*

'Must stir the judicial conscience.'—*Law Guardian.*

'Any book by John Watson is worth reading and this is no exception.' —*The Magistrate.*

Price £2 *post free from*

GEORGE ALLEN & UNWIN LTD.
40 Museum Street
London W.C.1

(or from any Bookseller)